Frontispiece: An Adam half-round commode, c.1785. See 'Colour and Patination'.
Courtesy of Norman Adams.

BRITISH
ANTIQUE
FURNITURE

PRICE GUIDE & REASONS FOR VALUES

JOHN ANDREWS

ANTIQUE COLLECTORS' CLUB

ISBN 1 85149 090 6

First edition published under original title
'The Price Guide to Antique Furniture' in 1968

Second edition 1978
Prices revised 1982, 1985
Reprinted 1985, 1986, 1987, 1988

This revised, expanded and retitled
edition first published 1989, reprinted 1992

British Library Cataloguing-in-Publication Data

A catalogue record for this book is available from the British Library

Published for the Antique Collectors' Club
by the Antique Collectors' Club Ltd.

Printed in England by
the Antique Collectors' Club Ltd., Woodbridge, Suffolk IP12 1DS
on Consort Royal Supreme Matt from Donside Mills, Aberdeen, Scotland

The Antique Collectors' Club

The Antique Collectors' Club was formed in 1966 and now has a five figure membership spread throughout the world. It publishes the only independently run monthly antiques magazine, *Antique Collecting,* which caters for those collectors who are interested in widening their knowledge of antiques, both by greater awareness of quality and by discussion of the factors which influence the price that is likely to be asked. The Antique Collectors' Club pioneered the provision of information on prices for collectors and the magazine still leads in the provision of detailed articles on a variety of subjects.

It was in response to the enormous demand for information on 'what to pay' that the price guide series was introduced in 1968 with the first edition of *The Price Guide to Antique Furniture* (completely revised 1978 and 1989), a book which broke new ground by illustrating the more common types of antique furniture, the sort that collectors could buy in shops and at auctions rather than the rare museum pieces which had previously been used (and still to a large extent are used) to make up the limited amount of illustrations in books published by commercial publishers. Many other price guides have followed, all copiously illustrated, and greatly appreciated by collectors for the valuable information they contain, quite apart from prices. The Antique Collectors' Club also publishes other books on antiques, including horology and art reference works, and a full book list is available.

Club membership, which is open to all collectors, costs £17.50 per annum. Members receive free of charge *Antique Collecting,* the Club's magazine (published ten times a year), which contains well-illustrated articles dealing with the practical aspects of collecting not normally dealt with by magazines. Prices, features of value, investment potential, fakes and forgeries are all given prominence in the magazine.

Among other facilities available to members are private buying and selling facilities, the longest list of ''For Sales'' of any antiques magazine, an annual ceramics conference and the opportunity to meet other collectors at their local antique collectors' clubs. There are over eighty in Britain and more than a dozen overseas. Members may also buy the Club's publications at special pre-publication prices.

As its motto implies, the Club is an organisation designed to help collectors get the most out of their hobby: it is informal and friendly and gives enormous enjoyment to all concerned.

For Collectors — By Collectors — About Collecting

The Antique Collectors' Club
5 Church Street, Woodbridge, Suffolk IP12 1DS, England

Price Revision List

Published January each year at £2.50

The usefulness of a book containing prices rapidly diminishes as market values change.

In order to keep the prices in this book updated, a price revision list will be issued in January each year. This will record the major price changes in the values of the items covered under the various headings in the book.

To ensure you receive the price revision list, complete the pro forma invoice inserted in this book and send it to the address below:

ANTIQUE COLLECTORS' CLUB
5 CHURCH STREET, WOODBRIDGE, SUFFOLK IP12 1DS

Acknowledgements

A list of photographic credits appears at the end of this book, but in addition there are a number of people who have kindly assisted me during the preparation of the manuscript whom I wish to thank.

If perchance a reader finds fault in an area where I have thanked others for help, he must remember that the responsibility lies solely with the author who, if he included every point made to him, would find it impossible to write a book of this nature.

Guy Bousfield of Windsor	— Points on mahogany furniture
Graham Child, Sotheby's	— Help, advice and assistance with photographs
Bill Cotton	— Country chairs
John Creed-Miles of John Creed, Camden Passage, London	— Pine dressers
Tom Crispin of St. Albans	— Dressers, table furniture and Windsor chairs
David Gibbins, Woodbridge	— Helpful comments and advice generally
Derek Green of Cedar Antiques, Hartley Wintney	— Walnut and country furniture, help on prices and general advice
P. Hewat Jaboor, Sotheby's Bond Street	— Pricing, particularly pre-Victorian furniture
J.P.J. Homer	— Table furniture
Christopher Hurst of Anthony Hurst Antiques Ltd., Woodbridge	— For the Trade Terminology section
The late Edward Joy	— For so many helpful points and corrections
William Lorimer, Christie's	— Help, advice and assistance with photographs
Christopher Payne, Sotheby's Belgravia	— Pricing, particularly Victorian furniture
The late A.T. Silvester	— Help since the first edition
Diana Steel	— Help in production of the book
John Steel	— Help in revising text

John Andrews
November 1989

Contents

Preface to the Third Edition

When *Antique Collecting*, the monthly journal of the Antique Collectors' Club, was started in 1965, it was discovered that there was a huge demand for information about ordinary antique furniture from people who wanted to furnish with the relatively modest pieces that were, and are still, to be found in shops and auctions. The result was the first edition of *The Price Guide to Antique Furniture*, a small book of some 340 pictures of the sort of furniture that members of the Club had in their own homes. The photographs, gleaned from a few helpful dealers and from the limited number then used by auctioneers, were supplemented by our own photographic efforts. To keep prices up to date price revision lists were, and are, published annually. The result of the analysis of the movement in antique furniture prices is set out in the section entitled 'Antique Furniture Prices over Twenty Years'.

Despite its somewhat amateur appearance, the first edition was a great success. It was the first book to discuss furniture prices in any detail. Twenty years ago antiques magazines never mentioned values for fear of annoying their advertisers; books contained only museum quality pieces. The *Price Guide's* straightforward practical style and sensible advice make it unique.

In the early 1970s inflation hit Britain and antiques, including antique furniture, were caught up in the rush for good hedges against inflation. At the same time litho printing improved in quality and auctioneers began to publish a large number of photographs in their catalogues. The large range of photographs which accumulated gave us the opportunity to establish for each type of furniture a hierarchy of quality which enabled the reader to understand the points to look for and made sense of the consequent price structure. Added to each illustration were comments to open the collector's eyes to possible problems, both of design and condition. The result was the second edition, published in 1978, containing over 1,000 carefully chosen illustrations from the many thousands of photographs available. It is a book that has been invaluable, not just to collectors of antique furniture but to a generation of home-furnishers intelligent enough to realise that modern furniture is largely rubbish and will be valueless in a few years, while antique furniture goes up in value and gives great pleasure. It has also provided a means of communication between those interested in the subject, be they dealers, auctioneers or collectors.

At first *The Price Guide to Antique Furniture* had no competition, but the flood of auctioneers' pictures enabled books to be compiled for a wider range of antiques than just furniture. Some of these general price guides are sold on the premise that because new photographs are published each year they build up into a valuable collection of priced antique furniture. This may work for collectables but not for antique furniture. Antique furniture falls within a surprisingly small range of types (e.g. tables, chairs, desks) but within each type there is a vast number of alternatives because of the interactions of secondary factors (e.g. wood, width, height, depth, colour, date, design, condition, fittings) which can result in substantial variations in value and saleability. Thus it is essential that the collector understands how these factors influence values and as far as any book is concerned this is best achieved by the 'Look, this is good and that is bad' approach, not by supplying thousands of photographs with short, formal auctioneer descriptions. Furniture is more akin to sculpture or painting than stamps, pot-lids or Dinky toys, and the buyer needs to train his eye, not consult thousands of pictures in the vain hope of finding one that is identical. Another disadvantage of the 'Don't think, just turn the pages until you find one like it' approach is that the prices quoted are those fetched at auction. This of course ignores the vagaries of a system which offers an item for only a couple of minutes and ignores the depressive influence of the 'ring'. The basic unsoundness of legislation which attempts to force business colleagues and often friends to bid against each other was well summed up in 1904 long before such 'protection' was attempted. The position is as true today as it was at the turn of the century.

> ...but it appears to me that, within certain bounds, the members of any trade have the right to combine for their own protection, and to gain any legitimate advantage from their special knowledge and experience. The dealers have the right to buy as cheaply as they can, and as many of them know that amateurs follow their lead, bidding as it were on their judgement, they employ means to defeat these ends and get all the advantage that they can from the sale...
>
> ...It is evident that in some cases combinations of this kind must cause serious loss to the vendors of property, but it must be borne in mind that this is generally the fault of employing an auctioneer who does not understand his business, and numerous cases have been known where, for example, in the case of a silver article being sold, some one has challenged the fact of its being silver, and the auctioneer has allowed it to be sold as plated, in which case those in the 'knock out' would divide the difference in value between that of a silver and a plated article...
>
> *How to Collect Old Furniture* by Frederick Litchfield

So, if the second edition is so good and the prices for each piece in the book are revised annually, why produce a third? During the hyper-inflation of the 1970s anything sold; now the critical judgement that collectors have always exercised has become more necessary than ever. Money invested earns interest in real terms and the new high prices, largely caused by UK inflation, put off many overseas buyers. The market for antiques is still strong, but not everything sells. There is an increasing distinction in price between a dull object and one with some spark.

Two factors have emerged. First, the neo-classical furniture of the 1810-1840 period which was not greatly appreciated a decade ago has come into fashion and that has had a remarkable effect on prices. The second edition did not include enough photographs of the neo-classical examples; names like Bullock and

Morant were generally unknown, apart from to a few scholars and one or two progressive dealers.

Secondly, the increasing importance of informed taste in the market of the mid-1980s and later has resulted in patination and colour becoming sought after. They always were desirable to the collector but, as a generalisation, uninformed taste (and sadly that includes much overseas demand) wanted everything to be antique but look new, a challenge to which the British antiques trade boldly responded by stripping thousands of pieces of antique furniture of a substance which, ounce for ounce, is more valuable than gold. The fakers were of course overjoyed, for colour and patination are most difficult to counterfeit. Public awareness of the importance of colour and patination has been slow to emerge and there is not always agreement about what is the 'best' colour, but the price premium, sometimes up to five times the estimate, that is increasingly attached to good patination and colour at auction makes it an essential element in a discussion of price — hence it has a section of its own in this edition.

Just as the second edition was facilititated by an abundance of black and white photographs, so this third edition can include an overdue discussion on colour and patina because recently the leading auctioneers and some leading dealers have started to use colour and have kindly made their transparencies available to us. In any event, colour gives a better idea of a piece of furniture and so it has been possible to supplement the black and white examples which remain largely unchanged from the second edition, substitution taking place only where a new example would make a point that was missing previously. Some examples of more expensive furniture have been included as there are points of design, condition and colour which can best be made by looking at the good pieces. In most cases, however, no prices are given for these as the colour is designed to make clearer the reason for the range of prices, not supplement it.

This book and the annual price revision lists, which are published in January/ February each year, also serve the useful function of updating the results of market trends and changes in the market.

Quite apart from collectors, the study of antique furniture is one which will repay anyone furnishing a home, for leaving aside all financial considerations there is great joy in living with object lessons in good design which, by their very presence, train the eye. The task of this book is to make people look, know what to look for, and know how to assess what they have seen.

John Andrews
September 1989

Introduction

This book illustrates nearly 1,200 examples of the furniture still found in shops and auction rooms in Great Britain. It illustrates only a limited number of really fine objects — included because one can best learn by comparison of the best and the not so good — and no out-and-out junk. It does show a wide variety of quality of pieces made between 1650 and about 1860. We have, however, extended this date line where many similar types exist within a few years of each other and the omission of later types would cause confusion.

This is not an academic work, nor is it a primer. It is intended as a reference book for the practising collector and dealer, a work from which the memory may be refreshed and points checked. Accordingly, free use has been made of some of the expressions used in the trade. If the newcomer to the subject finds expressions such as 'right', 'wrong', 'honest' and 'marriage' confusing, he will find them defined in the Glossary. This book also gives, wherever possible, a guide to the date and original features of a piece. In the Glossary and section on Periods of Antique Furniture the reader may look up terms, design and construction features, periods and dates. The outstanding cabinet makers and designers are briefly mentioned with, where necessary, the principal features for which they are remembered.

Every item is referenced. These references are to enable the annual price revision list to be compiled with a ready cross-reference. This is made available in January/February each year on private subscription as described elsewhere in this book. Although the concept of valuing works of art no longer generates the sort of heat that results in letters to *The Times*, it is necessary to be clear about the limitations that exist in giving values and state the philosophy behind the thinking.

First let us be quite clear that there is no 'correct' price for a piece of furniture, or indeed any other antique for that matter. At school we looked up stamps in a catalogue and talked about them being worth a certain definite sum. Disillusion came when we tried to sell examples to the people who published the catalogues.

Many people persist in thinking that a certain price can be attached to a piece of furniture. In fact most people who handle furniture regularly think of an individual piece as being within a price bracket and you will hear these thoughts expressed in a number of different ways in conversation. '£1,500 was a bit steep for that, wasn't it?' or 'You were lucky to get that for £1,000' or 'It was better than the one that went for £1,200 at the sale last week'. Fortunately for collectors every piece is different and dealers have different tastes and overheads so that what to one dealer seems just buyable at £1,500 is to another outrageously expensive at £1,300.

Secondly the buyer of antique furniture must appreciate the extent to which quality influences value and how difficult it is, at the top level of quality, to anticipate how buyers will react. The understanding of how to assess quality is the single most important task to which this book addresses itself and why eleven hundred photographs have been selected from the thousands available to show gradations of quality.

Plate 1 instances the sort of results which, to varying degrees, happen two or three dozen times each London auction season. Here is a top quality example of its type (this is not the place to discuss it in detail). The distinguished London auctioneers who prepared the catalogue saw clearly the quality and suggested a price that took this into account, albeit perhaps at the lower end of the scale as auctioneers tend to do. In the event enough buyers recognised just how superb it was to send it to three and a half times the estimate.

Thirdly the reader must bear in mind that auctions can sometimes generate results which appear without logical reason. Plate 2 is perhaps an extreme example, but is by no means unique. A copy in mixed styles, it could probably now be made for £7,000 — £12,000 and yet it cost somebody £110,000.

While these two examples are out of the ordinary, they do illustrate that auction prices can be high and, of course, given the existence of the ring, prices can also be ludicrously low. Add to this the uncertainty generated by offering a piece for a brief two minutes and it is clear why the prices quoted are those that you might be expected to pay if you buy a piece in the sort of shop in which such a piece would normally be stocked. This of course adds an additional premium to quality for you find junk in a low priced shop and top quality in an expensive establishment, unless of course you have taken the trouble to learn the subject and are lucky enough to find a piece as it makes its way upwards through the trade.

Finally remember that the price quoted in this book is for something in showroom condition. A piece in rough condition passing between dealers would be very much less. An area of concern for buyers of antique furniture must be restoration. Clearly antique furniture is likely to have been damaged at some time in the past, so it is almost inevitable that some otherwise desirable piece will have been restored and clearly what is acceptable must in the last analysis be a matter of personal opinion.

Bargains still exist. They always have and presumably will continue to do so. Traditionally a bargain came from some rural shop where the dealer was ignorant of what he had bought. This may still happen but most dealers have a nose for quality, even outside their own line of country, and put the piece in the car, visit the London auctioneers and perhaps hawk it round the specialist trade. Bargains nowadays arise either from lack of knowledge about a newly discovered field of collecting like neo-classical or gothic revival or else, and this is more likely, from dealers who know exactly what they have bought but have failed to keep up to date with rapidly rising price levels. For example, in 1986/87 marble top furniture took a sudden upward move. The price of such pieces sitting in provincial shops suddenly became a bargain, even in the most expensive areas.

Once you have decided to buy, insist on an invoice and make sure that it gives the approximate date when the piece was made. The word 'style' or 'type' should not appear on an invoice for period furniture. The words 'Old English' amount to an admission of ignorance or even dishonesty. Your invoice should read:

'Chippendale chair in mahogany c.1760'

not

'Chippendale chair' or 'Chippendale style chair'.
In addition any repairs should be clearly stated.

'Chippendale chair in mahogany c.1760, with one replacement arm'

not

'Chippendale chair repaired' or

'Chippendale chair with all faults' or 'W.A.F.' (with all faults) or

'Chippendale chair as found'.

The invoice should be signed and dated, ideally on the letter heading of the dealer. If any dealer refuses you an invoice on these lines, don't buy. No reputable dealer will refuse to give an invoice to a private buyer. The documentation of sales transactions between dealers is outside the scope of this book.

What if one wishes to sell the furniture seen in this book? The book is designed for buyers and the prices quoted are those which it is felt will have to be paid and, of course, as in every other subject, there is a gap between the buying and selling price. However, it must surely be the acid test of a book for buyers that it is also of use to sellers and we believe this to be the case. But what percentage should be deducted by the seller from the price for buyers? The answer lies in the method of sale. Most of the large London auction houses charge ten per cent to the buyer and up to fifteen per cent to the seller and they sell the bulk of their lots to the antiques trade. This means that the prices realised have to stand at least two hefty margins, those of the auctioneer and the dealer. As a broad generalisation it is true that poorer pieces sell often at surprisingly modest prices in these rooms. On the other hand, the expertise of the staff and the international connections of the firm ensure the best possible market for high quality goods. In these cases the price realised more than compensates for the costs involved, and in any case at high values commissions are negotiable.

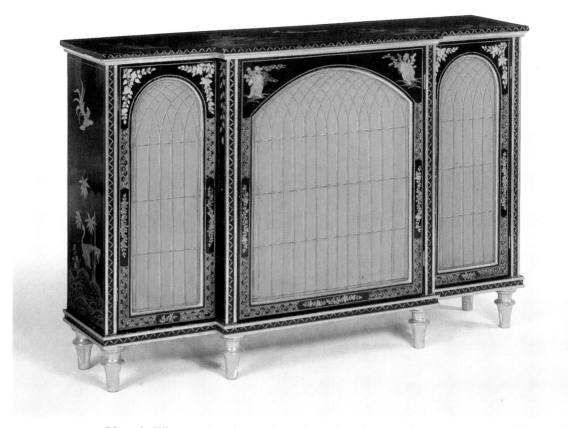

Plate 1. When a piece has style and quality, determining price can be difficult. This japanned breakfront side cabinet has a very common form but the delicate chinoiserie decoration, the subtle brass trellis and excellent condition make it very desirable. The auctioneers saw the quality, realised that it would cause a lot of interest and estimated it at £8,000 — £12,000, a figure which in 1987 seemed about right. In the event competition pushed the cost to over £35,000. A lot of money, perhaps, but one can understand the reason. Had it been a dull, plain mahogany example of exactly the same shape, with reproduction brasswork, the estimate would have been £1,500 — £2,000; a price of £6,000 would be unbelievable.

When selling at auction, ensure that a sensible reserve is fixed and ascertain the handling charge if the reserve is not reached. Many auctioneers are sufficiently confident in their judgement not to charge if they agree before the sale that the reserve is reasonable.

Another method of sale is to place a piece with a specialist dealer to sell on your behalf. Remember this may take time and you should agree on the price he will ask and the percentage he will take.

Remember also that when thinking about the value of a piece of furniture outside influences intrude. These include the general financial position and the overhead structure of the dealer or his financial strength. They can be simply summed up by the concept of demand. During a slump prices tend to steady or even fall while during a boom they rise. The subject is dealt with in more depth in the section 'Antique Furniture Prices over Twenty Years'.

Plate 2. Despite the mixture of styles in which William Kent type lion masks appear with neo-classical ovals, this is an impressive piece of office furniture. Almost certainly made in the last hundred years, its utility and cost of making today confirm the auctioneers' estimate of £15,000 — £20,000. Competition forced the cost to the staggering figure of £110,000, which acts as a salutary reminder to us all that the prices made at auction can be a function of competition rather than a reflection of generally held views on value.

This book is unique in discussing individual pieces in the down-to-earth terms that buyers use. No other book on the subject illustrates undesirable pieces and berates them, yet how else can one make the points of what to look for and what to avoid? It is only too easy to slip into the dead-pan language of the auctioneer's catalogue which is entirely unhelpful for the collector trying to understand why values can vary so much. In this connection I hope that any owner whose piece is included and described in less than congratulatory terms will accept that my reason for so doing is to try and make distinctions in quality as clear as possible and is not merely the result of a warped sense of humour. I am well aware that, for example, a table I describe as being a 'complete misalliance of top and bottom condoned by two elegantly turned legs of superior antecedents' may in fact be a description of the cherished possession of its current owner who sees in it nothing more than warm memories of happy times now passed. If this is the case I am sorry and can only plead that this sets out to be a technical book. As collectors our possessions all have memories and indeed collecting would be a joyless pastime if this were not the case. I hope this book will enable collectors to add to their enjoyment by giving fuller understanding of just what they are buying.

John Andrews
September 1989

Colour and Patination

When a piece comes up at auction with a good colour and patination the price realised usually goes well over the estimate and yet auctioneers rarely include this desirable attribute in their catalogue descriptions and books largely ignore the subject; indeed this book is the first to tackle it in any depth.

Clearly experts recognise a good original surface, and in departments like metalwork it is highly esteemed and catalogued; not so with furniture — officially anyway. Because the tastes of customers vary it is difficult for dealers to establish a consensus on what is desirable or undesirable. If a German customer requires his mahogany partners' desk to look like the contents of a newly opened chestnut, that is what he will be offered. If an American wants a faded look, then that is what the piece will be given. It will not look like the real thing but it will be a passable imitation. The dealers' problem is therefore not to determine if the surface is desirable and original but who is the most likely to buy. Packaging, as we all know, is one of the keys to success in marketing. But it is no accident that the homes of dealers who collect antique furniture are full of beautifully coloured and naturally patinated pieces and that when such pieces come up they carry a large premium. Even if a collector doesn't value such extras, he should be aware of them.

Increasingly there is a view that good natural colour and patination, the result of age and the attention a piece has received, is desirable. Certainly it is a wonderful protection against fakes because it is practically impossible to reproduce. Therefore the collector would do well to understand what is involved for three specific reasons:

1. Aesthetic appreciation
2. Protection against fakes and improvements
3. The extra value which is increasingly involved

Very little has been written about the nature of patination and colour and often the two are linked together under patina, the *Concise Oxford Dictionary* suggesting '. . .a gloss produced by age on woodwork'. However, what the furniture collector values includes colour as well. The problem is that the two are interrelated.

Plate 3. A mahogany tallboy of the 1760s but more desirable than most because it has an attractive curved pediment with a fretted decoration. However, the top moulding has faded much more than the rest of the piece which suggests a later 'improvement' in poorer wood which has not held the stain used to match it up with the rest of the piece.

New unpolished wood tends to have uniformity of colour. The difference between hard areas like knots, burrs, flecks, hard grains — natural features and distortions in the wood — and soft areas of straight grain and sapwood can be accentuated by adding a polish. Linseed was one of the oils used which sank into the wood in different degrees and, with added colour, helped accentuate distinctions and thus make the piece more interesting. Sheraton went so far as to suggest the use of powdered brick dust. The result was polished and often varnished. The owner was encouraged to see that a wax polish was applied and rubbed well down. This kept the piece clean and added to the protective layer (often accurately referred to by dealers as 'skin'), which in turn oxidised.

However, this hard, impervious, protective layer served another function. The bleaching effect of strong light gradually wastes out the colouring in the grain, producing different shades, and varies with the type of wood. The oil being applied in new polishing cannot permeate the patina ('the gloss produced by age') so the bleaching effect continues slowly and at different rates on the surface.

The result produced is often varying shades of colour which it is next to impossible for the faker or restorer to simulate. This is why a surface which carries an undisturbed and uniform colour suggests repolishing, which may have been carried out to facilitate a customer's requirement or hide some alterations, or both. However, this can vary with different woods and conditions so it is best to consider some actual examples.

Plate 3 is a George III tallboy of around the late 1760s. It has a fancy pediment, of which the front is a different colour, both from the sides and the rest of the piece. The implication here is that it was improved some years ago by the addition of a carved pediment replacing the original plain one which was probably rather like figure 361. However, the cabinet maker used a different quality of wood from the rest of the piece which was probably completely repolished at the time and sold with a uniform colour. The piece was placed in strong light which gradually bleached out the stain used to match up the colour of what was probably a softer, less dense wood. Now the difference is blatant and the improvement exposed.

One would also take a hard look at the blind fret on the angle of the top. Has it too been added? The handles could have been an improvement as well. This piece will now be repolished and the process recommence.

The point needs to be made that no moral judgement is offered. The chest-on-chest is a perfectly good, usable object of antique furniture. All that is necessary is that the collector should be aware that he is buying a piece which has been altered in an attempt to enhance its desirability and hence value.

Plate 4 shows an elegant mahogany breakfast table of the first years of the 19th century. It has stood in strong light over a period of time. In the middle was placed a square or rectangular object which has protected the surface from light and left a light brown patch. The rest of the table has gradually gone down to a silver grey, as has the crossbanding. Indeed, such has been the effect of heat that the animal glue holding the veneered crossbanding has melted at the point nearest the camera which now shows a crinkled broken surface.

What will be dealer who buys this do? He has a range of choices.

1. Rub down the top hard and repolish — perhaps even repolish the whole table so that the colour matches the present colour of the legs.

2. Rub down gently attempting to make the whole top the light brown colour of the centre piece.

3. Break the hard edge of the brown area on the left so that it merges in with the silver grey gradually, as does the colour on the right foreground.

4. Give it a good polish as it is, leaving the shades of silver grey.

What actually happens will depend on the dealer and the tastes of his clients.

Plate 5 is a Georgian mahogany double-sided desk of the very end of the 18th century. Strong light (but not necessarily sunlight) has concentrated on the front, particularly on the left-hand side where the surface has gone grey and is starting to acquire the silver grey colour which we saw on the tripod. The right-hand side has not had the same exposure and retains the deep dark polish which, perhaps in darker form, was the colour of the piece originally. The right-hand door, particularly at the bottom, has not had the same degree of exposure to light and retains some colour.

The purchaser will be faced with the same range of alternatives as on the previous example, but there are some complications. First he will have to make a plinth to go round the base. He will have to patch the left-hand side and take a decision on how to deal with the extra holes made by the later wooden handles.

The preferred solution — to the admirer of patination anyway — would be to make the plinth out of old wood and bleach it down artificially, clean the bottom of both doors gently and try to achieve a gentle gradation of colour from the dark bottom to the silver grey top. That leaves the patching and the piece missing on the top left. Old faded wood, if it were available, would be ideal. If not, a piece would have to be bleached right out in an attempt to simulate the silver grey.

The handle holes remain an intractable problem and might well dissuade a purist from attempting the restoration. Almost certainly this piece will be stripped and repolished.

Silver grey is only one of several colours to which mahogany can fade. As a broad generalisation, the earliest used mahoganies like the dark, heavy Spanish

Plate 4. The effects of light are apparent on the top of this mahogany breakfast table. The central square has been protected from the bleaching effect of the sun. The problem now is how to repolish without giving the impression of a new top.

Plate 5. Missing its bottom moulding and plinth, this double-sided mahogany desk c.1800 has started to acquire a silver grey colour at the point of maximum exposure to light. The need to patch and repair will probably mean repolishing.

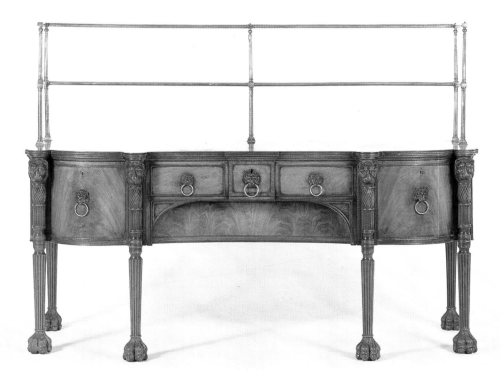

Plate 6. Only in the mid-1980s did designs like this neo-classical sideboard of the 1820s come to be accepted. The variation in the good, faded colour conforms to our expectation of how strong light would affect it, thus confirming its originality, adding value and enhancing the enjoyment of the piece.

San Domingo fade to a silvery grey. Cuban mahogany, which became popular in the mid-century, because of the fine line of the grain, goes down to grey-yellow (see Plate 6) and then almost white, while Honduras, which is a poor, inferior, grainless wood used extensively towards the end of the century, goes down to an unattractive yellow.

Plate 6 is in fact a good Regency mahogany sideboard of the 1820s with carefully chosen decorative veneers; by putting two consecutive curls opposite each other a 'feather pattern' is produced, a typical use of Cuban mahogany. You can see this dark swirl effect clearly on the edges of the low recessed central drawer where the effect of light has been least strong.

The dark colour has now gone from the bottom of the drawer fronts. (Incidentally, it is not unusual for time and light to lift and crack the dark areas and this should be seen as a plus, not a minus.) The edges of the curved side drawers show the light yellow colour with a touch of grey where the less dense grain has lost the most colour. Notice also the bleached lighter colour of the lions' pale noses, and the dark round the handles and where the projecting legs have shielded the wood. This piece has clearly not been altered or restored. For one reason, up until the mid-1980s it would have been worth only a few hundred pounds and been more likely to have been seen as a 'breaker' (broken up to provide wood) than 'improved'. With the move to the neo-classical the picture is very different.

Plate 7 is a double-sided library table, c.1820, in what auctioneers traditionally describe as 'distressed condition'. As it now appears the colour is not attractive, ranging from a dark reddish brown on the right-hand side drawer to a pale colour on the bottom rail. This piece has probably been french polished and the materials used have corrupted into a thick opaque layer which, instead of highlighting the wood as was intended and providing a shiny polish, now obscures it. At the rounded ends there are two distinct shades — the dark colour where the old polish still clings and the lighter where it has been dislodged. Also you can see in the area where the later Victorian knobs are now missing a lighter colour which is probably nearer to the original french polish finish. In this case there is no option but to clean and repolish.

Alterations can happen soon after a piece was made. The conversion from bun to bracket feet, a common early change, is discussed elsewhere. Others are less easy to follow. The breakfront secretaire bookcase shown as Plate 8 has the unusual feature of having the sides of the centre section veneered. This suggests that the wings were an afterthought, for veneer would not normally be wasted on an unexposed surface.

What other supporting evidence is there of the changes? There are two. First the thick stiles (the side verticals) of the lower part of the centre section are too large for a centre section — particularly with such narrow outside stiles. Secondly the wings are too high; the piece would look better if they were lower. But the most conclusive evidence would be if the wood was of different quality marked with different grain and was patinated differently. In the colour plate the wings appear lighter than the centre; this cannot be accounted for by sunlight otherwise the centre would be a lighter shade. It would be interesting to see how closely the patina corresponded, for that might provide an indication of how long the pieces have been together.

To conclude this section the frontispiece is an example of a glorious Adam half-round commode, c.1785. Although the surface has faded down to what might be described as a rich, faded chestnut, there is a considerable range of colour from the dark grey of the hard area of figure to the golden sheen on the broader grain.

Colour and patination are sometimes assisted by people in a more direct manner than polishing. It is important to look at the places where fingers will have deposited oily sweat, where dirt will have accumulated to provide a black layer on unpolished surfaces. The underside of a flap of a gateleg table should have a 'crossbanding' of such dark patina and if it is absent then questions arise. This human patination on unpolished as well as polished wood is usually present when a piece is in untouched condition. Small tables and chairs are lifted and carried, drawers are handled. Many old churches provide good examples of patina, often on the arms of chairs and stalls in the choir or near the altar. Notice how patina holds, even sometimes seems to project, light.

Old churches too have surfaces which have not been polished or handled and show how these surfaces oxidise to a pale old vellum appearance or, where exposed to weather, oak may take on a silvery quality. Hand patination on mahogany can be seen on the hand-rails of Victorian railway stations. The colour is different but the heightening of the grain and colour is there also.

When examining furniture, look for other forms of wear and use. The gate of a gateleg table will form a scratched arc on the underside of the table. Does the arc conform to the present movement of the leg?

An amusing example of patina in the broadest sense of the word arose when a broad gadrooned carving on the edge of a heavy Chippendale Pembroke table was under discussion. The expert opinion was that the crisp, assured carving was contemporary with the table. However, underneath, very close to the edge, about half an inch in, were several round indentations where the small pieces of equipment that hold lace-making equipment were secured. These fitted over the edge of the table and a screw below turned to give them a firm hold — just like a clamp. The distance of the indentations would have made it impossible for the equipment to have been held directly above on the rounded edge of gadrooning. It had obviously been added later.

In the colour captions you will find in a large number of cases comments about colour and patination. In the years ahead colour and patination will increasingly

Plate 7. The double-sided library table was probably stripped and french polished. This has now deteriorated to show an opaque layer of what looks like paint which has fallen off in places to give a blotchy effect.

dictate the value of furniture. There will be a basic price for repolished pieces and a healthy premium for those that can prove their age. Even top auctioneers do not always give credit for colour and patination and as a result actual prices can sometimes go thousands of pounds over the estimate. If top auctioneers can get it wrong, just think of the scope for mistakes elsewhere!

Plate 8. Alterations to furniture are not uncommon. Here wings have been added but made too tall. The sides at the bottom of the original piece are too broad by comparison with those of the additions. Are the woods the same? Certainly the grain is different and the degree of fading confirms this. One would have to consider the thickness of veneer, the subsidiary woods and the depth of patina to take a view on how much later the wings had been added.

Furniture Buying — Some Thoughts
by James Storm

As pointed out in the Introduction it is essential to develop one's eye when looking at antique furniture (or, come to that, any antiques). It may be tempting to buy a book which proclaims that each year there are entirely new photographs, and that the prices are 'not simply' an up-date, but each piece of furniture is different and until you understand what features to look for and what to avoid you can search through millions of photographs and remain ignorant.

The comments in this book are designed to help you to understand why some pieces are more desirable than others. There are certain general principles to remember. Colour and patination are dealt with in a separate section, but here are some more points to bear in mind.

Improvements ('What we do with *them* is this...')

There are several ways of looking at a piece of furniture. Somebody who wants furniture to fit into their home, or to make a focal point in a prestigious room, views a piece accordingly. They calculate how much they want it and if that is more than the price they buy it. Some changes are inexpensive but add hugely to the desirability of the piece in the eye of the customer. The result is that pieces are changed and adapted.

Changes have been made for centuries. A walnut bureau with bun feet would have looked very old fashioned in the 1720s and many were fitted with the new bracket feet; that is an acceptable alteration. At the other end of the spectrum are the changes discussed below. Buying from a reputable dealer provides a safeguard, for he would not pass off an improved piece; it would be recognised and his reputation damaged. The increased influence of auctioneers means that some of the altered pieces passing through the rooms of the less knowledgeable provincial auctioneers are not correctly described and indeed many dealers take the view that buying in auction is governed by *caveat emptor* and put into auction pieces they would not care to sell from the shop and have to guarantee with a written invoice. They simply deliver the piece, state the reserve they want and leave the auctioneers to do the cataloguing.

Auctioneers used to be considered as wholesale sources of supply but, like the cash and carry and D.I.Y. stores, the public increasingly gain admittance. Indeed, the auctioneers encourage the private buyer. Against this background it becomes even more essential that potential buyers learn to look at pieces and make their own judgements.

As you will find in the book, writing tables of the early nineteenth century are very expensive, especially if decorative. However, they are simply made and large, heavy examples are common. The example illustrated in Plate 10 has a later Greek key pattern carved in the frieze and brass masks screwed on to the

Plate 9. Clearly these two will part at some point. The bookcase alone could, when feet have been added, sell for the price of the total cost of the piece.

corners. The tapering legs may well be original but if they had been the same thickness all the way down it would have been a simple task to alter them to their present more elegant shape. The improvements might in total cost £2,000; the addition in value could be £5,000 — £10,000. The auctioneer pointed out the changes but will they be described in detail on the label if the piece is sold in an antique shop? Often they are, but not always. In some cases there may be an honest disagreement with the auctioneer's opinion and the dealer may feel that some, at least, of the decoration is original. As has already been stated, but cannot be emphasised enough, it is vital to get an invoice with a full description so that in the event of a dispute there is no element of doubt as to what you thought you were buying.

You should develop your eye by looking at what appears an uninteresting piece and try to imagine what could possibly be done with it. As a first simple example,

Plate 10. The popularity of writing tables, combined with their simplicity of construction and the ready availability of the cruder variety, makes them a good subject for improvement. The Greek key pattern and the brass masks were added later and provide an elegant piece at a relatively small cost.

take this Regency style double-sided bookcase on stand which sold for £1,500 at auction in 1989 (Plate 9). The bookcase will be lifted off the stand and given carved hairy feet; the stand will be given a top and proposed as a slightly low library table. There is little expense on the conversion and there is every hope of being able to double your money. The bookcase is a very popular form and the library table would sell eventually.

Now let us consider a more advanced example. The rosewood secretaire cabinet c.1835 shown in Plate 11 was of no distinction and sold in 1987 for £1,210. The cabinet maker, whose classic and oft repeated quote heads this section, would, faced with this piece, have in his mind's eye the drawing from Thomas Hope's *Household Furniture and Interior Decoration* (Plate 12). If he were up to date in his thinking (which fortunately most skilled old cabinet makers are not) he would also embrace the cabinet by Bullock for Napoleon's breakfast room in St. Helena (Plate 13), one of a pair shown in the original design sketch.

First he would build up the frieze to get the typical Thomas Hope ears. These he would decorate with similar brass decorations from the Hope pattern. At the same time he would be tempted to order from the brass founder eight winged hairy paw feet for the base, but would hesitate. If he is going down that road he will have difficulties because he'll be committed to the simplicity of Thomas Hope and that will mean doing away with all of the centre section which will leave too much new exposed wood on the side. Better stick with the Bullock

A George Smith design of 1808.

Plate 15. Victorian rococo, 1840-1850. Of immense quality but until the late 1980s not generally appreciated and therefore undervalued.

Plate 17. A Victorian neo-Elizabethan library table of c.1840 to a design by Bridgens. Not a style which in the 1980s commanded any interest. Will the fashion in the 1990s embrace it and send the value from £3,000 — £5,000 to £10,000+? It will be interesting to see.

Plate 11. Not a popular model but perhaps (so the faker thinks) worth the £1,210 it fetched at auction for the possibilities it presents. Almost a contemporary of the Bullock piece opposite. Alteration will cause no damage to the unpolished interior and back which will be examined with minute care.

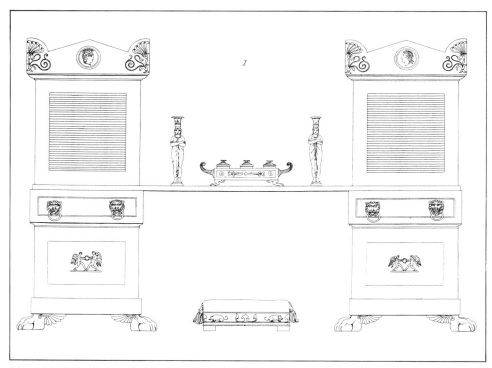

Plate 12. From Thomas Hope's Household Furniture and Interior Decoration, *which Hope calls 'a large library or writing-table, flanked with paper presses or escrutoirs'. The problem is how best to make the adaption.*

Plate 13. The bookcase made by Bullock for Napoleon's house in St. Helena. Following this design is easier than going direct to the Hope illustration. The latter would leave too much surface to re-veneer.

Below. Plate 14. The faker's solution which would not fool the expert for a minute but might trap the speculator or the decorator who is only seeking the Bullock 'look'. Even though the faker has Hope's pattern for the frieze in front of him he still gets it wrong. Apollo should be looking at Minerva, not away from her!

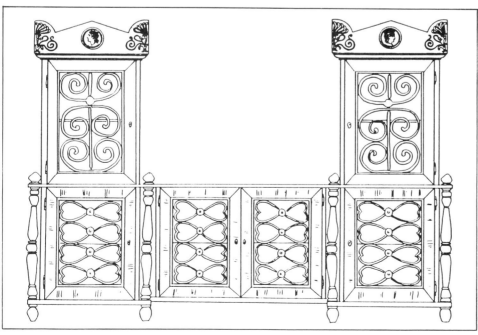

Plate 18. The maker of this early 18th century stool had the idea of extending the line of the knee of the cabriole and bringing it up under the seat. It was a bold concept and he carried it off well, with the result that walnut collectors got excited and the piece made seven times the auctioneer's estimate.

approach. So, with some reluctance (for brass winged hairy feet save a lot of work and command a good premium), he settles for turned pillars.

The doors present little problem. Take out the centre sections and put them on the sides to hide the removal of the top. Any space round the edges will have to be crossbanded using the wood from the top of the fall. The only problem is that Mr. Bullock hasn't crossbanded the sides, which is a pity.

The blocks at the sides of the centre section look Victorian so they have to come off. The pillars will help hide the change.

So he proceeded, and the result may well look like the drawing in Plate 14.

Why go to all this bother? Why not knock the piece to bits or use old wood rather than start with a £1,210 carcase? The answer is that the carcase is almost contemporary with the piece the cabinet maker is trying to copy and so all the old surfaces, both the inside and the back, will look right, which gives him a head start for it is much easier to simulate polished than unpolished surfaces (this traditional reasoning ignores patination which is one reason why patination is so important to the collector).

The economics are interesting. His labour will be worth about £2,000 and he will use up about £500 on wire and pieces from his precious wood store (breakers are hugely expensive for what they are) so the cost will be almost £4,000. Success depends primarily on the cabinet maker's skill but even more on the polisher's. If he can get the colour on the turned pillar right and age up the wood convincingly they could make a killing. When you think (they will reason) that at the Great Tew Park sale a dull looking 'Victorian' sofa made £33,000, what price an unrecorded bookcase? In reality the top dealers who pay the big money would look at it, recognise instantly what had happened and walk away chuckling silently to themselves. The faker's best hope would be a greedy unknowledgeable 'runner' who at £30,000 would see a huge profit and so be prepared to buy it against the ring at a provincial auction.

Fashion

Fashion has a profound effect on values but it is not easy to predict how it will move.

There is overseas demand, where enthusiasm is linked to the prosperity or particular interests of a group of buyers. In the 1970s the Dutch and Germans bought oak furniture and metalwork in quantity, but by the mid-1980s that market had contracted severely so that these pieces were out of fashion. Variations in overseas demand can change in a matter of months. An example comes from a shipper (someone who sends container loads of cheap, later pieces abroad) who bemoaned a particular overseas buyer's approach.

> Last year he bought all my carved oak (i.e. pieces of the 1870-1920 vintage) so I filled the warehouse up with more carved oak. Last week he came and said that carved oak wasn't selling and he wanted flat oak (i.e. not carved) so now I have a warehouse full of carved oak I can't sell, and no flat oak which everybody wants.

The example could just as well have come from a top gallery owner complaining about lack of interest in a more exotic commodity.

Where fashion is more predictable is in acceptance of later pieces. At the start of the nineteenth century Roman sculptures and medieval objects were seen as a fit subject for the collector; by the end of the century British oak furniture was in vogue. Victorian furniture was out of favour until the early 1960s and the Arts and Crafts Movement only achieved general acceptance in the late 1970s. It took the 1980s for people to see any virtue in furniture made between the wars and only now is interest turning to post-war furniture. The gap between what is acceptable or not is contracting but the rate is uneven between different groups. The rich, old collector may never move past 1760, most home furnishers now accept Edwardian furniture, but it takes an impoverished couple setting up a new home to look seriously at post-war furniture.

This move forward is a function of money. The cost of an object is driven up so that it appears overpriced by comparison with something made only a few

Plate 16. Not a favourite 'model' for a display cabinet. The rococo decoration is not contorted enough, nor of sufficient quality. It takes up rather a lot of space and the overtones of a reliquary are as offputting as the feet. Not a piece with a huge investment potential.

years later. This syndrome is particularly apparent in furniture made between the years 1790 and 1850. A sideboard of the late eighteenth century may fetch £10,000, one of the 1850s £1,000. Evidence of this move forward comes from Britain's most prestigious antiques event, the Grosvenor House Antiques Fair, held annually in London in June. Since it was founded in the 1930s the date line for furniture was 1830; nothing after that date could be shown, for to the purist it just was not acceptable. In 1983 the date restriction was removed so that furniture up to the First World War could be offered, *but* it had to be of sufficient quality. This reflected the change which had had to be made in the date line for pictures which until 1983 had excluded the French Impressionists.

Quality, therefore, rather than date, is becoming the key to acceptance. Consider Plate 15, a table which is the product of the Victorian rococo revival of the mid-

Plate 19. Again not an appealing 'model' though undoubtedly useful. Probably it was especially designed to give extra desk storage, which it undoubtedly does. The problem is that the eye used to the conventional form rejects the small bookcase.

nineteenth century. The massive hairy paw feet derive from the neo-classical revival of the second decade of the nineteenth century. They have the realistic but oversize quality that one associates with George Smith (see inset). However, in the rococo version they drip with luxuriant fruit and foliage, which in this example support reptilian life — a marvellous rococo conceit. Now, just as in the 1970s, when fine Regency pieces like Plate 1 sent a frisson of forbidden excitement down the spine, so Plate 15 cannot be ignored. In late 1970 it might have been several hundred pounds but today, given a decent provenance and maker's name, it might fetch £10,000 if not more, *simply because of its type*; it is super quality. To hammer home the point, compare it with Plate 16. Not only

Plate 20. A delightful small mid-Victorian pedestal sideboard, useful, decorative and well made. It is the sort of underestimated piece that is likely to move steadily up in value as new collectors, unbiased by anti-Victorian prejudices, come into the market.

is a display cabinet less utilitarian than a dining room table, but within display cabinets it is not a good 'model'. Better are the tall, thin, space-saving ones with plenty of drawer space. The design is not florid enough for good rococo and the execution does not have the workmanship of the table. It made £2,800 in 1989 which, at the time, seemed excessive, but perhaps I am blinkered to its virtues as I was a decade ago to those of Plate 15.

One has to be careful to readjust one's opinions of existing pieces as fashion moves. Consider Figure 901, reproduced in the Regency I price table as 56 (see pages 58 and 59). When the second edition was written the caption stated: 'It really is hard to be charitable about this horrible little table' and we ended up '. . . not only is the top plain but out of proportion to the base and the decoration seems mindless'. The price of £30 — £35 was prefaced by 'Presumably somebody likes it . . .'

That was ten years ago. Over the years it has increased more or less at the average rate. However, we all now respect the value neo-classicism has given to marble tops. So suddenly in the 1988 revision list it moved sharply up to £800 — £1,200 because it was obviously a neo-classical base suitable for holding a new imported marble top and would be snapped up for that purpose. So equipped it might make £2,000 — £3,000, hence the price increase.

When the history of art, fashion and decorators all get together the mixture is potent and secondary names can move up in the wake of genuine discoveries. George Bullock's name has long been underestimated and his work is rightly held in high esteem and makes huge prices. However, one of his associates turns out to be Bridgens, whose name has long been associated with the production of dark carved oak in the neo-Elizabethan style, like the library table in Plate 17 made c.1840, long despised by collectors and exported in container loads to overseas buyers who presumably enjoy dull, carved black oak. Five years ago such a piece would not have been put in a top London auctioneer's main sale, but after the Great Tew Park sale it was and made £4,620 in 1988. Inevitably another appeared but this time failed to make the estimate. The question now arises, has Bridgens been rehabilitated to become an accepted name of the future, a leading designer of Victorian Revival Elizabethan oak, an important figure in the development of British furniture design, or is he just another maker of boring black carved oak? Time will decide, but if he is accepted, it will be by new collectors who see with fresh eyes the beauty of his genius, not by old collectors who have despised his work for decades.

Conventional Images

Because we have conventional ideas of how a piece should look, when something unusual comes along we have to make up our minds if it is a brilliant extension of an old theme or a boring mistake. The former is illustrated by the stool in Plate 18. It was quite brilliant in conception and made a huge appeal to those of us who love fine examples of early walnut. When it came up in July 1988 the auctioneers estimated £2,500 — £3,500, which was clearly inadequate; the pre-sale opinion was £8,000 — £10,000. It in fact cost £24,000 which by comparison with the amount paid for Regency furniture was not expensive.

The secretaire in Plate 19 falls into the second category. Good mahogany secretaires don't have the extra bit just under the bookcase. It might be a practical idea to have an extra space to put papers in, rather like an old type of bureau bookcase/cabinet with a fitted top; indeed, that's what the man who ordered it probably had in mind. But to the collector's eye it just doesn't work on a secretaire, nor is it easy to improve because one needs about one-third to half of the extra bit to include in the top to get the bookcase part in the right proportions.

Plate 21. A mahogany and sycamore bureau from the 1780s, perhaps by a Swedish cabinet maker working in this country. Though useful, it lacks popular recognition and it belongs to no recognisable philosophy of design. The sycamore is a trifle dull too so it loses out on the purely decorative appeal.

That means extending the glass doors, or rather remaking the stiles (the vertical bits) because if you don't the joints will be obvious. That means changing the whole glazing pattern, extending the dividers for the bookshelves to rest on. At auction the piece was bought in against an estimate of £2,000 — £3,000 and a reserve of possibly £1,800. Nobody thought the effort of conversion worth while.

Looking into the Future

When the 1978 edition was published it was suggested that, following the years of high inflation, buyers in the 1980s would become more selective, with the result that the gap in value between high and low quality would increase.

As you will find as you go through this book, this is what has happened and there is no reason why the gap will not continue to grow. There is a great deal of money available to people who understand quality and enough people understand quality to shun what is not good. The result will be that poor quality pieces will compete with modern equivalents, while top quality pieces will move out of the patronising category of 'applied art' allocated to them by art historians and produce the sort of price made by 'fine art', i.e. paintings and sculptures. In 1989 the first piece of English furniture to make more than £1m was sold at auction (ironically it had been altered since made) and there is every reason to expect this figure repeated with increasing regularity in the 1990s.

Between the two extremes there will be some delightful pieces to be found by collectors who learn the subject, take in late periods but, above all, develop an eye for what is a good design. For me the little Victorian pedestal sideboard (Plate 20) is a delight. At 3ft.7ins. it is minute by sideboard standards, the wood is well chosen, the balance between height and width is well conceived. In 1987 it made £825 at auction, in 1989 it is probably worth £1,000 — £1,300; by the early 1990s I see no reason why, in good condition and with a good colour, £3,000 — £4,000 would be unreasonable. Is there any reason, outside historical prejudice, why it should not be more valuable than Plate 21?

Increasingly the auction houses will be the principal source of primary supply and, because auctioneers offer a piece for sale for a very limited period of time and the smaller ones do not have the facility to research, bargains will continue to appear for those who can recognise them.

James Storm regularly contributes articles on the practical aspects of buying antique furniture in Antique Collecting, *the journal of the Antique Collectors' Club.*

Antique Furniture Prices over Twenty Years

by James Storm

Late in 1968 the first edition of *The Price Guide to Antique Furniture* was published. The author, John Andrews, a founder member of the Antique Collectors' Club, came up with the idea that it was possible to predict the prices that antique dealers would ask for the range of antique furniture that could be found in the moderately priced provincial antique shops. Even more revolutionary, the prices would be updated each year so that the book wouldn't go out of date.

Looking back it is hard to recall the novelty of the idea. It was long before Lyle and, later, Miller swept the market with their general price guides and it was open to serious question whether or not one could provide a helpful guide. Two important points emerged from the hours of earnest discussion. Firstly if it was going to be any use to collectors, the illustrations should not include too many 'fancy' high quality pieces and should concentrate on what we could then afford or optimistically hoped we might eventually acquire. This was fortunate because it was only at that level that practicability was possible; once one got into the range of connoisseur items, values became more problematical — the price achieved when two wealthy collectors fight over a unique object is unpredictable and of no relevance to home furnishers. Secondly, if the book was going to be any real use, we would have to put collectors on their guard against alterations, improvements and fakes. It would also be necessary to make aesthetic judgements, to stand up and say that something was lumpy and ugly, or that it had charm. It was obviously going to be a very different book from what was currently available. Books on antique furniture then were full of museum photographs and auctioneers in the late sixties didn't publish highly illustrated catalogues; that came later. It is this practical aspect of the Price Guides which has ensured their popularity with the new generation of antique collectors who realise that anodyne auctioneers' descriptions are useless. You have to have a thorough understanding of what to look for before you can hope to value a piece. The extent to which two apparently similar objects can vary in value is a point consistently underestimated by the novice.

The second edition appeared in 1978 and while the selection was increased from some 370 to a thousand pieces, the criterion for selection remained much the same. The reason for adding a few really fine pieces was that collectors needed to have standards of excellence to enable them to make sound judgements. This has been extended in the third edition as the availability of colour printing has opened the subject of patination and its related colour.

TABLE I
ANTIQUE COLLECTORS' CLUB ANTIQUE FURNITURE INDEX
AS AT FEBRUARY EACH YEAR

YEAR	OAK	WALNUT	EARLY MAHOG.	LATE MAHOG.	REGENCY	VICT.	COUNTRY	AVERAGE
1968	100	100	100	100	100	100	100	100
1969	116	133	119	118	127	117	119	121
1970	120	151	126	125	137	124	126	130
1971	129	137	125	124	135	126	121	128
1972	154	195	143	140	171	170	175	164
1973	251	278	210	171	226	245	254	233
1974	361	352	282	225	273	304	358	308
1975	324	311	260	203	257	297	324	282
1976	333	341	323	252	313	359	385	329
1977	508	409	437	388	454	508	586	470
1978	748	487	576	504	592	685	767	623
1979	870	442	769	578	775	765	844	749
1980	1281	773	985	624	788	879	1084	916
1981	1186	766	985	619	859	926	1064	915
1982	1210	870	1046	723	935	879	1064	961
1983	1197	987	1212	749	958	897	1081	1011
1984	1212	1050	1266	774	1188	945	1144	1083
1985	1379	1198	1631	1112	1249	1201	1381	1307
1986	1595	1557	2174	1185	1535	1389	1886	1617
1987	1676	1628	2405	1375	1850	1569	2072	1797
1988	2093	1924	2809	1725	2267	1898	2489	2172
1989	2437	2014	3265	1799	2535	2244	2853	2449
% Increase over 1988	16%	5%	16%	4%	12%	18%	15%	13%

Every spring the current values of each item illustrated are given in a *Price Revision List* circulated in the form of a small booklet (it costs £2.50 including postage from the Club). This material has been put into the form of an index of eighty pieces of furniture, selected from each of the main divisions of English furniture. The result, as you can see from the tables that follow, is fascinating. Few people can have realised the extent to which the bits and pieces in their houses have gone up in value.

How much has antique furniture increased in price in the last two decades? The answer comes from Table I. If you'd bought an 'average piece' in 1968 for £100, something simple that could be bought in any shop, you would now have an object which would cost you about £2,450 to replace. That is an annual increase of over 100% on the original investment and does a great deal more than compensate for the drop in the value of money. If you go out now and buy a basket of groceries which would have cost you £100 in spring 1968 it will now cost £611.

But of course there is no such thing as an 'average piece' and the table shows how a small representative batch from each type (the make up of which is illustrated in another section) has fared for each of the last twenty years. It is clear that fashion plays a part in the relative increases in price. Take oak as an example. In 1976 at 333 it was only 1% more than the average of 329. Six years later in 1982 it was over 25% ahead but four years later it had dropped back to below average. The oak boom was over. But remember these statistics are based on a batch of quite pleasant but ordinary pieces; had a very good example of oak

TABLE II
COMPARISON OF DIFFERENT FORMS OF INVESTMENT

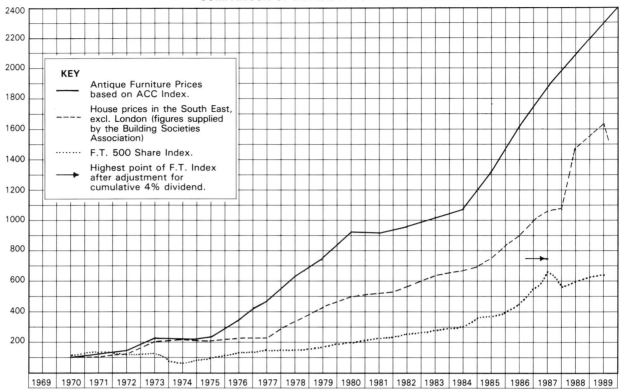

turned up at any time over the period the price would in all probability have been enormous. Good things do well, boom or slump. There has always been plenty of money for quality pieces and enough competition to send the price skywards.

But how good an investment has antique furniture been compared with other forms of investment? Leaving aside the fact that modern furniture loses virtually all its value once it becomes secondhand and therefore there is a negative factor to consider, antique furniture has been a wonderful investment.

Table II makes the obvious comparisons between antique furniture, stocks and shares, and houses in the South East of England. No comment is necessary. Significantly furniture was, and I suggest is, a much safer investment so long as you protect yourself by either knowing what you are buying, or else demanding an invoice which states clearly the date and condition of what you are buying. This gives you reasonable protection in law. No such protection exists on the Stock Exchange. (If your transaction note read 'Slater Walker' or 'London and Counties Securities' you would have ended up with little more than an involuntary investment in scripophily.) Thus armed, the worst that could have happened to you investing in furniture would have been that you'd paid £875 for A, a walnut kneehole desk, which would now be worth £6,000, a rise on the index of only 100 to 686, not much better than the retail price index. More likely you didn't have £875 in 1969, and instead bought something more useful like B which would have set you back an affordable £100 but now would have to be insured for £5,000, a fifty-fold rise.

Next we have to take into account that you might not have wanted to make a twenty year investment. What would have happened if you had wanted to sell

42

A

B

C

during one of the quiet patches, with selling costs of about 15%? It appears that you would have sacrificed no more than a year or two's profit, except in the early 1980s when prices went flat for three years. Then you could have lost even over a four year period but, as the figures show, this was exceptional.

Of course not all antique furniture has changed in value at the same rate. As you will see from Table I, different types of furniture have moved at different rates. Early mahogany and country furniture have performed particularly well. Oak has done better than one might imagine considering two years ago it was seen as being in the doldrums. Walnut appeared to do badly in the early years perhaps because it was relatively expensive, even in the late 1960s, and therefore the increase shows up poorly against the lesser priced pieces that had more room to rise but it came back strongly in the last decade to do only marginally worse than the overall index. The losers have been the late periods except, of course, Regency which has come to the fore, a fact that has been widely publicised. Bear in mind that our Regency selection — indeed, all our selections — being of a modest nature did not have makers' names attached (except of course in a general way such as Chippendale which, used in this sense, means general design and not the maker; to achieve that you need provenance). If they had the index would have shown even more dramatic results.

To sum up, over the years anyone that knew anything about the subject was presented with some wonderful bargains. But a collection put together painstakingly by a knowledgeable collector will show much greater returns than are set out here, probably by a factor of two or three. Exceptional collectors' items too will far outshine the index which, it is worth repeating, is largely for standard objects — or at least they were in the 1960s when we photographed them in the houses of our friends.

Shortage of supply is likely to be a major factor in pushing up prices, not just because people pay more for a piece when it turns up, but because increasingly one has to go to expensive shops as the only source of supply for things that in the 1960s and early 1970s were to be found in trade shops that traditionally only took a small profit margin and could afford to do so because of the volume they handled. All that is gone now. You rarely find a good piece, needing a little work, in a scruffy shop. If you do, the price is likely to be more than the same object in a good shop because the smaller dealer sees good pieces so infrequently he thinks them worth more than they are, especially at the lower end of the scale. This explains why provincial auctioneers often get higher prices than could be achieved in London for second rate objects, and why the large auctioneers are happy to see ordinary furniture sold in their provincial branches rather than incur expensive London overheads.

But to return to the relative increases in value. Another key factor is utility. Kneehole desks are pigs to use, and don't even make good dressing tables. It seems entirely reasonable, therefore, that an expensive walnut one should have performed so badly, and equally reasonable that something as elegant and useful as C, the bergère chair, should come into its rightful place as Regency furniture comes to the fore and William IV comes out of the closet. When the *Price Guide to Antique Furniture* was first published, no dealer outside the West End of London ever spoke of William IV — most of them had never heard of him. Anything made in that period was Regency. Now of course the picture has changed. Bullock, Morant *et al.* are names to be reckoned with. The rise in *their* prices since 1968 outshines everything but like everybody else then, we'd never heard of them either. Early mahogany leapt ahead of walnut in the late 1970s (is there significance in the fact that this has always been an American taste and that the dollar strengthened in the late 1970s?), while oak fell back relative to most other types in the mid-1980s. There are so many mysteries and interpretations. Why for example has late mahogany furniture fallen behind the rest. It was meant to be so much in fashion? Could it be that 'fashion' is in fact a euphemism for what can be bought relatively cheaply by the home furnishers, and that the

TABLE III
ANNUAL % CHANGES IN FURNITURE PRICES AND BUSINESS OPTIMISM

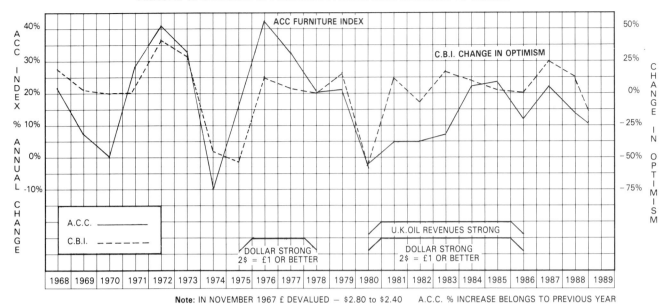

Note: IN NOVEMBER 1967 £ DEVALUED — $2.80 to $2.40   A.C.C. % INCREASE BELONGS TO PREVIOUS YEAR

equivalent of the person who bought inexpensive late mahogany and Victorian in the early 1970s now can't afford it, and buys stripped pine instead?

One of the mysteries which surround the ACC furniture index is the erratic way in which it moves forward. It rushes ahead for a cycle of three to five years then rests for a short while before charging on again as you can see in the graph which shows the annual percentage change, Table III. It also clearly illustrates just how violent some of these increases are. In the period of twenty years under review exactly half have shown increases of 20% or more.

TABLE IV Table of Events

1971/72	The Barber Boom
1973	Miners' strike leading to three-day week
1974	Harold Wilson won the February election and attempted to spend his way out of depression.
1975	Inflation 25%
1976	Inflation 16%
	By the autumn IMF team arrived and loans were made in return for cuts in public spending.
1977	Dollar strong
	Restriction on level of bank loans
1978	Iranian revolution. Second oil price shock.
1978/79	Winter of discontent
1979	May — Mrs Thatcher elected
	June — Oil at $34.40 p.b; the price had nearly trebled in nine months
1980	U.K. oil revenues start to flow in bulk.
1982	Falklands War
1983	Mrs Thatcher elected for second term
1987	Mrs Thatcher elected for third term

I have puzzled over these changes. Gold doesn't follow the same pattern and although there are some similarities with movement in the Stock Exchange, the comparison is not close. The first hints came when I re-read the economic history of the last two decades. The extraordinary rise in the 1971-73 period clearly equated to Anthony Barber's race for prosperity when the money supply (M3) increased by 28% a year for two years, and the new lending by banks to the private sector was:

1970	£1,320M
1971	£1,860M
1972	£6,430M
1973	£6,830M

It ended in tears. The property boom and threats of inflation caused the bank to tighten the supply of money, and this was followed by the secondary banking crisis of late 1973 when London and County Securities went under, and even the major clearing banks were the subject of rumours. To add to our problems at that time oil started to rise in price:

early 1973	$2.59 per barrel
October 1973	$5.11 per barrel
by early 1974	$11.65 per barrel

Having realised this relationship, it was an obvious move to see if there was any connection between the percentage changes and the Confederation of British Industry's survey of the optimism of British businessmen. It corresponded closely. The sets of figures are shown together as Table III.

Collectors with long memories will need little reminding of the events which followed (see Table IV) and which are reflected in the movement on the graph.

The places where the two graph lines part are in 1969 after Roy Jenkins' deflationary budget in March 1968; and in 1976 and 1977 when the dollar was strong for the first time and a lot of American buying occurred; and again in the 1980-1984 period after the March 1981 budget which has been described as the most stringent of any post-war budget when in eighteen months manufacturing output dropped a record 17.5%. At that time the dollar was strong.

The closeness of the two sets of figures is quite uncanny. It really looks as though people buy furniture — and hence push up the price — when they feel optimistic, and refrain when times are hard. Private collectors still buy British furniture; what they buy depends on their taste and their pocket. The people who bought expensive antique furniture in 1968 may not be the same people or even the same type of people as those buying furniture now, but others have come along who have the money and good sense to invest in furniture that appears to have lasting appeal.

Oak

OAK PERIOD		1968	1969	1970	1971	19
1. Simple Chair Late 17C	£	28	28	35	40	
(No. 109)	Index	100	100	125	143	1
2. Wainscot Chair Late 17C	£	110	125	125	125	2
(No. 105)	Index	100	114	114	114	2
3. Court Cupboard Late Mid 17C	£	175	225	200	200	2
(No. 436)	Index	100	129	114	114	1
4. Coffer Late 17C	£	40	52	55	75	
(No. 299)	Index	100	130	138	188	1
5. Dining Table Late 17C	£	110	125	150	175	2
(No. 730)	Index	100	114	136	159	2
6. Dresser Late 17C	£	375	425	450	450	5
(No. 466)	Index	100	113	120	120	1
7. Chest of Drawers Late 17C	£	95	100	105	105	1
(No. 318)	Index	100	105	111	111	1
8. Side Table Early 18C	£	62	70	75	115	1
(No. 839)	Index	100	113	121	185	2
TOTAL OAK	£	995	1,150	1,195	1,285	1,5
Group Index	Index	100	115	122	142	1
Group Ave. Value (8 items)	£	124.4	143.8	149	161	192
OAK INDEX		100	116	120	129	1
Oak % change			16%	4%	8%	2(

The numbers in brackets refer to illustrations in the book

1   2

4

3   5

1973	1974	1975	1976	1977	1978	1979	1980	1981	1982	1983	1984	1985	1986	1987	1988	1989	No.
80	90	85	85	105	150	213	250	250	240	260	260	300	350	400	400	400	1.
286	**321**	**304**	**304**	**375**	**536**	**761**	**893**	**893**	**857**	**929**	**929**	**1,071**	**1,250**	**1,429**	**1,429**	**1,429**	
325	700	600	600	800	1,150	1,250	1,400	1,200	1,200	1,200	1,200	1,400	1,750	2,250	3,500	5,000	2.
295	**636**	**545**	**545**	**727**	**1,045**	**1,136**	**1,273**	**1,091**	**1,091**	**1,091**	**1,091**	**1,273**	**1,591**	**2,045**	**3,182**	**4,545**	
400	525	475	525	850	1,000	1,375	2,500	2,000	1,875	1,875	1,875	1,875	1,875	1,875	2,500	2,500	3.
229	**300**	**271**	**300**	**486**	**571**	**786**	**1,429**	**1,143**	**1,071**	**1,071**	**1,071**	**1,071**	**1,071**	**1,071**	**1,429**	**1,429**	
130	250	220	215	325	450	475	650	500	500	500	500	700	700	800	1,500	1,600	4.
325	**625**	**550**	**538**	**813**	**1,125**	**1,188**	**1,625**	**1,250**	**1,250**	**1,250**	**1,250**	**1,750**	**1,750**	**2,000**	**3,750**	**4,000**	
400	475	450	525	700	1,750	1,750	2,250	2,350	2,750	2,600	2,600	3,000	3,000	3,000	3,500	4,000	5.
364	**432**	**409**	**477**	**636**	**1,591**	**1,591**	**2,045**	**2,136**	**2,500**	**2,364**	**2,364**	**2,727**	**2,727**	**2,727**	**3,182**	**3,636**	
800	1,000	900	800	1,400	1,800	2,150	4,250	4,000	4,000	4,000	4,000	4,750	6,250	6,250	7,000	8,000	6.
213	**267**	**240**	**213**	**373**	**480**	**573**	**1,133**	**1,067**	**1,067**	**1,067**	**1,067**	**1,267**	**1,667**	**1,667**	**1,867**	**2,133**	
160	250	215	237	400	540	750	700	700	625	625	725	700	700	700	825	1,000	7.
168	**263**	**226**	**249**	**421**	**568**	**789**	**737**	**737**	**658**	**658**	**763**	**737**	**737**	**736.8**	**868.4**	**1,053**	
200	300	275	325	475	600	700	750	800	850	850	900	1,000	1,250	1,400	1,600	1,750	8.
323	**484**	**444**	**524**	**766**	**968**	**1,129**	**1,210**	**1,290**	**1,371**	**1,371**	**1,452**	**1,613**	**2,016**	**2,258**	**2,581**	**2,823**	
495	**3,590**	**3,220**	**3,312**	**5,055**	**7,440**	**8,663**	**12,750**	**11,800**	**12,040**	**11,910**	**12,060**	**13,725**	**15,875**	**16,675**	**20,825**	**24,250**	
275	**416**	**374**	**394**	**575**	**861**	**994**	**1,293**	**1,201**	**1,233**	**1,225**	**1,248**	**1,439**	**1,601**	**1,742**	**2,286**	**2,631**	
1.9	448.8	402.5	414	631.9	930	1,083	1,594	1,475	1,505	1,489	1,508	1,716	1,984	2084.4	2603.1	3,031	
251	**361**	**324**	**333**	**508**	**748**	**870**	**1,281**	**1,186**	**1,210**	**1,197**	**1,212**	**1,379**	**1,595**	**1,676**	**2,093**	**2,437**	
2%	44%	-10%	3%	53%	47%	16%	47%	-7%	2%	-1%	1%	14%	16%	5%	25%	16%	

6

7

8

Walnut

9

10

11

		1968	1969	1970	1971	1
WALNUT						
9. Dining Chair	£	35	35	45	45	
(No. 122)	**Index**	**100**	**100**	**129**	**129**	
10. Wing Chair	£	250	300	300	338	
(No. 260)	**Index**	**100**	**120**	**120**	**135**	
11. Card Table	£	700	1,250	1,250	1,050	1,
(No. 696)	**Index**	**100**	**179**	**179**	**150**	
12. Dressing Table	£	350	375	450	450	
(No. 824)	**Index**	**100**	**107**	**129**	**129**	
13. Tripod Table	£	105	125	150	150	
(No. 888)	**Index**	**100**	**119**	**143**	**143**	
14. Chest of Drawers	£	200	250	300	300	
(No. 332)	**Index**	**100**	**125**	**150**	**150**	
15. Chest on Chest	£	300	375	425	350	
(No. 357)	**Index**	**100**	**125**	**142**	**117**	
16. Bureau	£	450	575	600	525	
(No. 36)	**Index**	**100**	**128**	**133**	**117**	
17. Fall Front Secretaire	£	350	450	550	450	
(No. 600)	**Index**	**100**	**129**	**157**	**129**	
18. Bureau Bookcase	£	1,250	1,750	2,250	2,250	3,
(No. 60)	**Index**	**100**	**140**	**180**	**180**	
19. Kneehole Desk	£	875	1,000	1,000	750	1,0
(No. 525)	**Index**	**100**	**114**	**114**	**86**	
TOTAL WALNUT		4,865	6,485	7,320	6,658	9,
Group Index	**Index**	**100**	**126**	**143**	**133**	
Group Ave. Value (11 items)	£	442.3	589.5	665	605	86
WALNUT INDEX		**100**	**133**	**151**	**137**	
Walnut % change			33%	13%	-9%	4

The numbers in brackets refer to illustrations in the book

12   13   14   15

973	1974	1975	1976	1977	1978	1979	1980	1981	1982	1983	1984	1985	1986	1987	1988	1989	
110	110	110	105	140	160	225	300	300	320	350	375	475	600	675	900	900	9.
314	314	314	300	400	457	643	857	857	914	1,000	1,071	1,357	1,714	1,929	2,571	2,571	
550	725	675	750	1,025	1,250	2,500	2,750	2,750	2,625	2,625	2,625	3,000	3,250	3,500	3,500	4,000	10.
220	290	270	300	410	500	1,000	1,100	1,100	1,050	1,050	1,050	1,200	1,300	1,400	1,400	1,600	
000	2,500	2,200	2,200	2,500	3,000	2,850	3,000	3,000	3,500	3,375	4,000	5,000	9,000	9,000	16,000	16,000	11.
286	357	314	314	357	429	407	429	429	500	482	571	714	1,286	1,286	2,286	2,286	
750	875	725	900	1,000	1,400	1,900	2,500	2,500	2,500	2,500	2,750	3,250	4,250	4,750	5,000	6,000	12.
214	250	207	257	286	400	543	714	714	714	714	786	929	1,214	1,357	1,429	1,714	
260	375	360	550	575	700	700	1,000	1,000	1,050	1,050	1,200	1,400	1,600	1,750	2,125	2,500	13.
248	357	343	524	548	667	667	952	952	1,000	1,000	1,143	1,333	1,524	1,667	2,024	2,381	
400	525	425	450	750	875	1,000	1,300	1,300	1,300	1,350	1,750	2,125	2,750	3,500	5,000	5,000	14.
200	263	213	225	375	438	500	650	650	650	675	875	1,063	1,375	1,750	2,500	2,500	
650	800	725	975	1,500	2,000	2,900	3,750	4,000	4,500	4,500	4,500	6,000	6,000	7,000	8,000	8,000	15.
217	267	242	325	500	667	967	1,250	1,333	1,500	1,500	1,500	2,000	2,000	2,333	2,667	2,667	
850	975	875	1,050	1,400	1,800	2,900	3,500	3,875	5,500	6,250	6,250	7,000	8,750	9,500	9,500	12,000	16.
189	217	194	233	311	400	644	778	861	1,222	1,389	1,389	1,556	1,944	2,111	2,111	2,667	
700	900	875	1,350	1,500	1,750	2,500	3,000	3,500	4,000	4,000	5,000	6,000	6,000	6,000	6,000	6,000	17.
200	257	250	386	429	500	714	857	1,000	1,143	1,143	1,429	1,714	1,714	1,714	1,714	1,714	
000	8,000	7,000	7,000	8,000	9,000	10,500	13,000	11,500	14,000	19,000	19,000	19,000	27,500	27,500	31,500	31,500	18.
480	640	560	560	640	720	840	1,040	920	1,120	1,520	1,520	1,520	2,200	2,200	2,520	2,520	
250	1,350	1,150	1,250	1,500	1,750	3,250	3,500	3,500	3,000	3,000	3,625	5,000	6,000	6,000	6,000	6,000	19.
143	154	131	143	171	200	371	400	400	343	343	414	571	686	685.7	685.7	686	
520	17,135	15,120	16,580	19,890	23,685	31,225	37,600	37,225	42,295	48,000	51,075	58,250	75,700	79,175	93,525	97,900	
246	306	276	324	402	489	663	821	838	923	983	1,068	1,269	1,542	1,676	1,992	2,119	
229	1,558	1,375	1,507	1,808	2,153	2,839	3,418	3,384	3,845	4,364	4,643	5,295	6,882	7197.7	8502.3	8,900	
278	352	311	341	409	487	642	773	766	870	987	1,050	1,198	1,557	1,628	1,924	2,014	
3%	27%	-12%	10%	20%	19%	32%	20%	-1%	14%	13%	6%	14%	30%	5%	18%	5%	

6

17

18

19

Early Mahogany

		1968	1969	1970	1971	197
EARLY MAHOGANY						
20. Dining Chair c.1735	£	55	70	100	100	11
(No. 129)	Index	100	127	182	182	20
21. Dining Table c.1740	£	100	200	225	225	30
(No. 739)	Index	100	200	225	225	30
22. Card Table c.1745	£	200	212	212	212	25
(No. 699)	Index	100	80.9	81	81	95
23. Tripod Table c.1745	£	60	60	60	60	8
(No. 891)	Index	100	100	100	100	13
24. Bachelor Chest c.1745	£	500	525	525	525	52
(No. 354)	Index	100	105	105	105	10
25. Bureau c.1745	£	125	160	160	163	17
(No. 47)	Index	100	128	128	130	14
26. Bureau Bookcase c.1750	£	460	550	600	600	70
(No. 65)	Index	100	120	130	130	15
27. Corner Cupboard c.1750	£	50	70	70	70	8
(No. 419)	Index	100	140	140	140	17
28. Night Table c.1760	£	65	70	70	53	7
(No. 797)	Index	100	108	108	82	11
TOTAL EARLY MAHOGANY	£	1,615	1,917	2,022	2,008	2.30
Group Index	Index	100	123	133	131	15
Group Ave. Value (9 items)	£	179.4	213	225	223	255
EARLY MAHOGANY INDEX		100	119	126	125	14
Early Mahogany % change			19%	5%	-1%	15

The numbers in brackets refer to illustrations in the book

20

21

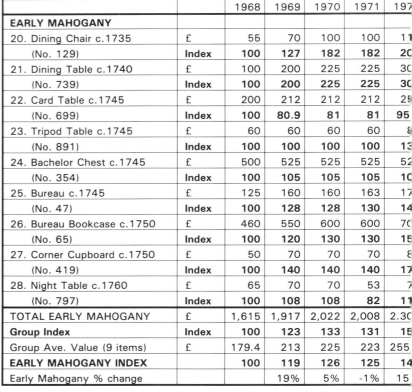

23

22

24

973	1974	1975	1976	1977	1978	1979	1980	1981	1982	1983	1984	1985	1986	1987	1988	1989	No.
275	300	300	325	475	325	325	400	425	625	725	725	1,000	1,150	1,300	1,600	1,750	20.
500	545	545	591	864	591	591	727	773	1,136	1,318	1,318	1,818	2,091	2,364	2,909	3,182	
350	400	450	625	675	850	1,250	1,750	2,000	2,200	2,050	2,050	2,600	3,125	3,500	5,000	5,000	21.
350	400	450	625	675	850	1,250	1,750	2,000	2,200	2,050	2,050	2,600	3,125	3,500	5,000	5,000	
350	400	350	550	675	800	800	1,500	1,500	1,650	1,650	2,375	3,500	4,500	4,500	5,500	5,500	22.
134	153	134	210	258	305	305	573	573	630	630	906	1,336	1,718	1,718	2,099	2,099	
100	115	100	150	238	400	475	625	800	825	825	900	1,050	1,750	1,875	2,500	3,500	23.
167	192	167	250	397	667	792	1,042	1,333	1,375	1,375	1,500	1,750	2,917	3,125	4,167	5,833	
850	1,250	1,050	1,250	1,750	2,000	2,050	4,000	4,000	3,500	3,500	3,500	5,250	8,000	9,000	9,000	12,000	24.
170	250	210	250	350	400	410	800	800	700	700	700	1,050	1,600	1,800	1,800	2,400	
350	500	475	525	675	800	1,800	1,800	1,850	2,500	2,500	2,500	3,000	4,250	5,000	5,000	6,000	25.
280	400	380	420	540	640	1,440	1,440	1,480	2,000	2,000	2,000	2,400	3,400	4,000	4,000	4,800	
900	1,350	1,250	1,500	2,100	3,500	5,000	5,000	4,500	4,750	7,500	7,500	8,750	11,000	12,000	14,000	16,000	26.
196	293	272	326	457	761	1,087	1,087	978	1,033	1,630	1,630	1,902	2,391	2,609	3,043	3,478	
125	125	120	150	250	300	350	425	425	375	375	375	475	600	700	1,600	1,600	27.
250	250	240	300	500	600	700	850	850	750	750	750	950	1,200	1,400	3,200	3,200	
80	105	95	130	200	300	338	375	375	425	400	475	650	650	875	1,050	1,250	28.
123	162	146	200	308	462	520	577	577	654	615	731	1,000	1,000	1,346	1,615	1,923	
380	4,545	4,190	5,205	7,038	9,275	12,388	15,875	15,875	16,850	19,525	20,400	26,275	35,025	38,750	45,250	52,600	
241	294	283	352	483	586	788	983	1,040	1,164	1,230	1,287	1,645	2,160	2,429	3,093	3,546	
'5.6	505	465.6	578.3	782	1,031	1,376	1,764	1,764	1,872	2,169	2,267	2,919	3,892	4305.6	5027.8	5,844	
210	282	260	323	437	576	769	985	985	1,046	1,212	1,266	1,631	2,174	2,405	2,809	3,265	
7%	34%	-8%	24%	35%	32%	34%	28%	0%	6%	16%	4%	29%	33%	11%	17%	16%	

26

27

28

Late Mahogany I

29

30

LATE MAHOGANY		1968	1969	1970	1971	19
29. Chippendale Dining Chair	£	100	115	115	115	1
(No. 147)	**Index**	**100**	**115**	**115**	**115**	**1**
30. Hepplewhite Chair	£	80	90	90	90	
(No. 157)	**Index**	**100**	**113**	**113**	**113**	**1**
31. Adam Armchair	£	400	450	450	450	5
(No. 279)	**Index**	**100**	**113**	**113**	**113**	**1**
32. Pedestal Dining Table	£	475	675	675	675	7
(No. 759)	**Index**	**100**	**142**	**142**	**142**	**1**
33. Card Table	£	160	175	200	175	2
(No. 707)	**Index**	**100**	**109**	**125**	**109**	**1**
34. Satinwood Card Table	£	180	200	225	200	3
(No. 714)	**Index**	**100**	**111**	**125**	**111**	**1**
35. Dressing Table	£	175	200	225	225	3
(No. 516)	**Index**	**100**	**114**	**129**	**129**	**1**
36. Pembroke Table	£	100	125	145	145	1
(No. 812)	**Index**	**100**	**125**	**145**	**145**	**1**
37. Sofa Table	£	475	525	575	600	8
(No. 864)	**Index**	**100**	**111**	**121**	**126**	**1**
38. Dumb Waiter	£	105	140	105	160	1
(No. 539)	**Index**	**100**	**133**	**100**	**152**	**1**

The numbers in brackets refer to illustrations in the book

32

34

31

33

35

1973	1974	1975	1976	1977	1978	1979	1980	1981	1982	1983	1984	1985	1986	1987	1988	1989	No.
150	175	175	225	300	425	500	500	600	700	700	700	875	1,200	1,500	1,500	1,500	29.
150	175	175	225	300	425	500	500	600	700	700	700	875	1,200	1,500	1,500	1,500	
110	110	110	110	135	175	250	350	275	300	400	400	575	700	800	1,350	1,350	30.
138	138	138	138	169	219	313	438	344	375	500	500	719	875	1,000	1,688	1,688	
550	750	700	800	1,200	1,500	1,750	1,750	1,750	2,125	2,500	2,500	3,000	3,000	4,500	4,500	4,500	31.
138	188	175	200	300	375	438	438	438	531	625	625	750	750	1,125	1,125	1,125	
900	1,050	1,000	1,200	1,700	2,500	3,500	4,250	4,750	5,250	6,000	5,500	9,750	9,750	12,000	17,500	17,500	32.
189	221	211	253	358	526	737	895	1,000	1,105	1,263	1,158	2,053	2,053	2,526	3,684	3,684	
300	375	338	500	525	700	750	825	825	950	950	950	1,200	1,400	1,600	1,750	2,250	33.
188	234	211	313	328	438	469	516	516	594	594	594	750	875	1,000	1,094	1,406	
400	450	400	575	675	800	750	725	775	825	825	825	1,025	1,150	1,300	1,750	1,750	34.
222	250	222	319	375	444	417	403	431	458	458	458	569	639	722.2	972.2	972	
400	450	385	425	525	725	725	750	775	800	875	1,050	1,750	1,750	2,500	3,000	3,000	35.
229	257	220	243	300	414	414	429	443	457	500	600	1,000	1,000	1,429	1,714	1,714	
225	300	275	350	475	525	600	550	550	550	800	800	1,350	1,500	1,600	1,750	1,750	36.
225	300	275	350	475	525	600	550	550	550	800	800	1,350	1,500	1,600	1,750	1,750	
000	1,200	1,000	1,100	2,500	3,500	5,250	5,250	4,500	8,000	8,000	8,000	13,000	13,000	15,000	15,000	16,000	37.
211	253	211	232	526	737	1,105	1,105	947	1,684	1,684	1,684	2,737	2,737	3,158	3,158	3,368	
225	300	270	375	575	800	850	800	825	900	875	1,125	1,200	1,400	1,750	2,000	2,000	38.
214	286	257	357	548	762	810	762	786	857	833	1,071	1,143	1,333	1,667	1,905	1,905	

36

37

38

39

40

Late Mahogany II

39. Chest of Drawers	£	75	90	90	70	
(No. 386)	Index	100	120	120	93	1
40. Serpentine Chest	£	525	625	625	625	6
(No. 370)	Index	100	119	119	119	1
41. Chest on Chest	£	225	225	225	180	2
(No. 358)	Index	100	100	100	80	1
42. Wardrobe	£	175	225	275	225	2
(No. 408)	Index	100	129	157	129	1
43. Bureau	£	100	125	125	145	1
(No. 49)	Index	100	125	125	145	1
44. Bureau Bookcase	£	1,750	2,000	2,250	2,250	2,2
(No. 70)	Index	100	114	129	129	1
45. Sideboard	£	550	675	700	700	8
(No. 628)	Index	100	123	127	127	1
46. Corner Cupboard	£	50	55	55	55	
(No. 422)	Index	100	110	110	110	1
TOTAL LATE MAHOGANY	£	5,700	6,715	7,150	7,085	7,9
Group Index	Index	100	118	123	121	1
Group Ave. Value (18 items)	£	316.7	373.1	397	394	442
LATE MAHOGANY INDEX		100	118	125	124	1
Late Mahogany % change			18%	6%	-1%	12

The numbers in brackets refer to illustrations in the book

41

42

43

140	175	155	185	300	375	375	500	500	475	475	550	675	750	950	1,400	1,600	39.
187	**269**	**238**	**247**	**400**	**577**	**577**	**769**	**667**	**633**	**731**	**846**	**900**	**1,154**	**1,462**	**2,154**	**2,462**	
850	1,000	850	900	1,300	1,500	2,150	2,500	2,600	2,600	2,600	2,600	4,750	6,000	6,000	7,250	7,250	- 40.
162	**190**	**162**	**171**	**248**	**286**	**410**	**476**	**495**	**495**	**495**	**495**	**905**	**1,143**	**1,143**	**1,381**	**1,381**	
325	500	475	600	1,000	1,500	2,250	2,500	2,850	3,000	3,000	3,000	3,500	4,250	5,500	8,000	8,000	41.
144	**222**	**211**	**267**	**444**	**667**	**1,000**	**1,111**	**1,267**	**1,333**	**1,333**	**1,333**	**1,556**	**1,889**	**2,444**	**3,556**	**3,556**	
275	350	350	375	475	550	950	1,050	1,050	1,050	1,050	1,050	1,500	1,750	2,125	3,500	3,500	42.
157	**200**	**200**	**214**	**271**	**314**	**543**	**600**	**600**	**600**	**600**	**600**	**857**	**1,000**	**1,214**	**2,000**	**2,000**	
275	315	300	425	625	850	1,100	1,250	1,100	1,200	1,300	1,550	1,650	2,150	2,375	3,000	3,000	43.
275	315	300	425	625	850	1,100	1,250	1,100	1,200	1,300	1,550	1,650	2,150	2,375	3,000	3,000	
,500	4,000	3,600	5,000	8,000	10,000	8,000	8,000	7,000	8,000	8,000	8,000	9,000	9,000	9,000	12,500	14,000	44.
143	**229**	**206**	**286**	**457**	**571**	**457**	**457**	**400**	**457**	**457**	**457**	**514**	**514**	**514.3**	**714.3**	**800**	
,000	1,200	1,100	1,100	1,600	2,000	2,850	3,500	4,000	4,000	3,850	5,000	8,000	8,000	9,000	11,500	12,500	45.
182	**218**	**200**	**200**	**291**	**364**	**518**	**636**	**727**	**727**	**700**	**909**	**1,455**	**1,455**	**1,636**	**2,091**	**2,273**	
95	110	100	125	200	300	350	500	550	500	500	500	600	800	900	1,100	1,100	46.
190	**220**	**200**	**250**	**400**	**600**	**700**	**1,000**	**1,100**	**1,000**	**1,000**	**1,000**	**1,200**	**1,600**	**1,800**	**2,200**	**2,200**	
720	12,810	11,583	14,370	22,110	28,725	32,950	35,550	35,275	41,225	42,700	44,100	63,400	67,550	78,400	98,350	102,550	
186	**231**	**212**	**260**	**379**	**505**	**617**	**685**	**689**	**764**	**810**	**855**	**1,166**	**1,326**	**1,573**	**1,983**	**2,044**	
540	711.7	643.5	798.3	1,228	1,596	1,831	1,975	1,960	2,290	2,372	2,450	3,522	3,753	4355.6	5463.9	5,697	
171	**225**	**203**	**252**	**388**	**504**	**578**	**624**	**619**	**723**	**749**	**774**	**1,112**	**1,185**	**1,375**	**1,725**	**1,799**	
22%	32%	-10%	24%	54%	30%	15%	8%	-1%	17%	4%	3%	44%	7%	16%	25%	4%	

44

45

46

Regency I

		1968	1969	1970	1971	19
REGENCY						
47. Armchair	£	60	70	70	70	
(No. 173)	Index	100	117	117	117	1
48. Bergère Chair	£	30	35	35	40	
(No. 286)	Index	100	117	117	133	1
49. Breakfast Table	£	100	120	140	160	2
(No. 771)	Index	100	120	140	160	2
50. Circular Table	£	50	60	67	68	
(No. 782)	Index	100	120	134	136	1
51. Card Table	£	212	240	275	275	4
(No. 721)	Index	100	113	130	130	1
52. Sofa Table	£	325	375	450	350	5
(No. 869)	Index	100	177	212	165	2
53. Sofa Table	£	250	275	315	315	3
(No. 880)	Index	100	110	126	126	1
54. Library Table	£	325	500	500	525	5
(No. 938)	Index	100	154	154	162	1
55. Writing Table	£	80	90	105	105	1
(No. 928)	Index	100	113	131	131	1
56. Tripod Table	£	9	12	10	10	1
(No. 907)	Index	100	133	111	111	1

The numbers in brackets refer to illustrations in the book

47

48

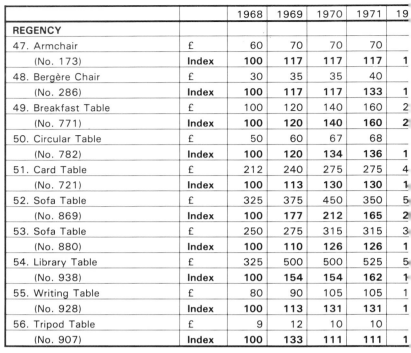

49

50

51

1973	1974	1975	1976	1977	1978	1979	1980	1981	1982	1983	1984	1985	1986	1987	1988	1989	No.
105	120	105	105	160	200	250	300	250	250	260	260	300	425	475	600	600	47.
175	200	175	175	267	333	417	500	417	417	433	433	500	708	791.7	1,000	1,000	
70	75	75	100	170	240	450	475	525	500	500	650	725	1,200	1,400	2,150	2,375	48.
233	250	250	333	567	800	1,500	1,583	1,750	1,667	1,667	2,167	2,417	4,000	4,667	7,167	7,917	
250	325	335	425	575	775	775	850	850	950	950	1,050	2,500	3,000	3,500	3,500	4,250	49.
250	325	335	425	575	775	775	850	850	950	950	1,050	2,500	3,000	3,500	3,500	4,250	
145	175	230	400	500	600	550	388	388	525	525	525	575	575	800	1,050	1,250	50.
290	350	460	800	1,000	1,200	1,100	776	776	1,050	1,050	1,050	1,150	1,150	1,600	2,100	2,500	
500	575	525	700	1,000	1,200	1,950	850	850	950	950	950	1,250	1,600	1,750	2,500	2,500	51.
236	271	248	330	472	566	920	401	401	448	448	448	590	755	825.5	1,179	1,179	
700	850	800	900	1,500	2,500	3,500	3,500	3,000	3,000	3,000	3,000	3,500	3,500	4,500	5,000	5,000	52.
330	401	377	277	708	1,179	1,651	1,651	1,415	1,415	1,415	1,415	1,651	1,651	2,123	2,358	2,358	
450	550	500	700	900	1,100	1.950	1,800	2,700	2,500	2,500	2,500	2,875	3,250	4,250	4,500	4,500	53.
180	220	200	280	360	440	780	720	1,080	1,000	1,000	1,000	1,150	1,300	1,700	1,800	1,800	
650	850	800	900	1,100	1,500	1,650	1,800	2,400	3,000	3,000	3,000	3,500	4,000	4,500	8,500	7,500	54.
200	262	246	277	338	462	508	554	738	923	923	923	1,077	1,231	1,385	2,615	2,308	
150	175	150	213	375	500	900	1,400	1,700	1,650	1,600	1,700	2,150	3,000	4,000	5,000	7,000	55.
188	219	188	266	469	625	1,125	1,750	2,125	2,063	2,000	2,125	2,688	3,750	5,000	6,250	8,750	
20	30	23	30	38	50	50	50	50	50	50	50	63	80	100	175	175	56.
222	333	256	333	422	556	556	556	556	556	556	556	700	889	1,111	1,944	1,944	

52

53

54

55

56

Regency II

57. Chest	£	60	65	75	63	
(No. 379)	**Index**	**100**	**108**	**125**	**105**	
58. Military Chest	£	90	110	130	130	
(No. 392)	**Index**	**100**	**122**	**144**	**144**	
59. Bureau	£	70	90	90	90	
(No. 53)	**Index**	**100**	**129**	**129**	**129**	
60. Davenport	£	115	175	175	175	
(No. 445)	**Index**	**100**	**152**	**152**	**152**	
61. Sideboard	£	125	150	175	175	
(No. 635)	**Index**	**100**	**120**	**140**	**140**	
62. Chiffonier	£	65	138	138	165	
(No. 399)	**Index**	**100**	**212**	**110**	**132**	
63. Work Table	£	125	165	90	88	
(No. 910)	**Index**	**100**	**132**	**72**	**70**	
64. Canterbury	£	115	138	175	175	
(No. 91)	**Index**	**100**	**120**	**152**	**152**	
65. Teapoy	£	50	65	70	70	
(No. 969)	**Index**	**100**	**130**	**140**	**140**	
TOTAL REGENCY	£	2,256	2,873	3,085	3,049	3,8
Group Index	Index	**100**	**132**	**133**	**133**	
Group Ave. Value (19 items)	£	118.7	151.2	162	160	20
REGENCY INDEX		**100**	**127**	**137**	**135**	
Regency % change			27%	7%	-1%	2

The numbers in brackets refer to illustrations in the book

57

58

61

60

59

85	100	95	125	238	275	275	388	400	350	350	350	400	475	475	625	725	57.
142	**167**	**158**	**208**	**397**	**458**	**458**	**647**	**667**	**583**	**583**	**583**	**667**	**792**	**791.7**	**1,042**	**1,208**	
250	300	300	375	525	650	750	800	875	575	900	900	1,200	1,350	1,600	1,750	1,750	58.
278	**333**	**333**	**417**	**583**	**722**	**833**	**889**	**972**	**639**	**1,000**	**1,000**	**1,333**	**1,500**	**1,778**	**1,944**	**1,944**	
140	145	140	200	400	475	650	650	700	625	675	750	800	1,000	1,000	1,250	1,250	59.
200	**207**	**200**	**286**	**571**	**679**	**929**	**929**	**1,000**	**893**	**964**	**1,071**	**1,143**	**1,429**	**1,429**	**1,786**	**1,786**	
500	600	550	500	625	725	675	1,000	1,000	2,000	2,500	2,500	3,000	5,000	5,000	6,250	7,000	60.
435	**522**	**478**	**435**	**543**	**630**	**587**	**870**	**870**	**1,739**	**2,174**	**2,174**	**2,609**	**4,348**	**4,348**	**5,435**	**6,087**	
300	350	325	425	600	800	950	750	850	850	850	850	1,050	1,200	2,125	3,000	3,500	61.
240	**280**	**260**	**340**	**480**	**640**	**760**	**600**	**680**	**680**	**680**	**680**	**840**	**960**	**1,700**	**2,400**	**2,800**	
250	325	288	300	425	500	850	1,250	1,250	1,250	1,250	1,550	2,000	2,125	2,500	3,000	5,000	62.
200	**260**	**230**	**240**	**340**	**400**	**680**	**1,000**	**1,000**	**1,000**	**1,000**	**1,240**	**1,600**	**1,700**	**2,000**	**2,400**	**4,000**	
175	195	180	175	350	425	350	350	350	800	425	475	475	625	750	1,050	1,200	63.
140	**156**	**144**	**140**	**280**	**340**	**280**	**280**	**280**	**640**	**340**	**380**	**380**	**500**	**600**	**840**	**960**	
225	275	240	270	400	425	425	675	750	750	800	950	1,250	1,550	2,250	2,500	3,000	64.
196	**239**	**209**	**235**	**348**	**370**	**370**	**587**	**652**	**652**	**696**	**826**	**1,087**	**1,348**	**1,957**	**2,174**	**2,609**	
125	150	140	210	350	425	525	500	500	525	525	525	575	675	750	1,000	1,150	65.
250	**300**	**280**	**420**	**700**	**850**	**1,050**	**1,000**	**1,000**	**1,050**	**1,050**	**1,050**	**1,150**	**1,350**	**1,500**	**2,000**	**2,300**	
090	6,165	5,801	7,053	10,231	13,365	17,475	17,776	19,388	21,100	21,610	26,810	28,188	34,630	41,725	53,400	59,725	
362	**418**	**265**	**327**	**496**	**633**	**804**	**850**	**907**	**1,186**	**1,211**	**1,479**	**1,328**	**1,703**	**2,042**	**2,628**	**3,037**	
7.9	324.5	305.3	371.2	538.5	703.4	919.7	935.6	1,020	1,111	1,137	1,411	1,484	1,823	2196.1	2810.5	3,143	
226	**273**	**257**	**313**	**454**	**592**	**775**	**788**	**859**	**935**	**958**	**1,188**	**1,249**	**1,535**	**1,850**	**2,267**	**2,535**	
2%	21%	-6%	22%	45%	31%	31%	2%	9%	9%	2%	24%	5%	23%	20%	23%	12%	

64

62

63

65

66

67

68

Victorian (Mainly Early)

		1968	1969	1970	1971	19
VICTORIAN						
66. Dining Chair	£	70	75	75	75	1
(No. 193)	Index	100	107	107	107	
67. Dining Chair	£	105	150	150	150	1
(No. 197)	Index	100	143	143	143	1
68. Button Back Chair	£	35	40	43	43	
(No. 293)	Index	100	114	123	123	2
69. Settee	£	80	90	105	105	1
(No. 612)	Index	100	113	131	131	1
70. Canterbury	£	35	50	50	43	
(No. 102)	Index	100	143	143	123	2
71. Wellington Chest	£	35	35	45	45	
(No. 397)	Index	100	100	129	129	2
72. Davenport Desk	£	55	70	70	75	
(No. 455)	Index	100	127	127	136	1
73. Desk	£	110	110	120	120	1
(No. 462)	Index	100	100	109	109	1
74. Chiffonier	£	28	40	50	63	
(No. 403)	Index	100	143	179	225	2
75. Work Table	£	50	55	55	50	
(No. 925)	Index	100	110	110	100	1
76. Whatnot	£	55	55	55	65	
(No. 1001)	Index	100	100	100	118	1
77. Teapoy	£	35	40	40	40	
(No. 970)	Index	100	114	114	114	1
TOTAL VICTORIAN	£	693	810	858	874	1,1
Group Index	Index	100	118	126	130	1
Group Ave. Value (12 items)	£	57.75	67.5	71.5	72.8	98.
VICTORIAN INDEX		100	117	124	126	1
Victorian % change			17%	6%	2%	3

The numbers in brackets refer to illustrations in the book

69

70

71

72

73

973	1974	1975	1976	1977	1978	1979	1980	1981	1982	1983	1984	1985	1986	1987	1988	1989	No.
135	180	180	195	240	420	420	500	550	550	550	550	550	725	800	900	900	66.
193	**257**	**257**	**279**	**343**	**600**	**600**	**714**	**786**	**786**	**786**	**786**	**786**	**1,036**	**1,143**	**1,286**	**1,286**	
300	360	360	375	480	600	690	750	975	900	900	900	1,050	1,175	1,300	1,600	1,750	67.
286	**343**	**343**	**357**	**457**	**571**	**657**	**714**	**929**	**857**	**857**	**857**	**1,000**	**1,119**	**1,238**	**1,524**	**1,667**	
105	135	135	175	275	325	325	425	438	388	363	450	575	750	850	1,200	1,250	68.
300	**386**	**386**	**500**	**786**	**929**	**929**	**1,214**	**1,251**	**1,109**	**1,037**	**1,286**	**1,643**	**2,143**	**2,429**	**3,429**	**3,571**	
200	235	215	350	500	550	650	700	600	650	650	650	825	900	1,050	1,200	1,500	69.
250	**294**	**269**	**438**	**625**	**688**	**813**	**875**	**750**	**813**	**813**	**813**	**1,031**	**1,125**	**1,313**	**1,500**	**1,875**	
85	125	115	125	170	213	300	213	260	350	350	500	575	575	625	700	850	70.
243	**357**	**329**	**357**	**486**	**609**	**857**	**609**	**743**	**1,000**	**1,000**	**1,429**	**1,643**	**1,643**	**1,786**	**2,000**	**2,429**	
125	175	225	300	425	500	550	625	625	575	575	575	725	725	725	1,050	1,200	71.
357	**500**	**643**	**857**	**1,214**	**1,429**	**1,571**	**1,786**	**1,786**	**1,643**	**1,643**	**1,643**	**2,071**	**2,071**	**2,071**	**3,000**	**3,429**	
140	200	185	250	400	725	625	700	625	600	600	600	775	1,050	1,200	1,600	1,750	72.
255	**364**	**336**	**455**	**727**	**1,318**	**1,136**	**1,273**	**1,136**	**1,091**	**1,091**	**1,091**	**1,409**	**1,909**	**2,182**	**2,909**	**3,182**	
275	275	265	275	400	575	800	1,250	1,250	1,100	1,250	1,250	2,000	2,250	2,750	2,750	4,000	73.
250	**250**	**241**	**250**	**364**	**523**	**727**	**1,136**	**1,136**	**1,000**	**1,136**	**1,136**	**1,818**	**2,045**	**2,500**	**2,500**	**3,636**	
85	120	105	120	175	200	250	250	300	300	300	375	400	400	400	500	700	74.
304	**429**	**375**	**429**	**625**	**714**	**893**	**893**	**1,071**	**1,071**	**1,071**	**1,339**	**1,429**	**1,429**	**1,429**	**1,786**	**2,500**	
60	75	70	63	105	140	140	130	130	130	125	150	160	250	300	350	350	75.
120	**150**	**140**	**126**	**210**	**280**	**280**	**260**	**260**	**260**	**250**	**300**	**320**	**500**	**600**	**700**	**700**	
125	145	135	160	175	250	300	350	463	350	350	350	475	525	575	800	800	76.
227	**264**	**245**	**291**	**318**	**455**	**545**	**636**	**842**	**636**	**636**	**636**	**864**	**955**	**1,045**	**1,455**	**1,455**	
60	80	70	100	175	250	250	200	200	200	200	200	213	300	300	500	500	77.
171	**229**	**200**	**286**	**500**	**714**	**714**	**571**	**571**	**571**	**571**	**571**	**609**	**857**	**857.1**	**1,429**	**1,429**	
695	2,105	2,060	2,488	3,520	4,748	5,300	6,093	6,416	6,093	6,213	6,550	8,323	9,625	10,875	13,150	15,550	
246	318	314	385	555	736	810	890	938	903	908	991	1,219	1,403	1,549	1,960	2,263	
1.3	175.4	171.7	207.3	293.3	395.7	441.7	507.8	534.7	507.8	517.8	545.8	693.6	802.1	906.25	1095.8	1,296	
245	304	297	359	508	685	765	879	926	879	897	945	1,201	1,389	1,569	1,898	2,244	
4%	24%	-2%	21%	41%	35%	12%	15%	5%	-5%	2%	5%	27%	16%	13%	21%	18%	

75

76

77

78

79

80

Country

		1968	1969	1970	1971	19
COUNTRY						
78. Chippendale Chair — Oak	£	18	22	25	25	
(No. 153)	Index	100	122	139	139	
79. Sheraton Chair — Fruitwood	£	8	8	8	8	
(No. 171)	Index	100	100	100	100	
80. Windsor Chair — Yew	£	65	75	75	80	
(No. 236)	Index	100	115	115	123	
81. Gateleg Table — Oak	£	45	60	60	60	
(No. 744)	Index	100	133	133	133	
82. Side Table — Fruitwood	£	68	70	75	75	
(No. 842)	Index	100	103	110	110	
83. Side Table — Elm	£	45	50	50	45	
(No. 852)	Index	100	111	111	100	
84. Dressing Table — Fruitwood	£	125	145	175	150	
(No. 831)	Index	100	116	140	120	
85. Mule Chest — Oak	£	30	40	43	40	
(No. 309)	Index	100	133	143	133	
86. Chest — Walnut	£	98	125	130	115	
(No. 347)	Index	100	128	133	117	
87. Bureau — Walnut	£	125	175	175	175	
(No. 44)	Index	100	140	140	140	
88. Dresser — Oak 18C	£	275	325	350	350	
(No. 497)	Index	100	118	127	127	
89. Corner Cupboard — Oak	£	65	65	65	55	
(No. 415)	Index	100	100	100	85	
90. Mendlesham Chair	£	55	55	55	55	
(No. 246)	Index	100	100	100	100	
TOTAL COUNTRY	£	1,022	1,215	1,286	1,233	1,
Group Index	Index	100	117	122	118	
Group Ave. Value (13 items)	£	73	86.79	91.9	88.1	12
COUNTRY INDEX		100	119	126	121	
Country % change			19%	6%	-4%	4

The numbers in brackets refer to illustrations in the book

81

73	1974	1975	1976	1977	1978	1979	1980	1981	1982	1983	1984	1985	1986	1987	1988	1989	No.
60	60	60	60	88	115	125	143	143	175	175	175	250	300	375	425	425	78.
33	333	333	333	489	639	694	794	794	972	972	972	1,389	1,667	2,083	2,361	2,361	
18	18	18	18	20	25	25	25	30	30	30	30	40	50	50	65	80	79.
25	225	225	225	250	313	313	313	375	375	375	375	500	625	625	812.5	1,000	
60	220	210	240	425	550	675	900	900	900	950	950	1,200	1,400	2,500	3,125	3,650	80.
46	338	323	369	654	846	1,038	1,385	1,385	1,385	1,462	1,462	1,846	2,154	3,846	4,808	5,615	
25	200	250	425	525	650	875	1,050	1,250	1,125	1,125	1,125	1,250	1,250	1,400	2,500	3,000	81.
78	444	556	944	1,167	1,444	1,944	2,333	2,778	2,500	2,500	2,500	2,778	2,778	3,111	5,556	6,667	
00	300	275	375	475	600	700	750	800	850	850	900	1,000	1,250	1,400	1,600	2,150	82.
94	441	404	551	699	882	1,029	1,103	1,176	1,250	1,250	1,324	1,471	1,838	2,059	2,353	3,162	
65	75	65	80	105	150	150	160	155	165	165	165	175	300	350	425	425	83.
44	167	144	178	233	333	333	356	344	367	367	367	389	667	777.8	944.4	944	
00	500	425	525	675	1,050	1,050	1,150	1,100	1,150	1,150	1,350	1,750	2,125	2,125	2,125	2,500	84.
40	400	340	420	540	840	840	920	880	920	920	1,080	1,400	1,700	1,700	1,700	2,000	
00	125	115	140	250	425	350	400	450	425	425	475	550	550	625	725	800	85.
33	417	383	467	833	1,417	1,167	1,333	1,500	1,417	1,417	1,583	1,833	1,833	2,083	2,417	2,667	
50	350	313	350	550	650	650	725	750	650	625	650	700	1,000	1,150	2,000	2,375	86.
55	357	319	357	561	663	663	740	765	663	638	663	714	1,020	1,173	2,041	2,423	
50	600	500	600	850	1,050	1,250	1,400	1,300	1,400	1,550	1,750	2,375	3,250	3,250	3,250	3,750	87.
80	480	400	480	680	840	1,000	1,120	1,040	1,120	1,240	1,400	1,900	2,600	2,600	2,600	2,800	
50	925	800	825	1,500	1,900	2,150	3,500	3,000	3,000	3,000	3,125	3,500	6,000	6,000	7,000	7,500	88.
73	336	291	300	545	691	782	1,273	1,091	1,091	1,091	1,136	1,273	2,182	2,182	2,545	2,727	
00	125	115	125	250	350	300	400	400	425	425	425	525	600	700	800	900	89.
54	192	177	192	385	538	462	615	615	654	654	654	808	923	1,077	1,231	1,385	
20	165	165	175	275	325	325	475	600	575	575	575	800	1,200	1,250	1,400	1,600	90.
18	300	300	318	500	591	591	864	1,091	1,045	1,045	1,045	1,455	2,182	2,273	2,545	2,909	
98	3,663	3,311	3,938	5,988	7,840	8,625	11,078	10,878	10,870	11,045	11,695	14,115	19,275	21,175	25,440	28,905	
52	341	323	395	580	772	835	1,011	1,064	1,058	1,072	1,120	1,366	1,705	1,968	2,455	2,820	
.6	261.6	236.5	281.3	427.7	560	616.1	791.3	777	776.4	788.9	835.4	1,008	1,377	1512.5	1817.1	2,065	
54	358	324	385	586	767	844	1,084	1,064	1,064	1,081	1,114	1,381	1,886	2,072	2,489	2,828	
%	41%	-10%	19%	52%	31%	10%	28%	-2%	0%	2%	6%	21%	37%	10%	20%	14%	

82

83

Totals

		1968	1969	1970	1971	1
TOTAL OF VALUE INDEXES						
a. Oak		99.98	115.6	120	129	1
b. Walnut		100.1	133.4	151	137	1
c. Early Mahogany		100.2	119.0	126	125	14
d. Late Mahogany		100.0	117.8	125	124	13
e. Regency		100.0	127.3	137	135	17
f. Victorian		100	116.9	124	126	17
g. Country		100	118.9	126	121	17
Total of Index		700.3	848.9	908	897	1,
TOTAL INDEX		**100**	**121**	**130**	**128**	
Total Furniture % change			21%	7%	-1%	2
BY TYPE						
h. Chairs	Index	100	113.9	122	125	17
i. Dining Tables	Index	100	134.9	145	151	19
j. Dressers	Index	100	115.8	124	124	14
k. Sideboards and Court Cupboards	Index	100	123.5	130	134	18
l. Sundry Dining	Index	100	133.3	100	152	16
THE DINING ROOM	**Index**	**100**	**124**	**124**	**137**	
m. Chest of Drawers	Index	100	113.8	122	114	12
n. Bureaux	Index	100	125.4	132	128	16
o. Davenports	Index	100	139.7	140	144	21
p. Card Tables	Index	100	118.6	128	116	16
q. Sofa Tables	Index	100	132.5	153	139	19
r. Tripod Tables	Index	100	117.5	118	118	16
s. Canterburies	Index	100	131.4	148	138	19
t. Teapoys	Index	100	122.1	127	127	16
u. Work Tables	Index	100	121	91	85.2	
THE SITTING ROOM	**Index**	**100**	**125**	**129**	**123**	
Retail Price Index		**100**	**106**	**108**	**114**	
R.P.I. % Change			6%	2%	6%	1

84

85

86

1973	1974	1975	1976	1977	1978	1979	1980	1981	1982	1983	1984	1985	1986	1987	1988	1989	No.
0.7	360.7	323.6	332.8	507.9	747.6	870.5	1,281	1,186	1,210	1,197	1,212	1,379	1,595	1675.5	2092.5	2,437	a.
8.1	352.4	311.0	341.0	409.1	487.1	642.2	773.3	765.6	869.9	987.2	1,050	1,198	1,557	1628.4	1923.6	2,014	b.
9.8	282.1	260.1	323.1	436.9	575.7	769.0	985.4	985.4	1,046	1,212	1,266	1,631	2,174	2405.3	2808.8	3,265	c.
0.5	224.7	203.2	252.1	387.9	503.9	578.1	623.7	618.9	723.2	749.1	773.7	1,112	1,185	1375.4	1725.4	1,799	d.
5.6	273.3	257.1	312.6	453.5	592.4	774.6	787.9	859.4	935.3	957.9	1,188	1,249	1,535	1849.5	2266.6	2,535	e.
4.6	303.8	297.3	359.0	507.9	685.1	764.8	879.2	925.8	879.2	896.5	945.2	1,201	1,389	1569.3	1897.5	2,244	f.
4.2	358.4	324.0	385.3	585.9	767.1	843.9	1,084	1,064	1,064	1,081	1,144	1,381	1,886	2071.9	2489.2	2,828	g.
634	2,155	1,976	2,306	3,289	4,359	5,243	6,415	6,405	6,727	7,080	7,580	9,152	11,321	12,575	15,204	17,122	
233	308	282	329	470	623	749	916	915	961	1,011	1,083	1,307	1,617	1,796	2,172	2,446	
2%	32%	-8%	17%	43%	33%	20%	22%	0%	5%	5%	7%	21%	24%	11%	21%	13%	
0.0	308.2	297.6	323.1	462.1	574.7	712.9	841.6	874.8	898.1	932.2	980.4	1,212	1,553	1875.7	2396.2	2,645	h.
4.9	346.5	377.5	520.0	651.4	944.8	1,082	1,260	1,407	1,494	1,477	1,477	1,949	2,123	2418.2	3228.9	3,586	i.
3.0	301.5	265.5	256.7	459.4	585.5	677.6	1,203	1,079	1,079	1,079	1,102	1,270	1,924	1924.2	2206.1	2,430	j.
1.1	269.9	246.2	287.3	452.3	575.4	688.3	860.5	883.8	850.6	846.7	914.8	1,107	1,234	1444.8	2048.0	2,255	k.
4.3	285.7	257.1	357.1	547.6	761.9	809.5	761.9	785.7	857.1	833.3	1,071	1,143	1,333	1666.7	1904.8	1,905	l.
241	302	289	349	515	688	794	985	1,006	1,036	1,034	1,109	1,336	1,634	1,866	2,357	2,564	
1.4	233.7	201.3	225.2	365.1	454.5	524.0	679.8	669.2	620.0	640.4	710.5	886.8	1,133	1280.5	1624.1	1,834	m.
9.1	303.7	280.8	354.3	502.8	633.0	936.4	1,073	1,088	1,225	1,310	1,425	1,740	2,183	2389.9	2530.2	2,915	n.
4.7	442.7	407.3	444.7	635.4	974.3	861.7	1,071	1,003	1,415	1,632	1,632	2,009	3,128	3264.8	4171.9	4,634	o.
3.0	253.1	225.8	297.3	357.9	436.4	503.5	464.1	469.6	526.0	522.4	595.6	791.8	1,054	1110.2	1526.0	1,589	p.
0.2	291.2	262.6	262.8	531.3	785.4	1,179	1,159	1,147	1,366	1,366	1,366	1,846	1,896	2326.8	2438.8	2,509	q.
2.2	294.0	255.0	369.0	455.5	629.6	671.3	849.9	947.1	976.9	976.9	1,066	1,261	1,776	1967.6	2711.6	3,386	r.
9.3	298.1	268.6	296.0	416.8	489.1	613.4	597.8	697.5	826.1	847.8	1,127	1,365	1,495	1871.1	2087.0	2,519	s.
0.7	264.3	240	352.9	600	782.1	882.1	785.7	785.7	810.7	810.7	810.7	879.3	1,104	1178.6	1714.3	1,864	t.
30	153	142	133	245	310	280	270	270	450	295	2,050	350	500	600	770	830	u.
220	282	254	304	457	610	717	772	786	913	934	1,198	1,237	1,586	1,777	2,175	2,453	
136	158	195	229	265	287	325	384	429	466	487	512	543	562	585	611	611	
9%	16%	23%	17%	16%	8%	13%	18%	12%	9%	5%	5%	6%	3%	4%	4%	0%	

88

89

90

Technical Terms

Acanthus. A leaf design used to ornament furniture in carving. Although used earlier, it is most frequently found in mahogany furniture from 1730 and continued to be popular among Victorians.

Amorini. Cupids or cherubs used in decoration. Popular in the late seventeenth and early eighteenth century as well as in Adam designs.

Anthemian. Another decoration, this time like the flower of the honeysuckle. Again used in Adam designs and also during the Regency period.

Arcaded Decoration. A series of arches on pillars or columns. Sometimes included on the cavetto of a top moulding.

Art Nouveau. A style of the late Victorian and Edwardian period. Its heyday was from 1895 to 1905 approximately, although the influence went on much longer. Very strong in Europe (see Paris metro stations and the Hotel Ceramic in the Ave. Wagram) and fostered by Liberty's in London. The inverted heart shape was much used in the furniture of this style and bronze beaten plaques were also popular as decoration.

Astragal. A moulding used on the glazing bars of bookcases.

Ball-and-Claw. A design incorporating a ball clutched by a claw, much used as a foot on cabriole leg furniture from c.1710 and reproduced into the present day.

Baluster. A turned shaping used on legs of furniture or centre columns. Usually rather bulbous but also in modified forms. See 735.

Bamboo. The bamboo form as a leg or otherwise was popular during the influence of Eastern designs in 1740-1760, and again at the turn of the eighteenth into the nineteenth century. It took the form of clustered columns in mahogany furniture, with small double collars turned to look like bamboo joints, or, later, single columns so turned. In the Regency period actual bamboo reproduction was made in other woods (or even iron, as the stair banister in the Brighton Pavilion). Bamboo furniture itself tends to be a Victorian manufacture, since much bamboo furniture was produced in the late nineteenth century perhaps as a feature of the heyday of Empire.

Banding. Used around the edges of tables or drawers for decorative effect, the art and proportion of the banding is vital to the success of the design. Straight banding is one which has been cut along the grain; crossbanding describes that where the wood has been cut across the grain. Very decorative effects were obtained by using different and exotic woods for crossbanding. Herring-bone or feather bandings were used in walnut furniture. See drawer fronts under 'Drawer' section.

Barley-Sugar Twist. See Spiral Twist.

Baroque. A style of richly ornamented type with flowing curves and masks of various heads. Late seventeenth and early eighteenth century furniture of European Continental makers used this style and its influence spread to England.

Bead Mould. Used for two types of moulding: either a small plain moulding of semi-circular section or one in the form of a string of beads.

Bearer. See Loper.

Bergère. An armchair, originally with upholstered sides, but now a term used to describe a chair with cane woven sides and back, usually post-1800 in date.

Birdcage Gallery. A construction used under the top of a tripod table to enable it to revolve as well as tip up. Formed by two squares of wood with four turned columns between, pivoting about the centre column. See 891.

Blind Fret. Fretwork glued or carved upon a solid surface. Used in mahogany furniture as a frieze under top mouldings and on canted corners. See 146 and 704.

Bobbin Turning. Turning of baluster in shape of bobbins, one on top of another. See 805 and 806.

Bow Front. The front of the piece follows the curve of a circle rather than a straight line. See 374 to 377.

Bracket. Used in chairs and tables to strengthen the joint between leg and supporting rails, often with decorative effect by means of fretting.

Bracket Foot. A type of foot for chests, bureaux and cabinets introduced c.1690. The outside bracket shape does not in fact support the weight of the piece which is taken on a wood block under the corner of the carcase on to which the shaped outside bracket fits. See 356.

Brass Inlay. Brass inlay and stringing became popular in the late Georgian and Regency period 1800-1840. Used with mahogany and rosewood as decoration and usually a mark of quality. See 774.

Break-front. A term usually applied to bookcases and descriptive of a centre section which protrudes out beyond the line of the sides. See 14.

Broken Pediment. A pediment above a piece of furniture which is usually classical in style with, of course, the centre point missing, i.e. 'broken'. Used particularly above bureau bookcases of the first half of the eighteenth century in both walnut and mahogany examples. See 15 and 17 for illustrations.

Bulb. The bulging or bulbous turned part of supports or legs of early furniture of the oak period, i.e. before c.1650. Also seen in later seventeenth century walnut turning.

Buffet. A term loosely used to describe a piece of furniture of the sixteenth and seventeenth century used as a sideboard, with open shelves supported on bulbous turned members. See examples 435-437.

Bun Foot. A turned ball-shaped foot of flattened form, like a cheese, used from c.1650-1710 particularly on chests and bureaux. The spigot by which the bun foot was attached to the piece was often turned with a coarse worm thread which matched that of the socket (under the corner of the piece) into which it fitted. See 315, 318, 321.

Cabochon. A design motif found often on the knees of chairs of the early mahogany period — c.1740, consisting of a ball shape usually surrounded by leaf ornament.

Cabriole Leg. See illustrations pages 53-56. Introduced to England in the early eighteenth century and originally terminating in a hoof foot, the cabriole leg was subject to many design variations and was produced with pad, hoof, claw and ball, paw and scroll foot according to taste. The design seems to have declined after 1750 until early Victorian times, when it was revived.

Caning. First used in chairs in the mid-seventeenth century, i.e. at the Restoration or Charles II period. Its use seems to have declined after the William and Mary period (1689-1702) and was revived again in the late eighteenth century. Hepplewhite and Shearer both illustrated carved chairs in the 1790s and subsequently, through Regency and Victorian periods, it was used in dining chairs and others.

Canted Corner. Bevelled or chamfered corners, found on carcase furniture — chests, bureaux, etc., sometimes decorated with a blind fret, reeding, fluting, etc.

Canterbury. A term used in the late eighteenth century for rather mobile furiture and said to be named after an archbishop of that See. Sheraton illustrated a 'supper Canterbury' which was the forerunner of the modern tea trolley, used for holding cutlery and plates. Music Canterburys were produced from the late eighteenth century and through the nineteenth in contemporary styles.

Carcase. A term generally used to describe the frame of which a chest of drawers, or bureau was built.

Cartouche. A decoration, usually in the form of a flat surface with shield or scroll shape on which an inscription or monogram can be placed.

Caryatid. A carved female figure used as decoration or support, i.e. a leg, on furniture of the early seventeenth century or again after 1800.

Castors. Early forms of castors were made — c.1700 — of wood, both wheel and axle. In the mid-eighteenth century leather rollers appear to have come in use but in the last quarter of the century brass castors with stylised motifs made their appearance. See Table Sections for typical examples.

Cavetto. A hollowed, concave moulding of quarter-circle section. See 'Mouldings'.

Chamfer. A bevelled edge used to lighten the effect of a piece of furniture. Used on the back edge of square 'Chippendale' chairs.

Clubfoot. Virtually the same as a pad foot and most commonly found on cabriole legs. See 'Pad Foot'.

Clustered Column. A design of medieval origin used in the mid-eighteenth century consisting of several pillars clustered together. See 268.

Cockbead. A small bead moulding used on the edges of drawer fronts from 1725 onwards. See Drawers.

Column Turning. Turning in the form of a column used from the mid-seventeenth century onwards. See 729.

Commode. A term borrowed from France and used from the mid-eighteenth century to describe a piece of furniture for use in principal rooms. Very fine examples in Adam or prevailing styles with rounded or serpentine shaped fronts, and original French pieces, resembling finely decorated chests of drawers, with or without doors; represent the height of collecting, in both taste and purse. A term which should not be used as a Victorian euphemism for a piece of furniture designed to conceal a chamber-pot. See 365 to 369.

Console Table. A wall side table supported by brackets. See 855 to 859.

Cresting Rail. The top rail of a chair, joining the two back uprights at the top.

Crossbanding. See Banding.

Cross-grain moulding. See Mouldings.

Cushion Drawer. A drawer set in the upper moulding or frieze of a secretaire or chest having a convex, or 'cushion', shape to the front. See 600.

Cushion Mirror. See 558.

Dentil Frieze. The part of a frieze moulding of dentillated or 'square-toothed' form. Made up of a series of small rectangular blocks. See 'Mouldings'.

Diaper. A decorative pattern of diamond-shaped lines with dots or forms inside. Used for border decoration.

Dovetailing. One of the broad methods of dating a chest is by the dovetailing. In sixteenth and early seventeenth century pieces the drawer sides were nailed into a rebated front as shown in photograph 1. During the first half of the seventeenth century however, fairly crude dovetails were introduced as shown in photograph 2. Note that both these drawers have side runners, i.e. a groove let into the thick side linings, made of oak, acts as a bearing for rectangular section bearers inside the carcase, on which the drawer runs and is supported.

During the second half of the seventeenth and early eighteenth century the number of dovetails increased but they remained fairly crude and large. See photograph 3. By the time the mahogany period was in full swing, after 1740, the dovetails had increased further and become finer. See photograph 4. This form has continued up to modern times.

Dowel. A wooden peg used to fasten timber joints.

1

3

2

4

Drawers. A guide to dating furniture with drawers can be obtained from their construction. On the chests of the early seventeenth century the drawers were nailed together, with the side linings rebated into the front, as shown in Photograph 1 under the heading 'Dovetails'. Subsequently dovetails were used as shown in photograph 2 of that section. The weight of the drawers was taken on side runners which fitted into grooves cut in the thick sides of the drawer. This is also evident in photograph 2.

About the time of the transition to walnut, in 1680, the bottom runner appeared. This was a strip of wood — usually oak — fixed under the drawer at each end which ran on horizontal bearers on the interlinings of a chest. The drawer bottom, whether of pine or oak, ran from front to back as far as grain was concerned, as shown in photograph 5. Between the drawer fronts the carcase was flat.

However, when the change to veneered walnut furniture took place, a variety of possibilities came about. Initially it is probable that a vertically veneered front with simple diagonal grain crossbanding — a sort of half herring-bone — was used, as shown in photograph 6. This was in use from c.1680 to c.1710. However, herring-bone crossbanding, as shown in photograph 7, was used from c.1690 to c.1720 and probably was more common. A variation was the use of inlaid boxwood and ebony stringing lines from c.1690 to c.1710, as shown in photograph 8.

Between the drawers at this time the carcase fronts were covered by the half-round or D-moulding and the double half-round or double-D moulding, with the latter the rarer of the two. Usually double-D moulding, cut, like the single version, across the grian, was used to maintain the proportion on broader carcase front edgings. A country form of simple cross-banding to drawers was used, with the half herring-bone, well into the first half of the eighteenth century and is shown in photograph 9.

About 1710 an alternative form appeared. This was the drawer edged by an ovolo lip moulding which hid the gap between the drawer and the carcase edge. The carcase front edging was, in this case, flat veneered, obviating the need for D- or double D-mouldings. A disadvantage was that unless the stop blocks at the back of the drawer remained fixed, it was possible to break off the lip moulding by pushing the drawer in too hard. This is shown in photograph 10.

Concurrent with the lip moulding the cockbead appeared. This is generally assumed to have been widely adopted about 1730 and the walnut drawer front of photograph 11 with its herring-bone banding is of about this date. The cockbead solved the lip moulding breakage problem and was used on mahogany furniture from 1730 throughout the eighteenth and nineteenth century, although plain mahogany drawers without any beading were also common.

The linings used continued to be oak or pine and in later furniture, from about 1770, the bottom was made with the grain running across instead of front to back. About 1790 some drawer bottoms had a central bearer introduced and were made in two halves running across again. This continued up to the present day.

Ebonised Wood. Wood which has been stained black to simulate ebony.

End Standards. The supporting ends of a table or stool.

Escritoire. A word borrowed from the French to denote a piece of furniture at which one can write. Sometimes found in early accounts in the form 'scrutoire'. Synonym of secretaire.

Escutcheon. A motif used as a centre decoration.

Fielded Panel. A panel which has the edges bevelled or chamfered. See 622.

Finial. A turned knob used at the intersection of stretchers on tables, chairs and stools to complete a design effect. See 552, 553, 789. Also used on the hoods of longcase clocks.

Fluting. Grooving of semi-circular or concave section used as ornament or design on flat or turned surfaces, usually to lighten the appearance of a piece or to give a required proportion to the design. See 528.

Frets. Fretwork either applied or cut from solid and used as decoration. If presented on a solid surface, known as a 'blind' fret. If left as open decoration, known as 'open' fret. Used particularly in mid- and later eighteenth century in Gothic or Chinese taste. See 146.

Frieze. The surface below a table top or the part of a cornice consisting of the flat surface beneath the top moulding. See 358 where the blind fret is on the frieze.

Gadrooning. A carved edge of repetitive shapes usually convex curved form. See also 'Mouldings'.

Gallery. A term used to describe an arcaded, pillared, or columned open sequence of decorative surrounding or cloistered motif, which can be in wood, brass or other material.

5

6

7

8

9

10

11

Gesso. A sort of plaster composition or gunge, used as a base for applying gilding and usually moulded in bas relief on mirror frames or furniture, rather as plaster was in the nineteenth century.

Gothic. A style which keeps reappearing but which is derived from Gothic architecture and was used on furniture in the fifteenth and sixteenth centuries, again in the mid-eighteenth century, again in Regency times ('Strawberry Hill Gothic') and again in Victorian times by Pugin, etc. Characterised by curved pointed arches.

Hairy Feet. The publisher's derogatory slang for fine carved paw feet, mainly after Hope and Smith, c.1820. See 779.

Handles. Funnily enough wooden knobs were used on drawer furniture in the seventeenth century oak period until about 1660, when brass drops were introduced. Funnily, because one always associates wooden knobs with Victorians. However, brass drops rapidly came into use and oak and walnut furniture of the 1660-1710 period is usually found to have drops similar to those known in photographs 12 and 13. The handle on these pulls was linked to a double strip of brass or iron which passed through the drawer front and was then parted and turned over so that each end was pinned to the drawer back in opposing vertical senses. Modern reproductions have a threaded spigot with a nut to secure it.

From about 1690, however, the brass loop handle with solid back plate appeared, as shown in photographs 14 and 15. The back plate was shaped and could be engraved, as in photograph 15, and the loop was cast and perhaps moulded, as in photograph 14. Brass knob-shaped sockets on the face of bolts held the loop ends.

Pierced back plates were introduced about 1710 and showed many forms of which photographs 16 and 17 are but two examples. Both walnut and later mahogany furniture used the solid and pierced back plate, but by 1740 the 'swan-neck', which is often associated with cockbeaded drawers, had been introduced. This is shown in photograph 18. In this type the loop is thicker and there are merely two metal moulded circular roses behind each bolt head, without any back plate. It was a type capable of considerable ornamentation, as shown in photograph 19 and the later fine quality pieces — after 1750 — had very Rococo forms of this in cast and chased metal of a type found on commodes.

About 1780 the stamped brass back plate of oval or circular form associated with Hepplewhite or Sheraton furniture came into use. Photograph 20 is a typical example. This would be made from thin sheet brass, stamped to shape and hence hollow at the back.

About 1800 the turned wooden knob — photograph 21 — came into use and, although there was a period of overlap, by the time the Victorian period had set in, most drawer furniture used wooden knobs of varied simplicity or complication. Some had a simple wooden spigot to fit into the drawer front; some had a wooden threaded screwed spigot; some had a metal bolt set into them. Unfortunately the Victorians considered that the wooden knob was so desirable that they could not resist fitting it to furniture from other periods with the result that walnut and early mahogany chests in thousands have been despoiled by Victorian 'improvers'.

With the return of eighteenth century fashions, from about 1880 onwards, it was necessary to return to brass handles again, although wooden knobs continued to be fitted to ordinary furniture. Photograph 22 shows a late Victorian version of a brass loop and back plate fitted to a 'reproduc-

tion' of an eighteenth century piece. Photograph 23 shows an Edwardian Art Nouveau handle and stamped back plate as fitted to the 'simple' furniture of the period which strived to return to medieval simplicity of line!

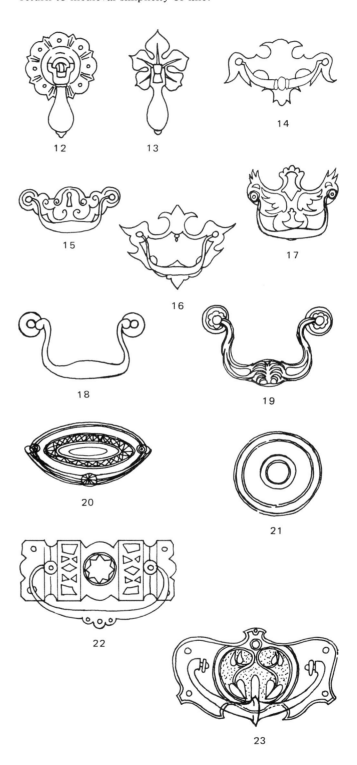

12

13

14

15

16

17

18

19

20

21

22

23

Herring-bone. An inlaid banding or border used in walnut veneered furniture for decorative effect. Also called 'feather-banding'. Made by laying two strips of veneer at right angles to each other in 'V' form to give a feathered or herring-bone effect.

Hipping. A form of cabriole leg extension used on rather better quality pieces, in which the leg continues at the top to a level above the seat rail. See 127.

Hoof Foot. An animal form of foot used on early, perhaps original, cabriole legs. The French name was *pied-de-biche*. See 739.

Husk. A decoration used in Adam and Hepplewhite designs of bell-shaped form frequently shown in festoons.

Inlay. A decoration which has been let into the solid wood. Used from mid-sixteenth century onwards.

Japanning. Another term for lacquering (q.v.).

Jardinière. A piece of furniture for containing flowers or plants indoors. Usually lined with lead or zinc to enable watering to be done without rotting the wood.

Lacquer. Lacquer furniture was popular from an early date, being originally imported during the sixteenth century but becoming more popular during the seventeenth. By the late seventeenth century it was being produced in England, but the vogue seemed to die down to lesser proportions in the second quarter of the eighteenth century. Nevertheless lacquering continued to be used as decoration into the nineteenth century.

Linenfold. A carved design used on panels of early sixteenth century date. See 297.

Linings. The interior parts of a drawer.

Lion Mask. A decoration of carved form popular in the early mahogany period, 1720-40, and again in the Regency period.

Loper. The rectangular section length of wood under a bureau fall which pulls out to support the fall when open. Many a fall has been smashed off its hinges by people forgetting to pull out the lopers before opening the fall.

Lowboy. A term, probably of American origin, now used to describe a dressing table or side table usually on cabriole legs.

Marquetry. Veneers of different woods cut into designs and fitted together to give a decorative effect. To be distinguished from inlays (q.v.) by the fact that design is veneered on to a carcase and not cut into the solid. See 328.

Mitre Joint. A joint made by fitting together two surfaces cut at an angle of 45°.

Monopodium. A carved support with a lion-mask top. The foot is usually of claw form and this type of support is of Regency period.

Mouldings. In the last analysis, perhaps the most important features which date a piece of furniture are its mouldings. More correctly, they are often the factor which ultimately determines its originality and extent to which it has been restored or 'improved' with a view to pre-dating or faking a later piece. In the eighteenth century and before, the mouldings used were based on architectural designs and had a boldness of shape and execution which nineteenth century makers with machines to do the work failed to maintain. The meanness and over-sophistication of the mouldings on Victorian reproductions gives them away instantly, quite apart from considerations of colour and ageing.

Mouldings of the oak period were bold and generally cut along the grain. It was in the walnut period that the cross-grained mouldings in small pieces, which generally shrink slightly apart and yellow so beautifully with age, came into their own. On the best walnut furnture the mouldings were always cut across the grain, although those along the sides of a piece of furniture might be cut along the grain on lesser quality pieces to save time and money. In mahogany furniture the applied mouldings are nearly always cut along the grain. Integral mouldings, of course, cut across.

Towards the end of the eighteenth century the mouldings became tighter and under the influence of Hepplewhite and Sheraton designs were curtailed or dispensed with altogether. Carcase edges were flat veneered, as were projecting edges. In the sketch illustrations we have shown a few of the principal types.

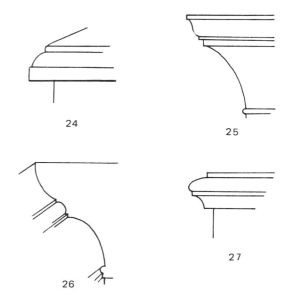

24   25

26   27

Ogee. A double curve, convex at the top and turning to concave below.

Open Fret. See 'Frets'.

Ormolu. A gilt composition metal used as a surface ornamentation on metal mounts, etc.

Ovolo. A moulding form of a convex quarter-circle section. Used around drawer edges to lip over carcase fronts in walnut and early mahogany furniture up to c.1745.

Oyster veneer. Oystershell veneering, or parquetry work, was produced by cutting the small branches of walnut, laburnum, olive and other woods across the branch to give a concentric ringed effect and laying these veneers in a decorative pattern. The form was introduced from Holland in the late seventeenth century. See 40 and 43.

Pad Foot. A round foot at the base of a cabriole or straighter turned leg. See 848.

Papier Mâché. See Clay, Henry, and Jennens and Bettridge in Cabinet Makers, Designers and Manufacturers Section.

Parquetry. A geometric pattern of veneers, often oysters, usually involving stringing and inlays. Contemporary with marquetry. See 327.

Patera. A round or oval decoration either applied, carved or painted on wood, used as an ornament.

Patina. The deep surface shine or gloss produced by years of undisturbed polishing and rubbing.

Paw Foot. A foot design used on cabriole legs in the mid-eighteenth century. Also see 'Hairy Feet'.

Pediment. A moulding or shape above the cornice of bookcases and other furniture. See 'Broken Pediment'.

Pie Crust. An edge carving of scalloped form used in the later eighteenth century, particularly on tea and tripod tables.

Plinth. The square base of a column; also used to describe the flat base support of a piece of furniture.

Polishing. In the seventeenth century it seems to have been the practice to polish oak furniture by means of rubbing in poppy or linseed oil, often dyed with alkanet root. Subsequently beeswax and turpentine polish was used to keep surfaces in good condition and to preserve the wood.

Walnut furniture of the late seventeenth and early eighteenth century was initially brushed with oil varnish to provide a surface for polishing with wax. The retention of this oil varnish, which provides a magnificently mellowed surface after years of polishing, is an important factor in patination.

Mahogany furniture of the eighteenth century was treated according to its type. Spanish or Cuban mahogany was either rubbed with linseed oil or wax and often stained with alkanet root or some other dye to obtain the red colour then very popular. Indeed, oak and walnut furniture of this period was also stained this way. Honduras mahogany was either oil varnished or rubbed with linseed oil and brick dust to give a hard polish. Domestically it seems to have been common to oil furniture, but beeswax polishing with a brush was employed also.

About 1810 the process of French polishing began by using shellac dissolved in spirit. This helped to seal off the wood and provide a bright hard finish. French polishing has developed much since then and is now a much shorter process than the original method. Nearly all furniture was French polished during the nineteenth century and few pieces from the eighteenth century have survived in an unstripped repolished condition. Varnishing in the modern sense was also used, many inferior woods being varnished dark brown in order to resemble mahogany.

Quartering. A means of obtaining a formal pattern in wood figure by taking four consecutively cut pieces of veneer, which have identical figuring, and setting them in opposing senses to give a mirrored pattern effect. Used in the walnut period 1680-1730 for tops of tables, chests and door fronts. See 329.

Rails. The horizontal part of a joined frame of a panelled piece of furniture. See 302. Also: Top Rail or Cresting Rail — used to describe the top wooden member between the uprights of a chair back.

Ram's Head. Decoration used by Adam in mask form.

Reeding. Convex raised beads on furniture: the opposite of fluting. Used on eighteenth century furniture and particularly later eighteenth and nineteenth century chair and table legs. See 184.

Rococo. An extravagant style, using much scroll work and of exuberant nature in its motifs, very predominant in the 1740-50 period and reappearing again in the 1840-50 Victorian era.

Rule Joint. An edge joint found on drop-flap tables from the seventeenth century, but pretty well superseding other plain joints in the eighteenth century. Used on gateleg and Pembroke tables.

Runner. The strip of wood on which a drawer runs.

Scagliola. A plaster and marble chip composition, made to imitate marble, used for table tops in the eighteenth century.

Scroll Foot. A cabriole leg termination of French origin used from mid-eighteenth century. See 367.

Scrutoire. Synonym for escritoire, secretaire or writing cabinet.

Serpentine. A curved shaping particularly valued in chest front forms. See 367.

Shell. The shell, or scallop, was a popular decorative motif in the walnut and early mahogany period, covering the years from 1700 up to c.1770.

Spade Foot. A tapered foot of square section used in the later eighteenth century and much associated with Sheraton and Hepplewhite designs. See 157.

Spandrel. A decoration used in square corners, usually on clock dials to fill the space between curved chapter ring and the corners.

Spiral Twist. A form of turning often known as barley-sugar twist very popular in the late seventeenth century. See 114, 840.

Splat. The vertical central upright of a chair back. It can be solid or pierced, plain or carved.

Split Baluster. Used as a decoration on chests of sixteenth and seventeenth century and made by splitting a turned baluster vertically in half to provide a flat surface for application. See 315 to 318.

Spoon back. Descriptive of chair back on which the splat curves like a spoon handle. See 120 to 124.

Stile. The vertical part of framing of a panelled piece of furniture.

Strapwork. Carved decoration used originally in the oak period from mid-sixteenth to mid-seventeenth century but again in Chippendale period.

Stretcher. The wooden connecting strut between legs of tables and chairs. See chair section for details of designs.

Stringing. Thin lines of inlay used as formal decoration, usually made in contrasting woods such as box, with possibly ebony and box patterning in later eighteenth century pieces. Used from early oak period — sixteenth century onwards.

Sunburst. A decoration of radiating lines or rays used particularly in the bottom drawers of tallboys and chests of the walnut period from 1700 to 1730. Made to look like the sun's rays and often inset in a concave shaping of the bottom drawer. See 583.

Swag. A decorative form shaped like a hanging festoon, often made up of husks or flowers. Popular in the late eighteenth century on Adam and other furniture.

Swan-neck. Term used to describe drop handles of eighteenth century form. See 'Handles'. Also used to describe the curve of a broken pediment cornice.

Tallboy. A chest upon a chest.

Tambour Front. A front made of strips of wood stuck side by side on canvas back to enable it to roll. A similar principle is used for a tambour shutter on sideboards and night tables. See 797.

Tenon. A joint form shaped to fit exactly into a cavity called a mortise. Used from the sixteenth century.

Tray-top. A top of detachable type usually with a fretted opening in the vertical sides to act as a carrying handle. Also loosely used to describe the top of a night table. See 795.

Veneer. A thin sheet of wood which can be cut from the tree in several ways. The first real vogue for veneered furniture came in the walnut period, 1680-1740, when the decorative effects of cutting veneers from walnut, laburnum, olive, tulipwood and so on, was appreciated. Originally these veneers were hand cut with a saw and were fairly thick — up to an eighth of an inch. They could be cut along the grain of the wood to give a straight, plain effect without much figure, or across the branches to form oysters (q.v.). Burr veneers were obtained by malformations of the grain due to injury, such as lopping.

Mahogany veneers of great decorative effect were also much used from about 1745, although the early Cuban mahogany was not much used for veneers. From the Victorian period paper thin veneers came into use and were obviously attractive because of the saving in wood. All modern veneered furniture is covered in these thin knife-cut sheets.

Woods

Amboyna. A yellowish-brown burred surface somewhat between 'bird's-eye' maple and burr walnut. Used in the eighteenth century and on into the nineteenth, both for cross-banding and for whole surfaces. Origin: East Indies.

Apple. One of the popular fruitwoods used in the solid country pieces in the eighteenth century, although it had some use as a veneer earlier. A light reddish-brown in colour with some mild figuring. Fairly close-ground and hard.

Ash. A whitish-grey fairly hard wood used in country furniture in the eighteenth century and for drawer linings.

Beech. A light brown surface with a distinctive flecked grain. Much loved by woodworm and used largely for chairs from the seventeenth century onwards. In the late Georgian and Regency periods it was painted, particularly in chair work. Early caned chairs of Restoration period were made from beech instead of walnut for economy and then ebonised.

Birch. A light yellowish-brown in colour and fairly soft. Used in eighteenth century for chairs and country furniture.

Boxwood. A whitish-yellow colour, without any figure. Used mainly as an inlay or for stringing lines from the sixteenth century.

Cedar. Reddish-brown, like a soft mahogany. Used for chests and interior work from the middle of the eighteenth century.

Cherry. Initially rather a pale wood but matures to a deeper reddish colour. Used for country furniture and for inlay or crossbanding from seventeenth century.

Chestnut. Horse chestnut is light, almost white and mainly found as a drawer lining material. Sweet chestnut matures to a reddish-brown and is reasonably hard for a country wood. Used for legs and in chairs from the seventeenth century.

Coromandel. A yellow and black striped wood used mainly for crossbanding from the late eighteenth century onwards.

Deal. Plain, straight-grained Scots pine. Used mainly for carcases (of chests, etc.) and drawer linings of lesser quality pieces. From seventeenth century onwards.

Ebony. Black, used for inlays.

Elm. Brown, with distinctive blackish figuring when old and ingrained with dirt. Another favourite of woodworms, and sometimes warps. Used extensively for country furniture and chairs, including seats of Windsors. Cut into burr veneers of fairly small sheets with extremely pleasing effect.

Harewood. This is just sycamore which has been stained to a greyish-green colour. Much used in later eighteenth century and Regency as a decorative veneer.

Holly. White, used for inlay and marquetry work from sixteenth century.

Kingwood. A brown and black striped wood like rosewood, particularly used for crossbanding on tables in late eighteenth century. Was used previously in late seventeenth century also as a veneer.

Laburnum. Cut as plain veneer, a yellow-brown with streaks of darker brown. Cut as an 'oyster' very dark rich blackish-brown. Used as veneer from late seventeenth century, particularly in parquetry.

Lignum vitae. Dark brown with black streaks. Very hard, used from seventeenth century as veneer and in solid.

Lime. Whitish-yellow; used by carvers.

Mahogany. Early mahogany, from 1720, was 'Spanish' or 'Cuban' from Cuba, Jamaica, San Domingo and Puerto Rico. Very dark, heavy with figuring. Later, 'Honduras' mahogany (originally called baywood) is lighter in colour and with a pinker tinge.

Maple. Light yellow; used as veneer and inlay. 'Bird's-eye' maple used more in the nineteenth century.

Oak. Early oak — before mid-seventeenth century — used in solid, has become usually very dark or plain brown colour. Later country oak furniture — of the eighteenth century — tends to be lighter and the distinctive 'wormlike' yellow rays are more visible. In fine furniture of late seventeenth and eighteenth centuries, oak was used for drawer linings in plain sawn form, and especially in inner drawers remains light in colour. Also used in veneer form.

Olive. Dark, greenish with black streaking. Used in parquetry, as 'oyster' and in veneers, from late seventeenth century.

Padouk. Red, with blackish figure. Used in solid from mid-eighteenth century and particularly from early nineteenth for military chests.

Pear. Yellowish-brown. Used for country furniture and for carving.

Plum. Yellowish-red. Used for country pieces and as an inlay from the seventeenth century.

Rosewood. Usually reddish-brown with black streaks, but fades to a greyer colour, still with dark streaks. Used from the sixteenth century but mostly found in Regency period in solid and veneer.

Satinwood. Yellow. Used particularly from the late eighteenth century in veneer and solid. Usually makes for price premium.

Sycamore. White with fleck. Used from the late seventeenth century as a veneer. Often found on sides or banding of marquetry furniture of the late seventeenth or early eighteenth century.

Tulipwood. Yellow-brown with reddish stripes. Used for crossbanding from the late eighteenth century.

Walnut. English walnut: golden brown with dark figuring. Much used in veneers from the sixteenth century but particularly 1660-1740. Also cut in burr and oyster form. Solid walnut used extensively in Tudor period. Black walnut: also grown in England from the late seventeenth century; usually called 'Virginian' walnut and much darker. Used in solid and can be mistaken for mahogany at first glance.

Yew. Reddish-brown, very hard, with some burr effects. Polishes magnificently. Used from the sixteenth century; often found in chairs of country origin. Windsors and tables but also used on fine furniture in burr veneer form.

Zebra-wood. Brown with dark stripes. Used as a veneer from the late eighteenth century.

PRICE GUIDE
& REASONS
FOR VALUES

BONHEURS-DU-JOUR AND CHEVERETS

A bonheur-du-jour is a Louis XVIth writing table of delicate proportions which seems to have been emulated in England from the last quarter of the eighteenth century. It is generally rather finely made by quality craftsmen.

A cheveret is a variant on the theme, having, usually, small drawers and a shelf in the upper portion.

Value Points: Satinwood and inlays + + +

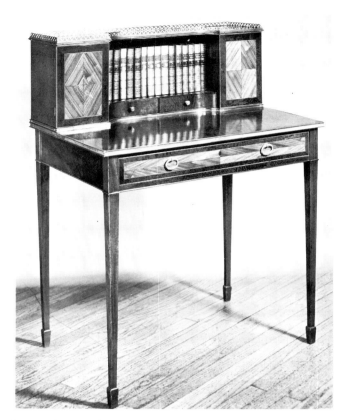

1 (left) A satinwood bonheur-du-jour on tapering square legs. The use of contrasting veneers on the drawer fronts and the doors, together with the extremely fine legs, all point towards high quality.

1780-1800
£7,000 — £9,000

2 A mahogany bonheur-du-jour with a brass gallery above.
1780-1800   *£7,000 — £9,000*

3 (left) A mahogany bonheur-du-jour with a tray shelf beneath. This is a type that was widely copied in Edwardian times.

1780-1800
£4,000 — £5,000

4 (right) A fine small satinwood bureau de dames with painted decoration of cherubs in flower decorated panels and swags on fine tapering legs with stretchers. Made over a long period but originating in the late eighteenth century. Wide range of value due to long period of production. Higher price if known painter.

If late 18th century   *£6,000 — £8,000*

5 A rosewood cheveret with inlaid stringing and banding, with a shelf beneath.

1790-1810   *£4,500 — £5,500*

6 (left) A mahogany cheveret with a hinged folding writing surface which opens to be supported on lopers. 1ft. 9ins wide.

1790-1810
£6,000 — £7,000

7 (right) A mahogany bonheur-du-jour, on turned legs, with painted decoration and with a brass gallery above. In this case the finely turned legs and good use of veneers help the price. Like many of these fine small pieces much copied in Edwardian times (see Agius).

c.1800
£5,500 — £7,500
depending on quality
of painting on
porcelain panels

8 A mahogany bonheur-du-jour on paw feet, with gadrooned edge on the principal surface, beaded edge on the base surface, fluted gallery, supports scrolled to give almost a 'lyre' shape.

1820-1840   *£3,500 — £4,500*

9 A rosewood bonheur-du-jour, with pillar supports, brass gallery — a typical piece of the period.

c.1830   *£2,500 — £3,500*

10 (left) A satinwood bonheur-du-jour by Waring and Gillow, somewhat Sheraton in style.

1850-1870
£3,000—£4,000

11 (right) A nineteenth century reproduction bonheur-du-jour extensively painted with Sheraton/Adam motifs. Note the 'bamboo' edge moulding to the mirror and edge of the table.

1860-1880
£5,000 — £6,000

12 (left) Another painted nineteenth century reproduction with floral decoration and satinwood. High quality. Made over a long period.

1860-1920
£3,500 — £4,500

13 (right) A fine satinwood bonheur-du-jour with excellent inlay work, made by H. Samuel. It is not unknown for nineteenth century cabinet makers who have restored a piece of period furniture to stamp it with their name! This one *could* be right.

If 1890-1910
£4,000 — £5,000

BOOKCASES — large

Bookcases fall into two main types, both the result of the requirements of the rich. The first from the eighteenth and early nineteenth century are floor to ceiling; the small very late eighteenth and nineteenth century examples were bought to preserve wall space for pictures — and even more expensive decoration.

Bookcases have been expensive for some time, whereas break-front wardrobes have been in demand only as embryonic bookcases. Conversion involves cutting about ten inches out of the depth, as clothes are that much wider than books. This and new astragal moulding to replace the solid fronts can leave tell-tale signs.

14 (above) A mahogany break-front bookcase of real quality. The glazing bars, the bracket feet, dentil moulding, decorated surrounds to the doors and matched veneers on the panels all combine to make this a fine example. The bookcase section dominates the lower portion.

c.1770 £20,000 — £24,000

15 (above) A more flamboyant example of the same period and again extremely well made with fine matched veneers, dentil moulded cornice and elegant moulding to the glazed doors.

c.1770 £24,000 — £28,000

16 (right) Here the two wings are gaining in importance. The diamond glazing bars are conventional, the quality of work and workmanship impeccable, but the top moulding, always wide on a good piece, seems to have taken off excessively.

c.1790 £10,000 — £14,000

17 (left) By contrast a small Hepplewhite design. The shaped apron, splay feet, the oval panels of contrasting veneer and the metal attachment to vary the depth of the bookshelves, rather than the regular rebate of the previous examples, all point to the later more refined version. The broken pediment looks thin.

c.1800 £5,000 — £7,000

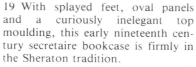

19 With splayed feet, oval panels and a curiously inelegant top moulding, this early nineteenth century secretaire bookcase is firmly in the Sheraton tradition.
c.1805 £10,000 — £14,000

18 A good honest late eighteenth century secretaire bookcase. The moulded bead round the top drawer and the dentil cornice lift it marginally out of the rut. It is typical of hundreds that were made over a long period.
c.1775-1795 £9,000 — £12,000

20 Much more straightforward is this functional piece whose only concession to fashion are the supports so typical of the period.
c.1830 £4,000 — £6,000

21 (left) Another example built on utilitarian lines, but the chamfered corners, well-panelled base, classical mouldings and break-front all lift it above the last example.
c.1840 £5,000 — £6,500

22 (right) Mid-Victorian with the very thin veneer of fine burr walnut that was so widely used at this date. Note the rounded moulding. A decorative and functional piece.

c.1860 £3,500 — £4,500

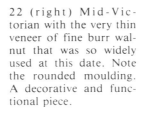

BOOKCASES — dwarf

The so-called dwarf bookcase came into vogue in Regency times. A patent for a revolving example was taken out in 1808. Being smaller they are desirable and hence relatively expensive for the workmanship in them. The very simple ones were also produced in Edwardian times. The distinction between side cabinets, display cabinets and bookcases is a fine one.

23 (above) An early nineteenth century example of Regency style with shell inlays in good quality mahogany veneer. The arches on the top of the doors, the use of applied decoration and the slightly high feet all point towards what will eventually become Victorian fussiness.

c.1820   *£4,000 — £5,500*

24 (right) A type which first came into favour in the last years of the eighteenth century. Very simple reeded moulding, turned legs and applied pillars. Sold at auction early 1978 for £1,250. So simple that logically fakes should abound.

c.1800   *£2,500 — £3,500*

25 Chiffonier or bookcase. Well-veneered in rosewood with pillars flanking and top mirror supported by well-executed scrolls.

c.1810   *£3,500 — £4,500*

26 A 'dwarf' break-front example with brass inlay on rosewood veneer. A good size with plenty of room for display on top.

c.1820   *£4,500 — £6,000*

27 A late Sheraton mahogany veneered example inset with a marble panel on top and two drawers under. Two decorated fluted pillars inset on either side — not a particularly successful design.

c.1820   *£2,500 — £3,500*

The bureau evolved from the simple portable boxes with sloping lids used by writers in the Middle Ages. With a certain stability coming to life, it was useful to have this on a stand rather than to keep using up valuable table space (although Victorians returned to the writing box much later). Towards the third quarter of the seventeenth century this form of desk appears to have been made on a stand as well as continuing in its portable form and our first illustrations show clearly this 'desk on legs', firstly in oak and, later in walnut.

Whilst these bureaux were initially on the turned legs and octagonal legs of the period, in due course they followed the fashion and were raised on cabrioles. This continued into the mahogany period — as the first section shows — but in later years they were put on square tapering legs but with modifications to the top desk section.

However, the merit of using the space beneath for drawers in chest form could not be ignored. In some early bureaux of the 1680-1700 period this form shows clearly the union between desk and chest by the moulding above the drawer section, which continues right round the sides and was retained, in an almost absent-minded way, either to appease traditionalists or as a decorative feature. The fall-front bureaux, originating as a simple desk, continued to be popular throughout the eighteenth and early nineteenth centuries. Walnut, then mahogany, were used, but elm, fruitwood, ash, oak and other available woods were quite often used by the provincial or country maker.

The style and construction of the drawers followed those of chests of the same period and the same constructional points apply.

Value Points:
All bureaux
1. Structural condition and originality + + +
2. Size: Width 3ft. or under + +
          Width 2ft. 9ins. or under + + +
          Width 2ft. 6ins. or under + + + +
3. Original brass handles and keyhole plates + +
4. Oak drawer linings +
Up to 1690 — The Oak Period
1. Colour and patination + + +
2. Original bun or bracket feet + +
3. Interior stepped + + +
4. Well + +
5. Quality of mouldings + +
1680-1740 — The Walnut Period
1. Quality and figure of veneers, colour and patination + + +
2. Herring-bone inlays and crossbanding + +
3. Stringing and other inlays + +
4. Marquetry + + + +
5. Original bun or bracket feet + +
6. Colour (faded) and quality of cross-grained mouldings + + +
7. Interior stepped + + +
8. Well + +

For oak and fruitwood of this period value points 3, 5, 7 and 8 as in the walnut period also apply plus the following:—
Choice of figured woods, colour and patination + + +
Quality of mouldings + +
1730 onwards — The Mahogany Period
It should be remembered that mahogany and walnut periods overlapped each other for about ten years from 1730-1740 and possibly longer. Value points for mahogany bureaux are:—
Quality and choice of figured wood, colour (faded or rich Spanish mahogany) and patination + + +
Interior arrangement + +
Quality of mouldings + +
Original bracket feet +
For oak and fruitwood examples of the period the above points also apply.

BUREAUX — on stands

28 Late seventeenth century oak bureau showing the evolution from a simple desk to more complex internal drawers and pigeon holes under the fall-front. The bureau is on a stand with a single drawer in it and on baluster-turned legs with square stretchers, one of which is missing (left-hand side). Note here the 'desk' section overlaps the stand.

1675-1700   *£2,000 — £3,000*

29 (left) Walnut bureau on stand with octagonal tapering legs ending in bun feet and linked by an X-stretcher. The fall is decoratively veneered with three sheets of walnut and cross-banded outside a 'feather' or herring-bone inlay. The 'desk' still overhangs the 'stand' part but the drawers have now increased to three. There is a book or bible rest moulding on the fall.

1680-1700 *£12,000 — £15,000*

30 (below left) A really superb arabesque marquetry bureau on a later stand with square chamfered legs and an X-stretcher. Note how the inside is 'stepped' to take advantage of the space under the fall.

1680-1700 *£16,000 — £22,000*

31 (below) A walnut bureau on stand with turned legs with inverted cup forms and bun feet with an X-stretcher. Note that now the bureau no longer hangs over the supports and that more locked space has been achieved by blanking off the top drawer and making access via the desk, i.e. a well.

1680-1700 *Assuming stand right £8,000 — £12,000*
If stand is wrong £3,000 — £4,500

32 (right) A walnut Queen Anne bureau on cabriole legs with trefoil feet. Note how the stand has become wider than the desk. A type much reproduced.

1710-1730   *If stand right £12,000 — £15,000*
If stand wrong and bureau is the sawn off top of a conventional bureau (e.g. fig.36) £3,000 — £4,500

33 (below) A mahogany bureau on cabriole-legged stand. The cabrioles are good — nice scroll behind the knee, good balance down to the pad feet.

1730-1745   *£5,000 — £6,000*

34 (below right) Chippendale at work — how he liked carved cabrioles! A mahogany Chippendale-design bureau with a blind fret around the top of the stand (beneath the drawers, which are cock-beaded) and cabrioles with scroll and leaf carving ending in ball-and-claw feet.

1750-1760   *£8,000 — £12,000*

Early eighteenth century bureaux are highly prized as examples of cabinet making at its best. As can be seen from the value points listed at the start of the Bureaux section, the inside fittings are important in determining value, as is size. They are extremely useful in the modern home for, when closed, they hide all the mess and exhibit the fine veneers on the fall at just the right angle to reflect the colour of the wood.

The value of any late seventeenth or early eighteenth century walnut veneered furniture tends to be greatly influenced by original brass handles and untouched patination and could lift the values above those quoted.

35 The bureau as we know it today but a very grand affair in mulberry wood. The stepped interior and all drawers are shaped and there is a well. The mulberry is very striking and brass inlay heightens the effect. These pieces are nearly all ascribed to Coxed and Woster who are known to have made them. A 'C & W' label would help the price.

c.1740   *£25,000 – £30,000*

36 This Queen Anne walnut bureau would originally have had bun feet. It has a first rate interior with most likely the original brass buttons on the drawers. The double half-round moulding between the drawers and the herring-bone veneer on the drawer fronts are an indication of the late William and Mary and Queen Anne period, e.g. before 1720. The dark strip on the side shows this bureau once had a moulding around the carcase where the bureau part finished and the drawer began. A relic of the days when the bureau part just stood on the three drawer base. The signs of other handles can just be seen on the drawer fronts. This one is just 3ft. wide. At 2ft. 8ins. the price might be +£1,000.

c.1700   When restored £10,000 – £14,000
Colour very important

37 (left) The next development of walnut bureaux, showing ovolo lip moulding around the drawer edges and flat veneered carcase fronts. The interior now has fluted pillars — a touch of pre-William Kent — but is still stepped. The feet and the lower mouldings look original, as do most of the brass handles and the lock on the fall. A very nice bureau. About 2ft. 6ins. but high price only if of good quality.

c.1730   *Because of size £7,000 — £10,000*

38 (below left) Items in solid walnut like this very fine bureau used to be considered one down to veneered pieces but the increasing respect for good colour, patina and original handles is fast rectifying this position. Besides, so much 'wrong' veneered walnut exists and central heating without humidifiers plays havoc with veneers, that many collectors are showing interest in non-veneered pieces, especially when they are as good as this one.

c.1730   *£6,000 — £8,000*

39 (below) A small oak bureau on buns with the desirable feature of being under 3ft. wide. A stepped interior is also good to see as is the concave section of its drawer fronts. A simple half-round moulding on the carcase face of the chest is the only decoration. This is a good honest piece with a well and attractive interior. The drop handles are replacements as one can see the two round circles where swan neck handles were fitted.

1690-1700   *£3,500 — £4,500*
Because small; colour very important

BUREAUX — some more early 18th century

The bureaux set out in the last section are all good standard bureaux of some quality; most of them superb. However not every bureau you will meet is beautiful, or even honest, while some that will at first sight strike the newcomer to antiques as merely homely have a hidden quality that gradually becomes more appreciated — here is a selection. See also the Victorian 'carve up' section.

40 Until about 1965 oak bureaux were relatively cheap while the walnut version was expensive — a differential which some found worthwhile to exploit. This bureau is veneered in fruitwood oysters, though clams might be a better description. The 'improver' has missed the point that oysters should be arranged in some sort of artistic pattern, not laid like floor tiles.

c.1710   *£2,500 — £3,500*

41 This bureau has a well, and there are places for holes at the corners where the bun feet used to fit. Furthermore it has the clumsily solid look of a bureau pre-1700, and the drawer fronts show the marks where the original drop handles were fitted. Admitted it has Regency looking mouldings applied but then a lot of furniture has been through the mill over the years. The problem is that it is made in Honduras mahogany. In other words made in a style of c.1690 with a wood which wasn't available until about 1740. The buyer who should have had more sense got rid of it fast at no profit. It was early American; motto — think.

c.1740   *£4,000 — £5,000*

42 (below left) This is a totally honest walnut bureau but it is included here because of the very uninteresting grain used. Quite rightly the veneers on the drawers are from consecutive cuts of the log but the effect brings no joy. The colour also looks flat, and 'cleaned off' walnut (or for that matter any surface that purports to be 250 years old) should have a number of subtle shades, not look as though it was french polished yesterday. If this is the case the price will be affected.

c.1720   *£3,000 — £4,000*

43 (opposite, below right) Although restraint was the keynote of much early work, flamboyant pieces are not uncommon. However, in the coarsest there is a degree of restraint, particularly on the sides, which are simply veneered. Here there is oyster panelling and crossbanding but confined to the bottom half of the side. The excessive use of light coloured wood is also not common. A buyer should give such a piece very careful inspection.

c.1730   *If wrong £2,500 — £3,500*
                              If right £7,000 — £9,000

44 (below) Made in solid walnut and cross-banded on the outside drawers with a contrasting fruitwood, this simple country made bureau has a stepped interior, a well and decorative frets to the tops of the pigeon-holes. At the bottom there are original bracket feet and a good wide moulding. Thus it has many of the characteristics of earlier pieces.

c.1730   *£3,000 — £4,000*

45 (right) A very similar bureau though of less quality. The colour is quite good but the lack of stepped interior and bottom moulding tell against it, as does the slightly ungainly height. It has lip moulding to the drawers.

c.1740   *£2,500 — £3,500*

46 (below right) Finally a very modest little country oak bureau with a well and big deep drawers. The handles may be original and, together with the double-D moulding would suggest a date of 1720 but as the interior is so simple one normally adds a few years for the fact that town fashions took time to reach the country. But it is small.

Say c.1730   *£900 — £1,200*

BUREAUX — later 18th century

47 A small (about 2ft. 9ins.) example veneered in the dark heavy Cuban mahogany which was among the first of the many types of this wood to be widely used for cabinet work. After years of decorative figured walnut this simple grain must have made a pleasing contrast. The appearance is slightly spoilt by the replacement handles; the originals would have been the shape of the keyplate. With attractive interior it will be expensive.

c.1745   £5,000 — £7,000

48 A good quality cedar wood bureau with an interior typical of a good quality piece of the period. The drawers at the side are stepped and the inside divisions have a well-decorated edge. Another good feature is the curved front section of the two drawers flanking the central door. The two applied pillars conceal thin vertical drawers. In addition all the drawers and the door are inlaid with pale coloured stringing lines, probably holly or sycamore — in all a pretty little interior. Cedar can form a fine patination not unlike yew, in which case the price will be at the top end of the scale. This, together with the relatively small size, about 3ft. 1in., make it a desirable example.

c.1750   £5,000 — £7,500

49 A typical provincial mahogany bureau gradually becoming longer and with a plainer interior. The presence of a door and pillars is a redeeming feature. The mahogany being used is a lighter and redder colour, a characteristic which was encouraged.

c.1770 £2,500 — £3,500

50 This is an example of good quality as demonstrated by blind fret door and top to the pigeon-holes, the stepped drawers and the bold well-moulded ogee shaped feet. At 3ft. 6ins. wide it is moving towards the large size but is by no means large for the period.

c.1760 £2,500 — £3,500

51 The bureau becomes longer and more plain, nevertheless the lighter Honduras mahogany has good figure and the quality of workmanship is excellent. Very typical of many to be seen. Being over 4ft. wide has a distinct effect on price.

c.1760 £1,750 — £2,250

52 A late eighteenth century bureau in which the mahogany has been chosen for its decorative markings. The inside fittings, though nothing exciting, are decorated with satinwood veneers — a good point, which, together with splayed Hepplewhite feet, give it a lighter appearance. The handles are stamped out of brass sheet rather than cast.

c.1780-1800   *£3,500 — £4,500*

53 Again on splayed feet with a shaped apron and cross-banded with satinwood on the fall. Now rather moving up in height like the chests of drawers of the period.

c.1820   *£1,000 — £1,500*

54 The three rather than four drawer arrangement gives a dumpy appearance. The inside is a straight fronted series of drawers. Still the drawer linings are of oak and the piece is soundly constructed. Made in the provinces over a long period. The price is relatively high because bureaux are in demand.

c.1800-1820   *£900 — £1,200*

BUREAU BOOKCASES

In the main, the same rules apply to the value of bureau bookcases as are applied to bureaux themselves and the dating of them lies in an understanding of the mouldings and types of veneered decoration. However, for the bureau bookcase there are additional features, particularly the decoration of the top moulding and the way the door fronts are arranged which give further signs of quality.

The essential point is, of course, to make sure that the top and bottom were made at the same time and that there has not been a marriage of two separate pieces. Among the points to check are colour, arrangements of drawers, old screw holes where the top has been secured, any signs of new cabinet work where the top may have been thinned or narrowed, the quality of wood used at both front and back and drawer lining materials and workmanship. Look carefully at the decoration, has some been added to one half to make it look more like the other? Often very difficult to tell.

Value points: as for bureaux plus the following point which apply to the top half.
domed or broken pediments + + +
mouldings of high quality + + +
original mirror or glass + + +
glazing bar arrangement + +

55 This superb George I walnut and carved parcel gilt example is a first rate piece in which the fitted work on the top half has been taken to such an extent that it has made it into a cabinet rather than a bookcase. The use of pillars, fine carving both on the acanthus cartouche medallion and the massive paw feet make it a formidable example of English cabinet work. It is only marginally over 6ft. which further enhances its desirability. Still modestly priced in terms of Continental furniture.

c.1720 £240,000+

BUREAU BOOKCASES — walnut

56 (left) A walnut bureau bookcase of finely figured walnut, with double-D mouldings and a dividing moulding around the bureau section — relic of earlier divisions (see Bureau). There is a bookrest moulding on the fall. The top has candle slides below the shaped mirrored doors, which are edged with cross-grained mouldings.

1700-1720 *£18,000 — £22,000*

57 (right) A burr elm bureau bookcase with attractive deeply cut mouldings to the top of the bookcase and round the sides ('returns'). The doors have bevelled Vauxhall glass doors and fine mouldings missing only a pair of engraved stars to make it the classic example. It has, of course, candle slides and beautifully matched veneers.

1700-1720 *£50,000 — £70,000*

58 (left) The classic profile of the good quality bureau bookcase of the period with great deep top mouldings and 'returns' to balance them. Finely shaped and bevelled glass. But the bottom has cock-beading and flat veneering instead of double-D moulding, and brackets instead of buns. This is almost certainly a marriage. For further evidence look at the difference between the wood on the side of the bureau and the bookcase. Finally, the inside fittings of the top have double-D mouldings. Priced accordingly. The top price if you have a William and Mary bureau missing a top or vice versa.

Top c.1700
Bottom c.1730 £7,000 — £9,000
If right £16,000 — £20,000

59 (right) A single-width (2ft. 3ins.) burr walnut example with cock-beaded drawers. The price drops principally because of the plain moulding.

1720-1740 *£20,000 — £25,000*

Plate 22. A mulberry wood bureau. The solid design places it at the very start of the eighteenth century. The use of pewter stringing lines highlighting the inlay is a typical feature linked with the London firm of Coxed and Woster. The inside has a sliding panel to the 'well' beneath, a central door, curved fronted drawers under pigeon holes and stepped forward sides. The whole piece resonates quality. The colour here is typical; note the large amount of black blotches on the side where twin panels of lesser quality wood are used.
c.1700

Plate 23. In the fifteen years since the last example the bureau becomes slightly taller and thinner but the effect is exaggerated by the adoption of carefully graduated drawers, the tall simply designed bracket feet and the disappearance of the moulding below the well. The burr walnut is of high quality and carefully chosen, as may be seen by the design achieved on the writing fall by the use of four consecutively cut pieces of veneer joined so as to produce an effect similar to marbled paper. The drawers fronts too are cut from consecutive pieces of burr wood but the sides, following the common practice, are decorated with two plain matching pieces of vertically placed walnut. Note the crossbanding; if it wasn't there the walnut would tend to split along the vertical grain. The colour on the front is excellent, faded but warm. The sides show in the photograph the less desirable yellow tinge which may however be a colour distortion from the photographer's lights. A well made, elegant piece of quality. Note how the use of cockbeading round the drawers gives a clean finish; it is even used on the pull-out which supports the writing fall. This is a very desirable piece in fine condition, made by a very competent craftsman.
c.1715-1725

Plate 24. Typical of walnut bureaux made from about 1715 to perhaps the late 1740s by 'provincial' craftsmen who either didn't keep up with design changes or worked for clients who liked the William and Mary look. Straight grained walnut has been used which would have been much cheaper than the burr in Plate 23. Like the maker of figure 42, the craftsman tried to get decorative effect by using soft, yellow sapwood on the fall, something that the maker of Plate 23 would avoid if he could. Faced with inferior wood he would have cut it off or at least made sure that the sapwood on the right came up the couple of inches to match the left-hand side and produce some sort of pattern. Notice too the economy in using as small pieces as possible. On Plate 23 the walnut is the same right across the face of the drawers, the inlaid stringing lines merely for decorative effect. Here the broad crossbanding uses up small pieces and saves on the size of the central section. The same is true of the sides. The lip moulding will break off if the drawer-stops come loose or if the drawers contract, whereas in Plate 23 the cockbeading would not stop the drawer from moving inwards undamaged. The piece has probably been repolished this century (see 'Colour and Patination') and the feet have the lower, broader design associated with late pieces.

The above comments are designed to highlight the original difference in cost of construction and illustrate what is conveniently known as 'provincial' workmanship, though in fact future research may show that it is simply a cheaper model than Plate 23.

Plate 25. The three previous examples were made of veneered walnut about 1/16in. thick; this is made out of the solid wood. It has no decorative grain so wasn't worth putting through the expensive and wasteful process of sawing into veneers. The colour is typical. Note how light and polishing on the upper section have produced a honey colour, whereas below there is a greyer, dull colour mainly associated with dirt. The sapwood on the back of the side is clearly lighter. The missing moulding on the left-hand side exposes the unpolished wood.

Looking back over the three previous examples the mixed design is clear. The fall has a book-rest but the well has gone; however, the top two drawers retain their boldness so there is no gradation of drawer sizes. The bracket feet look too unsubtle for craftsmen who could put together such a well-made fall and moulded book-rest so one would take out the bottom drawer expecting to see the round holes for the shafts of the original buns. The applied double round mouldings between the drawers look back to an earlier period. The escutcheon plates could be right but the brasses on the lower drawers look out of keeping. Are there holes where the drop handles went? How did these handles fit on the top two drawers if the escutcheon plate on the right-hand side is original? Could the well have been converted to drawers late in the century, explaining the different handles? This is interesting but academic. Repaired, and the feet returned to buns or reshaped, this is a pleasant furnishing piece.
First quarter 18th century

Plate 26. Clearly British in design but oriental in decorative treatment, this padouk double-doored bureau cabinet (the correct title because it is not fitted out as a bookcase) was made in India. All the mountings are of silver and the inlay is ivory foliage set in ebony. The result is a rare and sumptuous piece of good Anglo-Indian work. The cartouche on the fall is engraved with the arms of the original owner and thus establishes provenance.

The profile is classic and, apart from the treatment of the top of the mirrors, which is a happy mixture of styles, the decoration has been largely confined to areas of crossbanding. The early design is confirmed by the typical William and Mary arrangement of drawers. Only the thin drawer immediately under the fall looks a little out of place — the handles and the escutcheons have had to be foreshortened. Can it really be a drawer? If so either the ends are a strange shape to cope with the fall supports or the crossbanding is not on the drawer side. But this is only a minor quibble about a very fine piece in original condition. Only the bun feet are later replacements. *Probably first decade 18th century*

Plate 27. A transitional form of bureau cabinet dating from the very late 17th century in which the cabinet is wider than the bureau on which it sits. This is not normally a very happy arrangement and is reflected by a generally lower price than for the later straight sided form.

But this piece was made by a skilled craftsman with a good eye for design and it exudes quality. He clearly wasn't happy with the normal top-heavy effect so he added small scrolls either side which ease the eye over the break in form. He made the top of the moulded arch in the cabinet with confident boldness and he got the gradation of the drawers right. His choice of veneers is inspired; look at the way the burr fits into the arch and at the bottom the crossed lines give a finished look. Is it too far fetched to visualise a comparison with contemporary crewel work representations of the tree of life? Perhaps.

Time appears to have given the piece a good colour and there is a suggestion of some patination, though it is not possible to say with certainty from the photograph. Notice how the wood supporting the veneer on the fall and the top of the doors has moved and cracked the veneer slightly. This does not matter. However, it is hard to believe that the man who put this delightful piece together was responsible for the ugly cannon-ball bun feet which are the only feature which jars

Plate 28 Commercially this form of double dome bureau bookcase (there are no inside fittings other than for books) is much more desirable than the one just described. This is a perfectly respectable example of its type but, from the photograph at least, it lacks flair. The execution is sound and it looks in immaculate condition, but the veneers, though carefully arranged on the drawers fronts, have no visible form on the fall, the grain is straight and lacks inspiration and the handles are too small. For me (and remember these comments are subjective) the piece stands awkwardly, the bottom moulding is too heavy and is emphasised rather than relieved by the design on the bottom rail which serves only to highlight the pedestrian design of the bracket feet. The section designed to hold the candle slides looks thick in proportion to their size.

But most damning, if the camera has got it right, is the dead flat colour which suggests that the piece has been repolished this century.
c. 1700

Plate 29. A walnut bureau bookcase of the 1720s, to which time has not been kind. It originally had lighter wooden doors or more possibly a pair of mirrors — glass being heavier would have required stronger support — and this may become clear when the piece is examined in detail. Certainly it would look better without the half view of the modest arrangement of drawers and pigeon holes.

Raised on shaped bracket feet which are out of proportion to the rest of the piece, the Chinese Chippendale handles could not have been added until thirty years after it was made, if indeed they are not modern reproductions.

The craftsman has done his best with modest veneers. He's used them sensibly on the fall and the drawers are properly proportioned. The well arrangement to which handles have been fitted is old fashioned at this date and the top moulding is far too thin, consisting of only a gentle curve.

The piece appears to have some colour and, when reglazed and polished, and the feet sorted, will be a useful furnishing piece.

60 A good walnut bureau bookcase with herring-bone banding to the drawers. When looking at any bureau bookcase one has to decide whether the two parts started out life together. However, when the quality of the piece is such that the top half if well fitted with drawers and doors that clearly match those in the bottom half, both in veneers and patination as in this piece, the originality is obvious. Notice the insides of the doors are well veneered. Apart from the plain moulding it lacks only a door and curved drawers to the inside to put it right at the top.

1720-1740 £28,000 — £35,000

61 A good solid walnut bureau bookcase with fielded panel doors, good mouldings and unusual drawer arrangement, shown open and closed. Single heavily moulded pediment and fine interior fittings. The price is lower because it is in the solid rather than veneered and it has no glass, but in fact it is a better quality piece than many veneered ones, i.e. the top mouldings and good interior fittings especially in the bureau.

1730-1745
£14,000 — £18,000

BUREAU BOOKCASES —
early mahogany

63 A Chinese lacquer double-domed bureau bookcase on serpentine bracket feet. Note how the constructional features are similar to those of walnut pieces — double-D moulding (gilded) etc. Finials are missing.

1720-1740　　　　*Assume original lacquer £40,000　　£80,000*
　　　　　　　　　　If lacquer 20th century £7,000　　£15,000

62 A magnificent mahogany bureau bookcase under the influence of William Kent's architectural style — fluted pillar decoration, splendid broken pediment, canted fluted pillar corners to the bureau, serpentine bracket feet. 8ft. 6ins. high. A very wide piece though — 5ft. 2ins. — and possibly designed for a specific room. The name rather than the quality or size makes it so expensive. Top price for documented piece or one with good provenance.

1740-1750　　　　　　　*£40,000 — £50,000*

64 (right) Another lacquer bureau bookcase of similar quality shown with the mirrored doors open. Again good mouldings and returns (i.e. the side mouldings).

1720-1740　　　　　　　*£35,000 — £45,000*

65 A mahogany bureau bookcase with broken pediment including dentil frieze, canted fluted corners. Note the use of small side drawers as supports for the fall.

1750-1760   *£14,000 — £18,000*

66 A George III mahogany bureau cabinet with panelled doors, showing an interesting grain and a plain frieze with dentil moulding. The interior is elaborately fitted. The fall is inlaid with the initials WM and the date 1767. This is a piece of reasonable quality but with a plain top is not particularly exciting. It is 7ft. 1in. high.

c.1767
£6,000 — £8,000

67 Bureau bookcase in mahogany veneer with glazed doors and broken pediment. A very standard piece which joins the utility of the bureau with the even more desirable feature of display.

1750-1770
£9,000 — £12,000

68 Mahogany à la Chippendale — fretted broken pediment and frieze; blind fretted carcase edges and even the bracket feet are carved. As elaborate pediments add to the price and as few Chippendale wardrobes still retain them, make sure the two parts started life together.

1750-1770
£14,000 — £18,000

69 Fretted broken pediment, elegant glazed doors, bracket feet, vase and ribbon inlaid into fall and a satinwood frieze under the top moulding.

1780-1790   *£14,000 — £16,000*
1880-1910   *£5,000 — £7,000*

70 Hepplewhite elegance in mahogany; splayed feet, veneered and inlaid doors, glazed top and fretted broken pediment and central platform for a finial, not present. Note how well the veneers are matched — just to show Grandad Walnut that the new boys could do it too — a highly considered piece.

1780-1790   *£12,000 — £16,000*

71 A highly decorated Sheraton mahogany bureau bookcase with nicely matched veneers and ornate inlays, on splay feet. Thought to be Scottish.

1790-1810   *£9,000 — £12,000*

72 A straightforward mahogany bureau bookcase of late Georgian period, without decoration. Made repeatedly up to and including the present day.

1790-1810   *£4,500 — £5,500*

73 A nineteenth century reproduction, worthy of Edwards and Roberts, in mahogany with satinwood cross-banding.

1880-1910   *£2,000 — £3,000*

BUREAU BOOKCASES — oak

Eighteenth century oak examples of fashionable objects like bureau bookcases are generally thought of purely as provincial or even country pieces; indeed many are, but the range of quality varies enormously. They were made throughout a very long period of time.

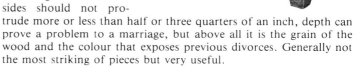

75 Very typical of the solidly well-made pieces produced in oak; like the previous example it has two candle slides. The fielded panels are well shaped and the top moulding is broad which helps to balance the bulk of the piece. Hundreds like it have been made and others married. Check that any screw holes in the bottom of the top half go through into the bottom. The moulding round the sides should not protrude more or less than half or three quarters of an inch, depth can prove a problem to a marriage, but above all it is the grain of the wood and the colour that exposes previous divorces. Generally not the most striking of pieces but very useful.

c.1750   *£4,500 — £6,500*

74 Here for example is a piece in oak which has almost everything one could ask of a walnut veneered example of the same period. One has only to look at the well-designed stepped interior and the fine double domed moulding of the bookcase, to appreciate that it was the customer who asked for a plain bookcase interior, not the maker who couldn't make one.

c.1710   *£8,000 — £10,000*

76 The shallow curved apron, the mahogany crossbanding and above all the dentil moulding and unimaginative arrangement of the glazing bars all point to a late provincial piece. Though probably original, the top looks small for the bureau compared with earlier examples, but this is quite usual and was probably accounted for by the lower ceilings of the more modest houses for which such bureau bookcases were intended.

c.1790
£3,000 — £4,000

105

BUREAUX — cylinder and tambour

The use of a sliding cylinder or tambour instead of a fall seems to have become most prevalent in the late eighteenth century and to have continued in use throughout the nineteenth, when the roll-top desk became widely used in offices.

This form of writing desk or bureau merits a section on its own although the value points, apart from the cylinder or tambour itself, are the same as those of bureaux and bureau bookcases of the same period. It should be noted, however, that since this is a more expensive way of covering the interior section than the fall front, these pieces tended to be of reasonably high craftsmanship.

77 (left and below) A high quality Sheraton cylinder writing desk and bookcase, shown both open and closed. The piece is in harewood, with oval mahogany inlaid panels of finely figured wood. Note how the writing surface slides out to give greater space.

1790-1810   *£17,000 — £22,000*

78 A burr yew writing cabinet, banded in satinwood and shown with its top open and the drawer, which is fitted like that of a dressing table or chest, also opened. The broken pediment has a vase-shaped finial. The glazing bars are arched in Gothic style. Both bureau and bookcase are fitted with carrying handles.

1790-1810   *£16,000 — £22,000*

79 A satinwood writing table with a dome-shaped tambour top and fitted with side slides. It is inlaid with marquetry and exhibits a very high degree of craftsmanship.

1790-1810   *£12,000 — £15,000*

80 A mahogany writing table with a dome-shaped tambour top, shown open to reveal the inner drawings and fittings. Like the previous example it is fitted with slides at the sides.

1790-1810   *£6,000 — £8,000*

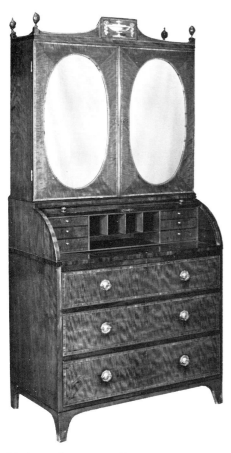

83 A mahogany cylinder writing desk on square tapering legs, inlaid with stringing lines. There is a brass rail, or gallery, around the top.

1790-1820   *£5,000*   *£7,000*

81 A mahogany cylinder bureau with glazed cabinet above, on splayed feet.

1790-1810   *£10,000 — £12,000*

82 A mahogany cylinder bureau bookcase with cabinet doors beneath, inlaid with stringing lines. The feet are a later Victorian replacement. Again the mahogany veneer is of very fine quality.

1820-1840   *£5,500 — £7,000*

84 A cylinder mahogany bureau on fluted bun feet, with a brass gallery. The quality of veneer chosen is very high.

1830-1840
£3,500 — £5,000

85 A kingwood cylinder bureau bookcase on square tapering legs, with much use of inset panel decoration.

1810-1830   *£7,000 — £9,000*

88 A cylinder lady's writing desk in mahogany, with a brass gallery. The columns at the front are decorated with twist and fluted carving. The piece is clearly influenced by French Empire neo-classical styles.

1810-1830   *£4,500 — £6,000*

86 A mahogany and satinwood cylinder desk and bookcase on turned legs. Castors on a cabinet full of porcelain! Would look much better with tapered legs.

c.1810   *If right £5,000 — £7,000*

87 A rosewood and brass-inlaid cylinder desk and bookcase on turned legs.

1820-1830   *£4,000 — £6,000*

89 (left) A late Victorian 'Sheraton' style satinwood cylinder lady's writing cabinet with oval panels. The Sheraton revival came late in the nineteenth century.

1870-1890   *£3,500 — £4,500*

90 (right) A late Victorian or early Edwardian cylinder-front bureau in the style known as 'Edwardian Sheraton'. Apart from the Gothic arching of the gallery around the top, the ivory and boxwood inalid decoration uses classical motifs in the Adam tradition. Note, however, the turned finials which are used to terminate the centre frame verticals and which are also used on the top corners of the gallery. These finials appear to have been irresistible to Victorian manufacturers. The slide, on which the baize inner writing surface is found, pulls out to provide more writing space.

1890-1910   *£2,000 — £3,000*

CANTERBURIES

The name Canterbury was originally given to a piece of mobile furniture named after one of the archbishops who liked the convenience this mobility provided for perhaps a rather sedentary nature. Sheraton illustrated a supper Canterbury which was the forerunner of the modern tea trolley, being equipped with sections for cutlery and plates. There were also atlas Canterburies and more importantly, music stands or Canterburies, which are now the most commonly found type.

The music Canterbury appears around 1800 and has the characteristic mahogany design features of that period — slightly severe outline often curving down in the middle, turned legs with perhaps a little turned decoration of collar or 'bamboo' double rimming and the legs ending in neat brass castors. Most Victorian Canterburies were made to fit under the pianoforte when it was not in use. They tend to be rather exuberantly if more flimsily made and to incorporate such usual decorative effects as scroll carving, elaborately turned uprights and burr veneers. Towards the end of the period they sometimes became dual purpose pieces, e.g. a writing slope being added to the top. Interestingly most forms had been established by the 1860s. W. Smee & Sons, 1850, and W. Blackie, 1853, show most of the types which follow (see *Pictorial Dictionary of British 19th Century Furniture Design*).

Although perhaps more useful for magazines and newspapers rather than the parlour ballads and sacred music they originally contained, Canterburies have.tended to be rather expensive pieces of furniture when assessed by the workmanship put in to them. However, they are small and often decorative so perhaps these desirable characteristics should be considered before we grumble at the prices. We have gone beyond the normal stopping date of about 1860 generally adopted in this book, because many of the designs continued on while others which look early did not arrive until late in the century.

91 A mahogany Canterbury of Sheraton design, a type he illustrated in his *Cabinet Directory* of 1803 and, apart from the turned legs identical to one by Gillows in 1793, considered a very restrained design which continued in broadly the same shape for forty years, by which time a rather bulbous turned collar appeared.

1800-1810   *£1,300 — £1,800*

92 (left) A mahogany Canterbury with turned corner uprights terminating in knobs.

1830-1860   *£800 — £1,100*

93 A rosewood Canterbury with turned uprights, flat divisions and a thin second drawer under the solid top. Not an elegant piece.

1830-1850   *£800 — £950*

94 A rosewood Canterbury with lyre motif in the divisions. Almost identical to one advertised in 1850 and typical of the period. Lyres seem to fetch money.

1850-1870 £800 — £1,100

95 A walnut example with the heavily decorated features of the period.

1850-1870 £900 — £1,200

96 Yet another design advertised in the 1850 catalogue of W. Smee & Co. He shows it as a single decker but given Victorian taste, it was no doubt ordered as a double to match the whatnot.

c. 1850 £1,000 — £1,300

97 This design is late 1860s. The top lifts up to form a writing slope; note the wide sections to the foot like the last example.

c. 1860 £700 — £900

99 A rosewood Canterbury with flat divisions of scrolled design incorporating Prince of Wales feather motif in low relief carving. A rather nasty crude looking piece, probably 1860s or later.

c.1860-1870   *£500   £650*

98 A burr walnut Canterbury with kidney or half round shape with fretted brass gallery to the top and decorative fretwork divisions below.

1860s   *£1,200 — £1,800*

101 (left) Bamboo furniture is a subject on its own but as one can clearly see from this example it is the decoration rather than the structure which is important. Hence this Canterbury is modestly priced.

c.1880   *£150   £200*

102 (right) Almost an exact copy from a catalogue of 1880.

1880   *£700 — £1,000*

100 Although a type which was used in a more refined form in the 1840s to the 1860s the rather heavier construction suggests 1870s.

c.1870   *£600 — £800*

CHAIRS — wainscot

Prior to the early seventeenth century the head of the house and his wife sat on chairs, the rest on stools. The chair was, therefore, a status symbol. By late Elizabethan times the chair had become the solidly constructed type illustrated, usually in oak, 1666 saw a furniture maker's dream come true — a fire destroying nearly all fashionable London without loss of life, and a new style lately arrived from the Continent with Charles II.

The oak panelled chair was dead in fashionable society but, judging by the number of these chairs dating as late as 1748, the style enjoyed continued popularity in the country, especially the north.

Value Points: Marquetry, good vigorous deep carving, inlay and, of course, patination. Ideally the chair should have a slightly high back with plenty of decoration on the top — the throne effect. The pattern should be clearly defined as a specific subject and not just general decoration.

103 A fine example, inlaid in flower patterns of various woods, and deeply carved. The decorative top rail and shoulder pieces combine to provide a suitably impressive back-cloth to the sitter's head.

If c.1600 (see Chinnery)   £9,000 — £12,000

104 An example with fluted legs and arm supports and carved panelled back with guilloche carving on the uprights and seat rails, but replaced top rail (see section on Victorian carving).

c.1625   Assuming 'right' £2,500 — £3,500

105 (above) A chair of a simpler but still well carved design incorporating birds which can be identified to a group made in South Yorkshire in the third quarter of the seventeenth century (see Chinnery). It is vigorously carved and retains the high top rail and supporting pieces of the earlier type.

c.1650-1675 £4,000 — £6,000

106 (above right) Comes from another well defined group in Cheshire (see Chinnery) and has very good carving with flowers and vines in an almost tapestry type outline. The pyramid finials on the top of the low back are typical of the group.

c.1660 £4,000 — £5,000

107 (right) Dated 1678 with baluster rather than straight turned legs and simple top rail, the back with shallow carving of decorated diamond form — probably South Yorkshire.

1678 £2,500 — £3,500

CHAIRS — oak dining, 1650-1700

By the mid-seventeenth century single oak chairs instead of stools came into vogue for diners other than the head of the house and his wife. They were similar in construction, often with vertical slats rather than panels in the back. Normally, the back uprights are of square section, whereas there is some turning on the front legs and a central, turned front cross-stretcher. These chairs did not have the same range of carving as the prestigious panelled chair.

108 This is a sophisticated walnut example showing Continental (mainly Dutch) influence on British post-Restoration design. This fine bold chair shows the walnut through the original ebonising, particularly on the moulded back and scrolled stretcher.

c.1670 £550 — £650

109 This is an early Carolean chair, with a high back and solid severe back uprights but turned front legs and cross-stretcher. Vertical back slats are moulded, the top rail carved with scrolls. The back uprights end in a scroll — a feature of these chairs.

c.1660-1680 £350 — £450

110 A highly distinctive Yorkshire/Derbyshire chair, typified by two or more horizontal back rails normally incorporating down turned crescents or open circles. Turned adornments, such as the acorns seen here, applied split balusters and curved tops to the backs are also found. The back rails are almost always carved or at least incised. The entire decoration is 'above table', presumably for show, for the bases are conventional, the occasional variation being a high rail to retain a cushion on the solid seat.

Mid-to-late 17th century £900 — £1,200

111 Shows later design, both in the back, which has a down curved centre in the top rail, and in the shaped centre splat which fits into a 'shoe' at seat level which suggests a post-1710 date. While the base is similar in design to the previous examples, the turning has lost its vigour and the central decoration on the underside of the front seat rail is a later concept.

Post-1710 £250 — £350

CHAIRS — late 17th century, lighter 'Anglo Dutch' designs

112 (left) In the 1650s lighter upholstered or, a little later, caned chairs came into fashion. The backs were supported not by a framed panel but by cross pieces covered in leather as in the case of this 'Cromwellian' example with bobbin turned base.

c.1660 £350 — £450

113 (right) Examples such as this chair are also found in which all the members are spiral turned and the seat and back caned. Generally structurally weak if in walnut and so the price is low.

c.1760   If sound £350 — £450

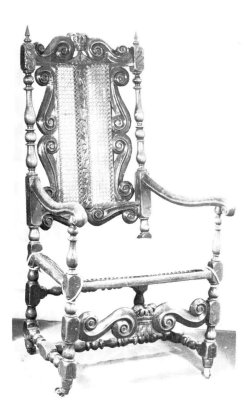

114 (left) The Dutch-inspired decorative excesses of the Restoration resulted in this type of chair becoming heavily carved, as in this excellent example. But despite the mass of decoration the basic construction was still the same, except for the bold sweep of the arms.

1675 If sound £1,200 — £1,800

115 (right) A good average example (to which castors have been added in the nineteenth century).

c.1685   £900 — £1,200

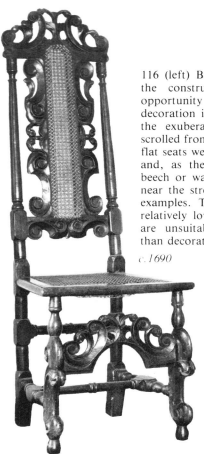

116 (left) Backs became high and the construction less solid. The opportunity for highly carved decoration is still seized upon; note the exuberant front stretcher and scrolled front legs. However, the thin flat seats were dowelled into the legs and, as the wood used was often beech or walnut, they had nowhere near the strength of the earlier oak examples. This is the key to their relatively low value; many of them are unsuitable for anything other than decorative purposes.

c.1690 £400 — £500

117 A more countrified example in walnut, none the less an interesting example for it has fine colour and shows the start of several future design trends. The centre of the top rail shows the tightly packed curve carved in the pre-Chippendale period and the simple front stretcher, the double bulge turnings found in country chairs of the early eighteenth century. The front legs end in scrolled 'Spanish' feet.

c.1690 £450 — £550

118 A design from the end of the century. The close carved vertical splats have replaced the long panelled cane backs. Note the graceful serpentine cross-stretchers with a centre finial. The bold curve of the arms helps the fine design but is expensive on material. The seat is now upholstered. Chairs of this type were designed by Daniel Mariot.

c.1690 £2,000 — £3,000

119 (right) The high back remains as does the decorated leg support which has moved back to become a stretcher. The legs have adopted the new cabriole form as yet without much confidence. Note the awkward square section at the top and the tentative carving on the knee which is in strong contrast to the assurance of the well carved back.

c.1700 £600 — £850

Plate 30. Turning is an ancient art and examples of turned chairs go back to medieval times. Scandinavia seems to have been a source of early forms of these chairs. They are also found round the Celtic fringes of Britain.

Until recently not popular with scholars, collectors or even decorators, they tend to be uncomfortable and, except in primitive surroundings, look out of place.

This is a particularly fine (i.e. highly decorated) example in ash from the early part of the 17th century; only the seat is oak. It has been used — look at the lighter colours of the centre of the back, the arms and the front rail

£6,000 — £9,000

Plate 31. Another foreign looking design. In this case a French design *caquetoire* which was principally used in Scotland. Most examples contain indication of ownership rather than decoration and on this example the arms are of a Devon family and it was probably made in the West Country. The wood used is a form of mahogany called 'mimsusopps' known as cherry mahogany and bullet wood from its hardness. It is thought to have been cut in the Amazon and imported through Dartmouth in 1617.

Such hardness combined with long wear gives a rich, slightly rubbed colour. The wear gives a reddish glow which contrasts with the near blackness of the unworn surfaces. Such pieces with strong historical backgrounds, fine construction and unusual form command a strong rarity premium.

c. 1617

Left. Plate 32. The strong architectural form of the decoration and the date 1616 suggest the influence of Inigo Jones and, because of the date, perhaps a metropolitan influence. A good deep oak patination with lighter colour in all the right places.

Right. Plate 33. From about the same date as the previous example. The cartouche carved in the back relates to an early group of furniture associated with Archbishop Laud. The colour suggests that over-cleaning has taken place.

The study of British oak furniture was greatly advanced by the publication a decade ago of Victor Chinnery's *Oak Furniture — The British Tradition*. Now much more is known about the regional origins of furniture.

Left. Plate 34. The strong similarity to figure 106 confirms the early 17th century Cheshire origin. It has the same stylised flower carving in which the design ensures that flowers or fruit appear at all corners. Notice too the broad overlapping seat and the small pyramids on the top of the stiles which proclaim a north-east origin for the piece. Good colour — note the cleaning of floors that has gone on round it over the years.

Right. Plate 35. A well carved back and unusual form of support to the base make this a desirable chair. It is not clear what, if anything, is missing from the top which would look a lot better with a top rail decoration. Nevertheless, another well patinated and interesting chair.
Early 17th century

Plate 36. This is several steps up in quality from figure 127 but is clearly related to it as a very good George I walnut chair. Compare the difference between the two. The hairy paw feet as against pads, the well thought out carving on the knee, as opposed to a stylised shell, the clever — almost fleur-de-lis — hipping. This is a very rare and attractive form — the lovely shoe where the splat meets the seat, the carefully thought out shell motif in the top rail, but above all the imaginative side connection on the splat. The fact that it has cracked does not detract from the excellent idea.
c.1725

Plate 37. So where does this chair fall in the scale of quality compared with the previous example?

It has to be said that judgement at this level becomes subjective because they are both excellent chairs but, as this book aims to develop the critical faculties, see if you can be persuaded to my view, which is that this is inferior to the previous example for these reasons:

1. Look at the meeting of the leg with the rail. A superbly executed decoration cries to go on to the rail, which it does on the previous example which works from both angles.
2. The shape of the splat is timid and as a result lacks the gusto of the last chair.
3. The carved decoration and the banding on the splat are timid, also the motif on the edge of the stiles, the carving on the shoe are nervously self-effacing. What is going on along the top rail? A few leaves and a squiggle?

Unfortunately this method of comparison is invalid. Of Plate 36 there were sadly only two, so they made £4,500 each. Of Plate 37 there were a useful eight, so they made £95,000 or nearly £12,000 apiece. Aesthetics don't stand up to usefulness.
c.1720

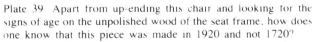

Plate 38 Dating from the 1730s comes this red walnut chair. The excellent colour photograph gives the tone and grain of this fine wood which is akin to mahogany but has a lightness of its own. Notice on the right side of the vertical which meets up with the back the typical dark 'bruising' that is sometimes apparent in this wood

This example gives a good impression of the restrained earlier Georgian furniture that one finds made of this wood which, though carved, relies more on form than surface adornment for its individual appearance

Plate 39 Apart from up-ending this chair and looking for the signs of age on the unpolished wood of the seat frame, how does one know that this piece was made in 1920 and not 1720?

There is no help from the colour photograph, though inspection would show the sharp, hard colour that comes from stain and french polish as opposed to the soft depth of polish and time, and there would be a lack of wear and gradation of colour.

The clues that it is not 'period' come from the thinness of the wood used at the bottom of the leg compared with the boldness of the knee. The hipping does not appear to go quite far enough up the frame of the seat, so that the seat sits on it instead of being an integral part of the construction. There is something 'over the top' about the birds' heads twisting round to form the ears at the side of the legs on a chair that in other respects is modest. The decoration from their heads doesn't flow properly into the decoration on the knee. It would be interesting to see how thick they are because the heads on the ends of the arms look thin too. Above all there is a thinness in the chair, a lack of boldness abouts its proportions, which is a common feature of so much reproduction work.

CHAIRS — cabriole leg, high back

It wasn't just the introduction of the cabriole leg, but the way it appears to have changed the thinking on how chairs should be made that caused so dramatic a revolution in chair design. In the next sections we have separated these chairs into two distinct categories. First, the group of high back chairs in which the back uprights and splats are highly curved. These chairs all have stretchers, most of them turned.

The second group have lower backs and some are less curved. Not all of them have stretchers between the legs and most of the better quality examples have flat or moulded faces to the back uprights, a feature which became almost universal as the century proceeded. Armchairs do not fit so easily into these distinct categories. It is a matter of conjecture whether the first group predates the second; there are several tempting theories to suggest that it does. We will leave this to be decided by the furniture historians... What is certain, however, is that the side views of the chairs below show the very marked difference in height and rake of the two types. Although most examples have drop-in seats, some certainly will have had rush seats.

The side view shows the main differences between the two types of early cabriole leg chairs. That on the left has a high, beautifully curved back with a simple splat. The one on the right has a shorter, stiffer, square back, much easier to make and cheaper on materials. The former type of chair is discussed in this section, the latter in the next.

As for most chairs the price escalates slightly for a pair. As a broad rule of thumb, a pair is worth three times the value of a single.

120 Cabriole legs all round and a serpentine stretcher to join them. The shape of the cabrioles is typical of the earlier type with a high knee; they are a bit thick near the foot because the maker felt he needed more support for the stretcher. Other early features are the thin front rail and, of course, the fine curve to the back. The two touches of seaweed marquetry make it appear a better chair than it is.

c.1700   *£2,000 — £2,750*

121 (left) A very cleverly designed chair, again with the thin vase splat and shaped top rail. Good use is made of the C-scroll motif on cabrioles but they are still corrupted by the cross-stretcher.

c.1710 £1,200 — £1,500

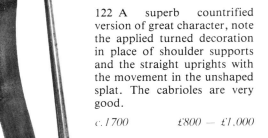

122 A superb countrified version of great character, note the applied turned decoration in place of shoulder supports and the straight uprights with the movement in the unshaped splat. The cabrioles are very good.

c.1700 £800 — £1,000

123 (left) A classic of the type but time has robbed it of its toes and drop-in seat. The thin rail, very high cabrioles, vase splat and high curved back are all there, as is the poor back of the cabriole where the stretcher meets it.

c.1700
£700 — £900 when repaired
and with drop-in seat

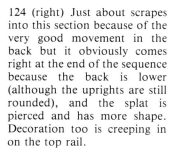

124 (right) Just about scrapes into this section because of the very good movement in the back but it obviously comes right at the end of the sequence because the back is lower (although the uprights are still rounded), and the splat is pierced and has more shape. Decoration too is creeping in on the top rail.

c.1700 £1,100 — £1,500

ARMCHAIRS

CHAIRS — cabriole leg, low back

Armchairs of the first quarter of the eighteenth century are not common and accordingly expensive. The same criterion applies in judging them. As for the type, both logically fall into the second category; low backs, deep seat rails, flat uprights.

The lower back chairs are normally associated with the George I period. Certainly the design settled down around the 1720s and carved decoration became increasingly used.

125 This very fine chair with the shepherd's crook arms has superb cabrioles with hipped decoration on the knee, ball-and-claw feet and despite the low back, superb movement. A collector's dream.
c.1720 £18,000 — £22,000

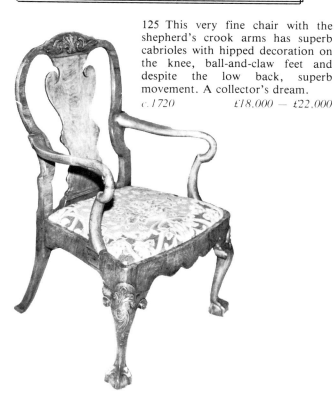

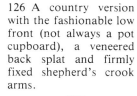

126 A country version with the fashionable low front (not always a pot cupboard), a veneered back splat and firmly fixed shepherd's crook arms.
c.1720
£6,000 — £8,000

127 A good George I example. The seat rail is much deeper than those of the previous section and the back is lower. The carved shell is hipped into the seat and the top rail is scooped into a definite hollow in the middle. The top rail is also more rounded in appearance and the distinction between it and the back uprights more difficult to define, as they flow into each other. The flat face of the uprights, splat and seat rails are veneered for decoration.
c.1725
Single £4,000 — £5,000
Pair £15,000 — £20,000

128 (left) A lesser quality chair on which the shell carving on the knee has an almost stuck-on appearance and looks out of place. Note that the chair is made of solid walnut and features no veneer, although the face of the back uprights is flat, as though to be veneered. See how material has been saved in producing the shaped back uprights — the lower inward curve of the left hand back upright is a different piece of wood joined to the main upright: the lighter colour betrays it.

c.1720   *£900 — £1,100*

129 (right) A mahogany high quality chair with carved decoration — see how the curving back uprights end in eagles' heads where they meet the top rail. Cuban mahogany encouraged a revival in the carver's art. Notice too that the seat has become larger and generally more solid. A move towards Chippendale.

1730-1740   *£1,500 — £2,000*
       Pair £5,000 — £7,000

130 (left) A fruitwood chair with rounded back uprights rather like chairs from the previous section. It has a rather country appearance despite the quality of the cabrioles and back splat, which is quite sophisticated.

c.1730
Rather wormy
so £600 — £800

131 (right) Although this chair has lost its front feet, it illustrates a stretchered type with flat-faced back uprights, the whole chair being made in solid walnut. It has little of the curvature of the back which the chairs in the previous section show, although akin to them below the seat level. Note that the shoulder piece is missing on the right hand cabriole.

c.1735
When restored   *£500*   *£600*

CHAIRS — corner, 1700-1750
(also known as writing chairs)

133 An interesting country version of 132, with cabriole legs ending in pad feet. Only the front cabriole has a shell carved on the knee; the turned uprights under the arms are not embellished with any shaping as in 132; the cabrioles do not flow as boldly, but the maker has added the precaution of stretchers between them for strength, and these are shaped where they join the leg just like the uprights of example 132. The decoration of a triangular inlay of boxwood on the seat rail and alternating box and ebony on the back rail is similar to that found on wainscot chairs.

c.1715

132 A fine quality chair, mostly solid walnut but with veneered seat rail and splats. The turned uprights are well shaped.

c.1715   *£6,000 — £8,000*

£3,000 — £4,000

135 A simple solid walnut corner chair with straight legs which belie the earlier date suggested by the shape of the splats.

c.1745
When restored   £500 — £700

134 An oak variation with only the front leg a cabriole which has simple thread and flower decoration on the knee.

c.1730   *£1,200 — £1,800*

136 A mahogany chair on square legs with cross-stretchers and pierced splats of the pre-Chippendale type.

c.1750   *£800 — £1,000*

CHAIRS — pre-Chippendale

> The Chippendale style didn't suddenly happen with the publication of the *Director* in 1754 — it evolved. These chairs, all of which have some of the features associated with Chippendale's designs, might usefully be grouped as pre-Chippendale. Many of them seem to contain a mixture of walnut and mahogany designs.

137 A mahogany chair with high quality cabriole legs ending in ball-and-claw feet. The carved decoration on the knee makes good use of the design possibilities of shoulder support which would not be out of place on a Chippendale chair but, despite its evident quality, the back has a straight cut splat which is still in the walnut period.

c.1740 £1,300 — £1,600

138 This chair might well be criticised on the basis of the exaggerated, heavy curls to the ends of the top rail but, to those who like it, the vigour of the workmanship gives a spring-like quality to the scrolling (which looks as if it might be uncoiled given a means of softening the wood!) The back is a bit heavy but the design sources of the chair would be evident (if you have read this book, that is).

c.1735 Assume right £2,500 — £3,500

139 A walnut example with a splat whose design is common to the first three chairs in this group, with slight variations. This chair is more restrained and the ankle of the cabrioles rather tentative.

c.1735 £1,100 — £1,500

140 (left) A country chair, whose back design belongs to the examples of 1710-30, but this chair is, in fact, 1740-50 with simple square legs and stretchers of the 'Chippendale' type.

c.1740-1750 £450 — £550

141 (right) Finally a top quality piece in walnut with a highly individual design of back and superbly decorated cabriole legs and ball-and-claw feet. It predates Chippendale's design by only a few years but shows clearly that richness of decoration and the overall shape were already well understood. It remained only for the designer to offer a variety of splats and personalised decorative design for his name to become the most famous in British furniture design. Much copied in the Victorian period.

c.1750 £4,000 — £5,000

CHAIRS — Chippendale, cabriole leg

Chippendale designed many chairs with cabriole legs. Country makers continued to use the cabriole with the newer type of Chippendale splat for some time, while a hundred years or so later Victorians made a wide range of imitations (see Chairs — Victorian reproductions).

142 (left) An elegant chair in which the moulded cabriole legs have been refined down as far as possible without either losing the cabriole effect or damaging the overall proportions. This together with the good broad shaped front seat, the carefully executed 'Gothic' splat, all point to a chair of quality.
c.1760   *If right £3,500 — £4,500*

143 (right) A poor photograph of a reasonable quality cabriole leg chair. The splat is typical Chippendale. It is restrained and, as it is not covered in carving like 146, does not fall into the grand class. Nevertheless, with its good carving, well-proportioned cabriole legs decorated with cabochon and leaves, the use of a decorated edge to the scroll round the shoulder and the top of the rail it is a highly desirable chair. The scroll foot is excellently carved.
c.1760   *£2,000 — £3,000*

144 (left) Chippendale mahogany chair with pleasing splat, good cabrioles and carving that is very similar to pre-Chippendale chairs, moulded sides and carved top rail — a pleasant chair.
c.1760   *£1,000 — £1,500*

145 (right) Of less quality than the last example and interesting to compare them. The simple shell on the back rail, the less complicated splat and the claw which does not quite grasp the ball, all point to a more simple (provincial?) approach, indeed the legs and back rail have not changed since the earlier part of the century, only the splat pronounces it Chippendale.
c.1765   *£750 — £1,000*

CHAIRS — Chippendale, straight leg

For convenience of comparison, this page discusses only examples with straight legs. Some of Chippendale's finest examples in fact utilised the cabrioles. Many of the backs are slightly lower and the seats slightly wide on some of the very good examples. The prosperous second half of the eighteenth century saw a proliferation of designs and some highly decorative workmanship. Styles include Gothic and Chinese and effects such as riband were used.

146 (right) A superb museum quality example with top quality splat, the stretchers have pierced frets, and the rest, except the back legs, is blind fretted. Odd chairs of almost this quality can still occasionally be found.

c.1760   *£7,000 — £9,000*

147 (below left) A good Chippendale chair, whose finely carved top rail and decoration on the splat give it style. The legs are moulded and decorated with carefully carved notches, and the boldness of the four intertwining loops in the splat corresponds to a design in Ince and Mayhew's *Universal System*, 1759-1763.

c.1760   *£1,200 — £1,800*
                                              Set of six £12,000 — £15,000

148 (below centre) A chair of considerably less quality, it has moulded legs and an elegant and reasonably intricate splat, but the top rail lacks carved motifs and the effect is one of solid comfort rather than impressiveness.

c.1760   *Single £700 — £900*
                                              Six £6,000 — £8,000

149 (below right) An almost country interpretation of the design; the Chippendale splat and legs are there but the main decoration comes from the curl at the extremities of the top rail and the base of the splat, hangovers from the pre-Chippendale period (for example 138). Compare the design of the splat with those of the three preceding examples. The interlaced strands are a bit close at the top and meet the top rather than flow from it. The chair is in walnut which supports the country made provenance.

c.1770   *£500 — £600*
                                              Six £4,000 — £6,000

Note 149 may not be aesthetically a success but financially it makes the grade. It is precisely this lack of equation between quality and price that makes it essential for the collector to learn to discriminate.

CHAIRS — Chippendale, provincial and country

Trying to arrange such a wide array of chairs in quality order is difficult, and dating even more so. Colour is important and personal preference plays a stronger part in assessment than for London-made pieces which can be judged against known standards. What is technically not very successful (i.e. 152) can prove very appealing to live with, hence values are surprisingly uniform. Sets of chairs of this period cost about six times the single price for a set of four, and around ten times for a set of six.

151 (left) One could speculate that the splat is a mixture of Chippendale (top half) and pre-Chippendale (bottom half), but the result is successful. The top rail flows convincingly into the splat. The shell is a pleasing touch and the cabrioles are very well made. The whole effect is successful.

c.1750   *Elm £550 — £700*

150 (above) Made in walnut at a time when most chairs of this quality were in mahogany. The splat is very successful — no carving except some simple gouging at the ends of the top rail. The deep rounded front seat rail and the solid but elegant cabrioles make this a fine chair. It could pass for a chair from New York State of a slightly later date, and no doubt many do.

1750   *£650   £800*

152 (right) Interesting provincial example. The maker has obviously seen a high quality example but has been afraid to do more than a pastiche of the splat design; rightly because his shoulder supports to the legs illustrate his limitations. What he has got gloriously right is the broad low back and big square seat that no Victorian would ever dream of producing.

c.1760   *£350 — £450*

153 (left) In oak, with fully upholstered seat. The maker has a reasonable grasp of the Chippendale idea but the splat is a little too broad and the effect is flat and stiff. Nevertheless a pleasing chair.

c.1760   *£350 — £500*
          Set of six £4,000 — £5,000

154 (right) A frequently encountered design which one might describe as provincial rather than strict country — in other words, rather a solid, solemn effect with neither the high decoration of the city example nor the character of the country.

c.1760   *£400 — £500*
          Set of six £3,500 — £4,500

Hepplewhite designs are found along with Sheraton in the 1775-1790 period. They were both influenced by classical designs — a search for elegance. The main Hepplewhite forms are shown in this section.

155 (left) A camel back design with serpentine front and drop-in seat. The legs are Chippendale in form except that they now taper instead of being the same size throughout their length. The splat is reminiscent of Chippendale and so are the small leaf carvings on the top rail. What could be the start of the Prince of Wales plumes (which Hepplewhite was possibly the first to use on chairs) are to be seen halfway up the splat — an elegant chair.

c.1775   £900 — £1,200
Set of six £10,000 — £14,000
Set of six + two £16,000 — £22,000

156 A fine chair almost straight out of Hepplewhite's design book but not a style normally associated with him. A high quality chair with tapering fluted legs, arms and back uprights. Leaf and swag carving in the square back are all classical motifs. (Just as Sheraton shows the shield back so Hepplewhite shows several of these square back designs.)

c.1780   £2,200 — £3,000

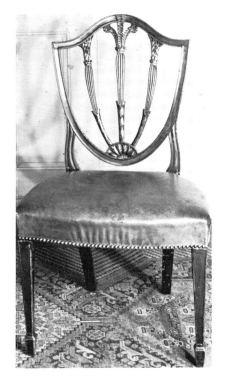

157 (left) A very good quality shield back chair. The Prince of Wales plumes and their supports are beautifully carved. The shield itself has a raised section at the edges which serves to emphasise the shape. This is repeated on the legs.

c.1780   £1,200 — £1,500
Set of six £8,000 — £10,000
Six + two £20,000 — £25,000

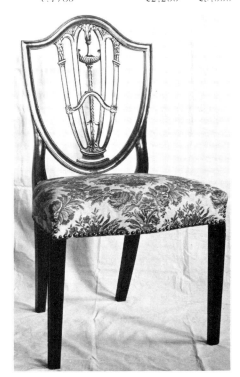

158 (right) The legs are plain tapered, but the well shaped and moulded shield back, the balanced arrangement of the splat and the carved decoration mark it as a chair of some quality but it clearly does not come up to the standard of the previous example.

c.1780   £700 — £900
Set of six £7,000 — £9,000

160 Another Hepplewhite variation, the hoop back. Note the continued use of the Chippendale moulding but on a well tapered leg. The hoop-back is decorated with carving and the splat, which is typical of the type, fits the hoop well. A successful chair.

c.1790   *£550 — £750*
Set of six £5,000 — £7,000

159 A shield back design. There is a striking contrast between the well carved splat with the Prince of Wales plumes and the dumpy legs which appear to taper too quickly (compare the last example). The lack of any decoration on the shield which is slightly awkward looking suggests a provincially made piece.

c.1785   *£400 — £500*
Set of six £2,500 — £3,500

161 The camel back is there, the splat works well and the bottom half is Chippendale. A rather stiff little provincial chair but the outcome is successful, particularly if the patination is good.

c.1790-1810   *£200 — £300*
Set of six £1,800 — £2,500

162 (left) An interesting comparison with example 161. It is more Hepplewhite in that the legs taper. But the splat is a near disaster: the outline is not true, the lower half is mean and its design poor. Most marked, however, is the contrast between the way 161 is successfully terminated at the top of the cuts in the splats and the way this fails.

c.1800   *£100 — £140*
Set of six £1,200 — £1,500

163 (right) A painted example of another popular Hepplewhite design and one which was extensively copied in late Victorian times. The quality of the painting determines the price.

c.1790   *£1,000 — £1,500*

164 A superbly executed Sheraton chair. The lightness of design and the sparing use of decoration further refines the move in this direction made by Hepplewhite. Compare 156 and note the gentle curve of the arm which emphasises the very delicate quality of the piece.

c.1790   *£3,000 — £4,000*

With Sheraton we cross the line between the eighteenth and nineteenth century. Sheraton chairs were produced in a wide variety of designs and, since Britain was involved in a war with Napoleon and its subsequent depression, so they lingered on well into the nineteenth century. Thomas Hope and George Smith are relatively little known and one does not see many claims to their designs outside the very fashionable furniture. Sabre leg chairs are covered in the next section.

Chairs with arms are considerably more expensive than those without. This is because, as well as being a comfortable dining chair, they can also be used as easy chairs. Not everybody likes soft, low chairs.

The rough rule for giving an approximate value for a set is to increase the price of a standard (not arms).

Pair — multiply by 3
Four — multiply by 6
Six   — multiply by 10

165 A somewhat Hepplewhite curve to the back, but the arm is definitely Sheraton. Much heavier and not in the same league as the previous example.

c.1800   *£1,000   £1,500*

166 Reasonable quality but heavier design, with a good double curve to the arm, which again gives it an elegant line. Going down the quality scale and moving on in time. The top rail is thickening up.

c.1805   *£700 — £900*
Set of six + two £7,000 — £9,000

167 A perfectly adequate cross-back design still retaining reeded legs and uprights, with an inlay in the top rail.

c.1810   *£350 — £450*

168 (left) Shows a much simpler treatment avoiding the use of any carving. The legs are now quite simple with no reeding or moulding.

c.1810
£200 — £300
Set of six
£2,250 — £3,000

169 (right) Shows a provincial interpretation of Sheraton design incorporating what might be thought of as a very simplified adaptation of the honeysuckle motif. Rather thick, squat and heavy with the back marginally small for the bulk of the seat.

c.1810
£250 — £350

170 (left) A country interpretation in beech or oak with drop-in seat and a simply formed decoration of horizontal splats.

1810   *£80 — £100*

171 (right) The simple country 'Sheraton' with dished solid wooden seat and stretchers. Decoration is confined to moulding lines with a veneered piece of mahogany in the centre of the splat.

1810   *£70 — £90*
But a set of six £900 — £1,200
if colour reasonable

CHAIRS — sabre leg, 1800-1840

Before the end of the Georgian-Regency era a profusion of chair designs appeared which seems to indicate an explosion in production. It thus becomes more difficult to classify chairs by quality although certain obvious features can be identified.

Sabre Leg Chairs

While variations in quality obviously exist, chairs with sabre legs do not go through the same gradations as previous types, perhaps because the country makers instinctively avoided them, mindful of the structural weakness implied in the sabre leg, which must be cut across the grain at some point. The scrolling arms, with their wide radius, suffer from the same inherent weakness. As a result, there are some very fine examples and the rest tend to be of good 'town' quality of execution. Those with brass inlay are considered the most valuable.

172 A fine quality example with rope-twist top rail and carved decoration.

c.1825   *£400 — £550*

173 Shows the same features of quality — rope-twist, etc. — with the addition of brass inlay.

c.1825   *£500 — £700*
Six + two £8,000 — £10,000

174 The thickening of the back top rail and the slightly heavy legs and arm supports suggest a provincial origin.

c.1830   *£500 — £600*

175 An interesting carved key pattern decoration in top rail.

c.1820   *£400 — £600*
Six £4,000 — £6,000
Six + two £7,000 — £9,000

176 A much broader top rail than the previous chair with leaf form carving.

c.1825   *£300 — £400*

177 The heavy rail is gadrooned at the top but brass inlay is clearly visible.

c.1820   *£400 — £500*
                                  Set of six £4,000 — £6,000

178 Probably about the simplest form of period sabre leg chair in mahogany, unpretentious and pleasing.

c.1825   *£250 — £350*

179 In contrast to the previous chair this one has gone rather towards the Victorian, in the exuberance of its carved top rail which has hints of the early balloon-back.

c.1830   *£250 — £300*

180 (below and right) A Regency sabre leg library step-chair in its open and closed positions. This type produced by Morgan and Sanders, c.1810 and illustrated in Ackermann's *Repository of Arts,* 1811.

c.1820   *£4,000 — £6,000*

CHAIRS — turned leg, 1800-1840

The turned leg chairs of the 1800-1840 period derive from late Sheraton and other, usually classical, design influences of the period. Whereas the overall shape is clearly recognisable, an infinite variety of decorative designs were used and it is again very difficult to range the quality of the enormous output.

181 A fine quality example with reeded arms and back. The top rail is also reeded and the legs reasonably restrained as far as the turning goes.

1810
£450 — £550

182 Another restrained chair of simple, quite elegant design.

c.1825   *£300 — £400*
Set of six £4,000 — £5,000
Set six + two £6,000 — £8,000

183 (left) This chair shows how the legs can become over-turned to the point of weakness. The violently striped covering is not, of course, contempory.

1835   Each £150 — £200

184 (right) An elegant later chair with fine quality work in the back and the expected reeded legs of William IV origin.

c.1835   £300 — £400
Set of six
£5,000 — £7,000
Set of six + two
£8,000 — £11,000

185 (left) Almost the classic dealer's mahogany dining chair of the late Georgian-Regency period. The arms now reach out to curve straight down into the front legs. The back centre rail is twist-turned and there is an inlaid brass stringing line in the top back rail.

1825   £450 — £600

186 A humbler example, where the legs are still elegant but the top rail of the back is wider and starting to grow into the heavier broad rail of the later part of the period.

c.1820   £350 — £450

187 This chair shows how events can take an unpleasant turn, with front legs becoming bulbous and unnecessary cross-stretchers appearing.

c.1835   £175 — £250

188 The broad top rail has started to be embellished by the Victorians, who were busy deciding to throw off such restraint as the severe straight tops of the previous examples, thus leading to 189.

c.1840   £175 — £250
                              Set of six £2,500 — £3,500

The rule for giving an approximate value for a set is to increase the single price as follows:—
Pair   — multiply by 3
Four   — multiply by 6
Six   — multiply by 10
but recently six has accelerated.

189 Here the top rail has broken out into a rebellion of a decidedly dashing nature.

c.1830-40   £150 — £200
                              Set of six £2,500 — £3,500

137

CHAIRS — towards the balloon back, 1820-1870

The nineteenth century saw the development of many new styles of which the dominant one from 1840-1880s was the balloon back with cabriole and turned legs. The evolution is clear but one has only to look at *The Pictorial Dictionary of 19th Century Furniture Design* to see how style persisted, often over several decades. Confusion on dating is therefore very easy. Prices are for sets of six. Single examples range from £40 — £70.

190 (left) The back rail is thin and no longer straight but the decoration on the splat still harks back to William IV (late Regency) as does the drop-in seat and decoration on the legs.

c.1835   *Set of six £1,200 — £1,800*

191 (right) Shows a simulated rosewood Regency bedroom chair made of beech in which the splat has developed and an early form of ballooning is evolving. This light and elegant chair contrasts sharply with the late ones.

c.1840   *Set of six each £175 — £225*

192 This design ran concurrently with the early balloon back and fits in well with cabrioles.

c.1850   Set of six £1,500 — £2,000

193 Almost a balloon back but not quite, nevertheless a good design with moulded edges to the legs as well as inside the back.

c.1850   Set of six £1,400 — £1,800

194 A later heavier type with solid turned legs and rather clumsy decoration on the splat.

c.1870   Set of six £800 — £1,000

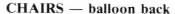

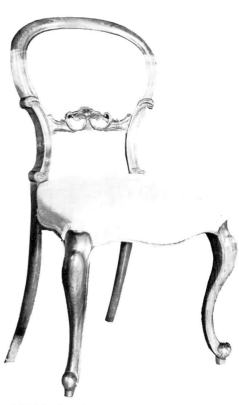

195 In walnut with a warm colour not obvious from the photograph. The slight shaping on the top and the small carved supports give the chair an elegant look.

c.1850   Set of six £1,800 — £2,400

196 Still a very good chair with an intricate splat which is in its favour, but less style than the previous example.

c.1850   Set of six £1,800 — £2,400

197 Moving down the scale, a simple splat and a not entirely successful attempt at decoration just above. The legs lack some of the elegance of the previous examples.

c.1850   £1,500 — £2,000

198 The later mechanical applied groove decoration and a very simple splat, the legs are pinched (see Agius). The price is relatively high because many people simply do not differentiate between quality.

c.1880   Set of six £1,200 — £1,600

Chairs 199 (above) and 200 (right) show how the balloon shape could infect other chairs of the period, even papier mâché as in 200. Note the difference between the Victorian idea of cabriole and that of the early eighteenth century; the former is bandy legged by comparison.

199: 1860   Set of six £1,200 — £1,600

200: 1850   If sound £700 — £900
If back broken — forget

CHAIRS — late Victorian reproductions of 17th and 18th century designs

The constant Victorian search for new designs ironically led to a revival of interest in eighteenth century designs. Contrary to popular myth, top quality Victorian craftsmen were just as good as their predecessors but, while they accurately reproduced the details of decoration correctly, they often lost the feeling of the original; for example, the Victorians seemed to dislike the large square seats and low broad backs of the Chippendale period, so their renditions are often lighter and more delicate. Similarly, the termination of the back legs, which were normally shaped in good quality designs prior to fashionable Chippendale, are often missing. More telling of course is the lack of age on the unpolished areas of the seat rails and the use of square corner supports rather than the open variety originally used (though these are often replaced, the old rebate marks should still be there). On top quality reproductions the shoulder pieces (supporting the tops of the legs to the frames) are often carefully shaped with a rounded tool, whereas the originals were quickly cleaned off with an ordinary chisel and here particularly age, in the form of dark patination of varying shades rather than stain, should be apparent.

As with Victorian carving originality meant the difference between high value or near worthlessness. Indiscriminating foreign demand has changed this in the last few years to the point where 'half age' pieces can be surprisingly valuable. A good long set of Victorian reproductions have increased in value to the point where they are almost worth as much each as a single original example.

201 A satinwood Hepplewhite-style shield back chair, very much in keeping with the original spirit.

In sets, each 600 — £800

202 A 'Queen Anne' chair in mahogany which, apart from the mahogany, gives away its Victorian origin by the seat rail (too shallow) and the cabriole legs (too thin behind the knee and a bit weak in the ankle).

In sets, each £450 — £600

203 Another mahogany 'Queen Anne' chair in which the lower half is quite successful but the treatment of the back is too clumsy by far — what is more the back is too high; this style of chair has a lower back if genuine — see the section on Chairs — cabriole leg.

Six + 2, each £300 — £400

204 Victorian 'Chippendale' chair of quite good quality as far as the back goes, but with golf-club-like feet on the legs, which are too thin and bandy.

In sets, each £200 — £300

205 (left) Quite a good Victorian 'Chippendale' chair, but, again, the seat rail and the legs are too thin for the real thing.

Each £200 — £250
Six + two £2,500 — £3,500

206 (right) Reproduction Chinese lacquer and walnut George I chair which has a lot thrown in by way of scrolls and an extraordinary central stretcher curving from the back stretcher up under the seat to the back of the front seat rail. The legs are bandy, and nearer to the Victorian baloon back than anything from the eighteenth century.

1920s   *Each £220 — £280*
In sets, each £500 — £700

207 (below) Victorian oak Charles II-style chair of quite faithful design — the colour and patination of the wood would be the give away here. Compare with 115.

In sets, each £250 — £350

208 (left) An upholstered version of a Queen Anne shepherd's crook armchair in walnut. Much too cosy and Victorian and on closer examination no age to the wood.

Late 19th century   *Each £400 — £550*

209 (right) The Victorians' love of decoration enjoyed to the full in this alleged Chippendale design. Rams' heads for the cabriole knees and naturally the same animals' feet. The riband back and the extremities of the top rail, the front serpentine seat rail, all carrying their full quota of carving. Why, one wonders, were the arms and their supports so neglected? The small size of seat is an easy give away to the later date. In terms of their value a few years ago the price is staggering.

Each £800 — £1,200
In sets, each £2,000 — £3,000

CHAIRS — children's low

210 Very well made walnut child's chair. Gloriously successful cabrioles, arms, legs and back. Only possible fault is that the back should perhaps be a fraction higher to be in proper proportion, but this is a very minor quibble about a superb piece.

c.1720   *£5,000 — £6,000*

Children's chairs naturally follow the same styles as those of their parents and one assesses them in the same way. The acid test is that if one sees a photograph without background it should not be obvious that it is a miniaturised version. Making a miniature in the correct proportions is extremely difficult and requires a very good maker to get them just right. As chair making itself is one of the most difficult arts, a good child's chair calls for a top craftsman.

To generalise on prices, fine town made examples of earlier types tend to fetch less then their adult equivalent while children's versions of country or late chairs fetch more.

211 An early eighteenth century child's country chair; from the photograph it looks as though the right hand arm and the top rail are oversized, but again this is a minor point, for the overall proportions are excellent.

c.1730   *£600 — £800*

212 (above) Ignore the fact that about 2ins. are missing from the bottom of the legs and holes drilled to provide support for a foot rest and this Hepplewhite example is another top quality piece. Look at the carefully moulded back, carved honeysuckle decoration and the excellent curve of the arms.

c.1770   *£600 — £800*
if in original condition

213 (below) Again the work of a competent maker, this Mendlesham chair can only be detected as a child's because the arms are a trifle thick and pinched inwards. A very rare and desirable piece.

c.1820
£900 — £1,200

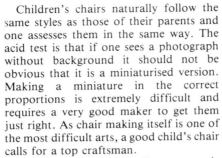

214 (above) A sweet little yew Windsor missing about an inch off the bottom of its feet. It has a slight Gothic appearance purely because the top rail would not bend so it cracked. Yew does not take kindly to tight curves.

1810-1840   *£1,000 — £1,400*

215 (below) An endearing child's Windsor rocking chair in ash. More simply made than the last example. The arms are a bit crude at the ends and the spindles have been tapered off slightly too much.

1820-1860   *£500 — £700*

CHAIRS — children's high

Here of course, one cannot judge a chair by its correctness of proportion as against the adult equivalent. Instead the test has to be how successfully the maker has elongated the piece while keeping in sympathy with the style of his period.

216 (left) In this fine child's oak chair the maker has got it just right. The design calls for stability and he has achieved it without losing the feel of the heavy panelled back. The simple turning on the front legs and the low stretcher work very well. As these chairs were very popular before the war one should always look at them very closely.

Second quarter 17th century   £3,000 — £4,000

217 (right) At first sight a late seventeenth century style but the outline of the splat and the shape of the turning suggest a later date. Lacks the stability and balance of the previous example, but then chairs of this period, dependent on turning, were rather square. Arms are good.

1690-1720   £1,200 — £1,700

218 (far left) A Hepplewhite design in which the back with its careful moulding and well-balanced splat is much more successful than the heavy front legs. The sweep outwards at the bottom gives an improved line.

c.1780   £1,000 — £1,500

219 (left) A strange crude little high chair which gives problems of dating. The dished seat suggests a Windsor chair origin but the scratch moulding and the crude little inset cross pleads for an earlier date. The top rail argues for an early nineteenth century date, as does the exaggerated chamfering of the side rails.

Probably early 19th century   £650 — £800

220 (far right) Very much the traditional Windsor design, good rake to back legs gives feeling of solidarity. The back is well made and the splat fits in well.

Early 19th century   £1,000 — £1,300

221 (right) Very appealing little piece, partly because it is a child's chair but also because of the generous sweep of the arms. Well turned front legs, the only drawback is the absence of a splat.

Early 19th century   £800 — £1,000

These chairs fall into distinct categories and can normally be allocated to various parts of the country. Basically, they are either ladderbacks, with or without a top rail, or backs made up of vertical spindles. A great deal of research has been and is being carried out on this subject. For more information see an article by Bill Cotton, who has studied this subject in depth, on 'Country Chairs', *Antique Collecting* Vol.8, No.6.

From left to right, top to bottom:—

222 Wavy line ladderbacks. A similar chair is in a Hogarth print c.1730. There are a number of variations of these Yorkshire chairs which are hardwearing and generally considered the best of the type.

1730-1800   *Armchair, each £500 — £600*
                     Set of two + six £3,500 — £4,000

223 A variation from the Midlands, missing half its top rail. Again, good quality but the back design is perhaps not quite as well balanced as the first example.

1740-1830   *Armchair, each £400 — £500*
                     Set of two + six £2,300 — £3,000

224 The Macclesfield variation of the second category. Again the rush seat comes over the front rail as with all chairs of this type.

1740-1840   *Each £400 — £500*
                     Set of two + six £3,500 — £4,000

225 The Wigan shape of ladderback is again seen on these wooden seated top-rail types with shaped front rail. A carver is very seldom found.

1760-1840   *Singles, each £150 — £220*
                     Set of two + six £2,500 — £3,000

226 The third main type, the spindlebacks predominantly from north Cheshire and south Lancashire. It is thought that the further north the chairs were made in Lancashire the thinner the spindles. Another variety has two lines of spindles with a top rail between the uprights often with some Chippendale design feature on it. They are lighter and are thought to come from Liverpool and Manchester.

1750-1840   *Armchair, each £400 — £500*
                     Set of two + six £2,500 — £3,500

227 Quite a different variety coming from Ormskirk or the Preston area of Lancashire. Very robust.

1840-1900   *Each £150 — £200*
                     Set of two + six £1,750 — £2,200

144

CHAIRS — hall and porters

Though grouped for convenience they are in fact complete opposites. The hall chair offers a rock-like resistance to the posterior and the back no comfort. It is almost as though they were designed to impress on those made to wait, the fact they were being made to do so. They were made in sets and were often carved with emblems of coats of arms as if to further enhance the superior position of their owner. The porter's chair on the other hand was made reasonably comfortable to protect him from the rigours of a job which condemned him to draughts, and if comfortable are very desirable.

Back patterns are normally little guide to date as they continued to be made over long periods. It is the legs which normally provide the key as to age.

Understandably the uncomfortable ones do not command large sums for they have a very limited application to the modern home.

228 A hall chair of a type usually made in sets — this was one of seventeen. This example shows a highly-carved shell back with a crest motif. The pascal lamb with halo might suggest a religious establishment. The legs are turned and reeded.

1820-1840   £700 — £1,000

229 A mahogany hall chair of whimsical design with a pierced back. The design for the base and seat with its curious round dished centre and eccentric stretcher is straight out of Bridgen's catalogue of 1838.

1838   £700 — £900

230 Typical of the many curved back designs which went on being made throughout the century. The hexagonal legs suggest the 1830s.

£600 — £800

231 A rather unfair porter's chair with an extremely hard solid seat, on cabriole legs, in mahogany.

1850-1870   £900 — £1,200

233 A design of wicker work hooded chair, Welsh ash frame with straw cover. They were made in most areas but survived longest in Monmouthshire and the Severn area.

Early 19th century   £250 — £350

232 Much more comfort; a deeply buttoned hall porter's chair, well designed to exclude those severe draughts. As the cost of deep buttoning in leather is very high, condition is highly relevant to price. A modern example costs £800.

Mid-18th century   £4,000 — £6,000

CHAIRS — Windsor and related types

234 An early comb-back version with shaped top rail and simple turned legs. It has a gloriously antique quality.

1760-1780 £2,000 — £3,000

236 A good quality yew Windsor, with ash back legs, well designed cabriole legs and crinoline stretcher. Identical to named example by William Webb of Newington, Surrey.

c.1770
£3,300 — £4,000
Set of six
Over £3,500 — £4,500

235 A comb-back with good cabriole legs, well-shaped splat and top rail. Thames Valley area — probably by Hewitt of Slough.

Mid-18th century
£3,500 — £4,500

236 A good quality yew Windsor, with ash back legs, well designed cabriole legs and crinoline stretcher. Identical to named example by William Webb of Newington, Surrey.

Windsor chairs first appeared at the beginning of the eighteenth century, but the bulk were made in the nineteenth century. These chairs were a cheap, comfortable form of seating made in the country for kitchen, tavern and general public use.

Tom Crispin, the well-known St. Albans dealer specialising in oak and country furniture, has photographed and researched the named examples he has handled over the last twenty years. He published his findings to date in Volume XIV of *Furniture History* the journal of the Furniture History Society. We are grateful to both the Society and Tom Crispin for permission to draw on his work in allocating makers and likely dates of manufacture to the pieces in this section. As a result of Tom Crispin's researches in parish records, census and trade directories, many dates are later than had hitherto been thought. The main indication of area of manufacture is to be found in the shape of the arm supports, legs from different areas often having similar designs. North Midlands used turned arm supports as in 241. East Anglia tended to use a shaped front arm support cut from the solid wood see 242 (a method widely used in late nineteenth century examples in the South), while in the Thames Valley, which includes the High Wycombe area, two methods were used. Early examples follow 235, later 236 which is made from a stick, a thicker version of the other sticks used.

Value Points:
Yew wood is important to high value but remember that seats are nearly always in elm, even in the finest examples. Cabriole legs also help value considerably as do some special shapes of splat. Perhaps the most sought after splat shape is the Gothic (not shown), but fine early comb-backs and original designs also command high prices.

237 A further development in the comb-back design, all the legs now exhibiting decorative turning and baluster shape. So-called Goldsmith type.

Early 19th century
£600 — £800

238 A classic form — an early nineteenth century yew chair with crinoline stretcher and typical turning. Made right through the middle of the century.

1820-1860
£1,000 — £1,500

239 A nineteenth century yew and elm 'Yorkshire' Windsor with decorative splat and characteristic 'smoker's bow' base chair to which the hooped back is fitted.

1840-1880   £1,200 — £1,500

240 A typical stickback Windsor of late eighteenth/early nineteenth century design with saddle seat but no splat. The curving arm supports indicate a pre-Regency date. This design appears in Gillow's cost books in the early nineteenth century, when Gillows offered them for sale in mahogany and elm with cherrywood.

1780-1810   Yew £750 — £1,000
Ash, elm £500 — £600

241 The lowback version of 238 made over a considerable period of time and until recently to be seen in sets. Very similar to named chairs made in the Worksop/Nottingham area.

1810-1840   Yew £1,000 — £1,300
Set £1,200 — £1,500
Ash, elm £500 — £700
Set £600 — £800

242 A good design with triple pierced splats, a type attributable to Robert Prior of Cambridge. An attractive yew design.

Early 19th century   £1,000 — £1,200
Sets about £1,200 — £1,500 each

243 Yew crinoline stretcher, front legs and bow. The splat is perhaps too timid. Attributable to John Amos, Grantham, Lincs.

c.1810-1840   £400 — £600
only because in yew

244 A very typical form of wheelback, mainly in yew. Light and elegant.

c.1820 onwards   Yew £800 — £1,000
Ash, elm £400 — £500

245 An interesting contrast with the last. It has a crinoline stretcher which should make it more desirable, but heavy legs and square arms and, above all, the lack of yew detract.

c.1820 onwards   £300 — £400
Set £400 — £550 each

Windsors did not have a monopoly on pleasing country chairs and designs and serious students of country chairs keep unearthing particular local examples, some of them very attractive. In addition, the nineteenth century saw the mass-production of many satisfying designs for the enormous demand from the manufacturing towns — for house, office and institution as well as tavern. As the price of poorly made modern chairs continues to rise, so more and more people see the sense in buying chairs of age and character. Prices have therefore shot up over the last few years. This is an area of British furniture where much research is still to be done.

246 A Mendlesham chair from the village of that name in Suffolk where the Days, father and son, worked. A superbly designed and executed example in fruitwood. The influence of Sheraton designs is strong.

Early 19th century   £1,400 — £1,800

247 A type known to have been made round Oxford in the mid-nineteenth century. This example in yew wood with the usual elm seat, solidly made (the circle portion is an inch thick), is of very similar design to one drawn by Sheraton, only with the circle enlarged. Yew, of course, increases the price.

c. 1850   £600 — £800

248 A typical 'kitchen' or institutional chair with pleasantly Gothic arched and spindled decoration in the back. Shown in several manufacturers' catalogues and a very similar design shown by W. Smee in 1850. Made of beech with an elm seat.

c. 1850s   £150 — £200
Set of six £1,200 — £1,400

249 A typical 'kitchen' armchair of the mid- to late-nineteenth century on turned legs, used in institutions and offices as well as homes. Usually made in birch or beech, with an elm seat and stained dark. When stripped, often a pleasant golden brown colour. Judging by the extreme difficulty of matching up sets — the turning on the back is nearly always different — they were made over a wide area.

Mid- to late 19th century   £130 — £170

252 (below) Another country variant which frequently turns up in East
Anglia. Sheraton design is apparent.

Early 19th century? £50 — £70
Sets £70 — £90 each

250 A pleasant nineteenth century
kitchen chair of the 'Roman spindles'
type with robust uprights and bold turning. The half-round cuts in the underside
of the top rail help to lighten the appearance. Badly undervalued. Similar to a
Worksop design.

Mid-19th century £120 — £180

251 A variant, but lacking the balance
of the previous example. The debased
Windsor splat seems upside-down and
sagging. Not a wild success.

1880s? £60 — £80
Sets £80 — £100 each

254 The 'blade' back has overtones of
249 but this chair is really a slightly more
ornate version of 253

Early 19th century £50 — £60
Sets £70 — £85 each

253 An even more simple design.
Nevertheless, there is a reeding line along
the back and uprights and the seat is
nicely curved.

Early 19th century £50 — £70
Sets £70 — £90 each

255 A deceptively simple little chair. It
has a well dished seat and a charming
horizontal splat which looks as though it
should be turned and dropped slightly in
this example. A good colour would make
a set very desirable.

1840-1860 £70 — £90
Sets £100 — £140 each

CHAIRS — upholstered 18th century, evolution of wings

Upholstery, like chairs, came late to the general ruck of people. Important personages, not obliged to sit on benches or stools, doubtless padded their important seats with a variety of coverings. For our purposes the upholstered chair can start in the late seventeenth century and go forward from there. The price of upholstered chairs is greatly influenced by the presence of original or contemporary covering fabric.

256 A walnut chair with needlework covering of fine proportion. The turning of the legs, which end in bun feet, and the stretcher and arm supports, is delightful.

c. 1670-1680   *£3,500 — £4,500*

258 A sophisticated walnut wing chair of the early eighteenth century with cabriole legs and shaped stretchers. There is a nicely scrolled curve inside the knee of the cabrioles, which end in pad feet.

1710-1720   *£5,000 — £7,000*

257 A late seventeenth century chair with typical scrolled feet and arm supports, with carved front stretcher again echoing these motifs. The silk covering could well be original. The straight high thin sides are typical.

1680-1690   *£3,000 — £4,000*

259 Another superb walnut wing chair on cabriole legs with scrolls at the top. The arms have an elegant outwards sweep. The only possible criticism is that the legs are, if anything, too thin, lacking the robustness of the period.

1710-1730   *£8,000 — £10,000*

260 A leather-covered wing chair on cabriole legs in walnut with pad feet.

1720-1730   *£4,000 — £5,000*

261 Better quality than the previous example with slightly hipped decoration and good ball-and-claw carving. The front cabriole seen on the right of the picture appears in the photograph to be too splayed out.

c.1730   *£7,000 — £9,000*

262 A Chippendale design with the typical square moulding to the front legs and stretcher. The wings curve out from the back of the arms and continue the serpentine form of the top rail in a most satisfying manner. A form much admired by reproduction manufacturers.

c.1760   *£4,000 — £6,000*

263 A slightly later type than 262. It lacks the broad roll of the arms and the straight top is less attractive. The castors are new — the originals would be broad and thin, and the seat looks out of shape.

264 The thinner tapering legs and lack of stretcher suggest a late eighteenth century date. The back and the wings have integrated into a single curve relieved by the pleating.

c.1780   *£2,500 — £3,500*

CHAIRS — upholstered,
with open arms

265 A walnut chair with shepherd's crook arms and cabriole legs of high quality carving incorporating shell motifs; hipped to the decorated seat rail. It has ball-and-claw feet. The termination of the back legs is interestingly designed.

1720-1730 *£14,000 — £18,000*

266 A leather-covered mahogany chair on cabriole legs with four ball-and-claw feet. Scroll and leaf carving completes the value points on this thoroughly robust piece.

c.1740 *£10,000 — £14,000*

267 A mid-century design of chair with a gadrooned leaf carved front rail and the fine decoration to the cabrioles which end in very successful scrolled feet, as used by Chippendale in some of his designs. Very elegant chair.

1750-1760 *£20,000 £25,000*

268 Another Chippendale motif, three clustered column carved front legs to give a slightly bamboo effect. The leaf carving on the reeded curved arms is a typical period design.

1750-1770 *£10,000 — £12,000*

269 Still fine quality but a much less grand piece. Moulded decoration on the arms and legs. The same solid four square appearance.

c.1765 *£4,000 — £6,000*

270 A variant in the style of the back which gives altogether a lighter appearance, which is however not supported by the thick Chippendale moulded legs; the arms by contrast are excellent. One can well see why the lighter neo-classical designs were so popular.

c.1765 *£2,500 — £3,500*

Plate 40. An example of a good library chair of the late 1740s of a type that was made in both walnut and mahogany, often referred to as a Gainsborough chair. This example is in walnut and is impressive for its well balanced boldness, which it achieves without looking heavy or dumpy

It stands extremely well on scroll feet which spread just enough to give a feeling of stability. The leg is well integrated into the body of the chair by being 'hipped' into the frame and the small scroll echoes the feet. The eye is drawn upwards by the curved arms which carry a simple leaf pattern; the top of the chair is devoid of all decoration.

The colour of the chair is good, the arm supports have a depth of colour and the carving on the knee has gradations of light and shade. Notice how the foot nearest the camera has suffered from passing feet and the bottom of the arm supports have been rubbed. Both show the light colour of the walnut which elsewhere on the piece is covered by a dark glowing patination. The needlework, though probably not original (lack of wear in the right places), gives a good colour harmony. A very desirable piece which sends the price over the range quoted for this type of chair (see figure 266).

Plate 41. This is not a library chair but a sofa so strictly it is not comparable with the previous example. Also in walnut and slightly earlier, it demonstrates how uninteresting a square design without movement can be. Look at the legs, too; well carved with a convincing ball and claw, they don't seem as much part of the piece as the legs in Plate 40; they seem to prop it up rather than provide part of the integrated design as in the previous example.
c.1730

Plate 42. First consider one of the great designs for a late 18th century English chair. Made c.1775, it encapsulates everything that this period stands for, good elegant design, super execution and comfort. It is almost circular in plan from whichever angle you look at it. The top is curved; consider the line of the arm and its termination and the way the arm support moves to pick up the top of the leg. The honeysuckle (anthemion) in the oval is a bold and graceful design, crisply carved. The elegant legs are strong enough for this purpose without overshadowing the central focus of the back.

It fetched £21,000 in mid-1989. The price caused little surprise, even though it was well over the auctioneers' estimate.

One of the problems that inevitably faces the collector attempting to appreciate variations in quality and hence price is to understand the extent to which what seem small variations attract massively disproportionate premiums. Here is a good example.

Plate 43. One of a pair of painted armchairs made c.1775, the same date as the previous example. Period painted chairs are in considerable demand so there is no objection for that reason. It's the same design, isn't it? Well no, it isn't. Look carefully at the difference in the anthemion; it is almost a pastiche of the first. Look at the arms, the lack of movement; the ends don't have the carefully continued drop. Apart from design, the detail is absent. The pair made £6,600 in 1986 which suggests that a single would fetch about £2,000 — £2,500 — a factor of ten times difference from the first example and a classic example of difference in quality.

Plate 44. Ebony inlaid mahogany bergère chairs typical of the heavy neo-classical fashion with which Thomas Hope's name is linked. (The inset illustrations are a chair taken from Thomas Hope's 'Second room containing Greek vases' in Duchess Street, London, and the ram's head which appears in other drawings of his furniture.) This, one of a pair, has a provenance, featuring in a painting of the library at Chesterfield House, the then residence of Lord Harewood.

These are fine examples of library furniture of the turn of the century, robustly made and conforming to how Thomas Hope saw classic furniture.

£20,000 — £30,000

Plate 45. A mahogany reading chair of ten years on from the above. The back with its three parallel bars is reminiscent of the Adam type chairs being made in the 1780s-1790s (see figure 165 for a near equivalent). A good robust piece, made to be sat at both ways round in a gentleman's library, it comes in a traditional form untainted by notions of neo-classicism.

Plate 46. A small six plank chest from the middle of the 16th century. Note the deeply carved leaf design and the faces at the corners. There is a careful confidence about this piece which makes it immediately appealing. If it has a good colour as well, then at about £3,000 — £5,000 it is typical of how undervalued oak remains

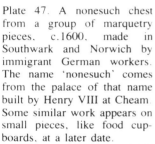

Plate 47. A nonesuch chest from a group of marquetry pieces, c.1600, made in Southwark and Norwich by immigrant German workers. The name 'nonesuch' comes from the palace of that name built by Henry VIII at Cheam. Some similar work appears on small pieces, like food cupboards, at a later date.
c.1600   £4,000 — £6,000

Plate 48. A hutch made of riven oak (oak split rather than sawn). A form of chest made in the late 16th and early 17th centuries which contained corn. Originally the top came off and could be used as a type of kneading trough. These should have a super dark colour. Note the early form of through tenon and the primitive shaping of the feet. Presumably they developed in the 18th century to the more familiar food bin on tall regularly set legs. It too has a removable top.

£2,500 — £3,500

This type of chair enjoyed a long period of popularity. At first the comfort and later the practicality ensured that with period features it continued to be made. The legs provide the clue to date.

271 The moulded cross stretcher and turned and carved legs indicate an early date. A good well-balanced chair.

c.1690   *£2,000 — £3,000*

272 Four good square cabrioles, C-scrolls, carved decoration on the knee. Of all these examples this is the only one with 'movement' in its back (see also 123 in Chairs — cabriole leg, high back). The period, or at least early tapestry, adds to the value even if it detracts from the usefulness.

c.1705   *£2,000 — £2,500*

273 Again legs here clearly proclaim a Queen Anne date and again the use of the C-scroll to decorate the outside of the top of the cabrioles and the use of the cabrioles on four legs is typical. But not the quality of the previous example.

c.1710   *£1,200 — £1,600*

274 A highly individual chair of great character made like the others in walnut. It has a more primitive quality as witnessed by the subdued use of the scroll decoration combined with a highly confident 'double cabriole'.

c.1710   *£2,000 — £2,750*

275 A late walnut example. Plain, but notice the less well made cabrioles terminating in high shaped oval pads.

c.1730   *£1,750 — £2,500*

276 The serpentine top rail is the only decorative feature on this simple square Chippendale period mahogany example.

c.1750   *£600 — £800*

CHAIRS — upholstered, neo-classical

The upholstered square shaped chairs in the earlier sections were peculiarly British. The high sophistication of the French designs towards the end of the eighteenth century were in strong contrast; and the introduction of the neo-classical designs of the Adams brothers; both resulted in demand from the rich for a less ponderous, lighter, more opulent design.

The examples that follow show the huge gradations in quality that were produced over a period. From sumptuous pieces, that in terms of quality are arguably the match of French designs, to the cosy Victorian mass-produced adaptations of the type. But even here quality varies to a surprising degree.

277 Adam carved wood and gilt elaborately decorated with paterae and husk. The shaped seats having a design of honeysuckle and scrolls on turned tapered legs carved with acanthus leaves.

c.1770   *£25,000+ if in pair*

278 Another Adam design chair with oval back and needlework covering. The fluting of the legs and frieze adds lightness and elegance to the design but it is nowhere near the same quality as the last example.

1760-1770   *£20,000+ if in pair*

279 A mahogany open armchair of Adam influence, with turned legs which are fluted and reeded. An elegant design not flattered by the upholstery.

1770-1780   *£4,000 — £5,000*

280 A Victorian walnut open armchair in the French manner — say Louis XVI — with scroll carving and of very high quality execution. One can clearly see the design moving towards the next example. Now much reproduced in Italy and Spain

c.1850   If right £1,000 — £1,500
If wrong £400 — £600

281 This chair clearly shows the development towards the typical Victorian upholstered chair, see the section on Chairs — upholstered, Victorian. Little remains of the neo-classical. Victorian comfort and the love of curves have taken over.

c.1845   *£900 — £1,200*

The vast majority of the furniture produced in the eighteenth century was restrained in design. Even the rococo extravagances made for the very wealthy had a sense of order. In the nineteenth century the mass market demand for more decorative furniture became increasingly strong but the results were not always successful.

282 A Thomas Hope chair in the grand Egypto-Classic manner with animals, paw feet, wings, coronet, gilding, ebonising, stars and leaves. A Brighton Pavilion fancy which is not altogether happy in the modern home.

1810-1820   *£20,000+*

283 A well-executed rosewood armchair but the splay effect of the highly decorated hairy feet is amusing rather than impressive. The long seat and high straight back make it look extremely uncomfortable.

c.1820   *£5,000 — £7,000*

284 Still hairy feet but some sense of movement on the arms and legs instead of the square constipated look of the previous two examples, decorated with simple reeding and thin veneered back rails.

c.1810   *£2,500 — £3,500*

285 The relatively heavy square section fluted legs point to a Regency date, the back is beautifully curved, the elegant little scrolls and rounded section to the back make this a very fine example of high Regency furniture at its best.

c.1810   *£1,800 — £2,500*

286 Clearly an evolution of the previous design, but while it lacks some of the subtlety, it is a solid functional attractive chair.

c.1815   *£2,000 — £2,750*

287 A rare form of Bergère chair with an unusual and uncomfortable shaped back. An extending footrest beneath the seat would add to the value.

c.1820   *£2,500 — £3,500*

288 An imposing highly-carved luxurious mahogany chair with much acanthus-leaf carving and scrolling. The turned legs are carved as well, only the back legs are left plain. Solid early Victorian prosperous comfort.

1840-1850   *£1,750 — £2,250*

289 Would-be impressive giltwood armchair. The carving on the end of the arms is lumpy, the mask at the centre of the top rail is unimaginative, the upholstered arm supports are equally inelegant and look like an afterthought.

c.1830   *£1,200 — £1,500*

290 An all-over deep-buttoned leather armchair with mahogany frame, moulded back and seat rail, short turned legs. A good design. Leather is expensive and this one is in excellent condition.

c.1850   *£1,000 — £1,400*

291 The neo-classical model based on French design of the eighteenth century (see Chairs — upholstered, neo-classical) has now almost evolved to the recognisably mid-Victorian style. The oval back is still a complete entity and is supported as previously. The legs and arms have fully evolved.

c.1840   *£900 — £1,200*

292 The evolution is complete in this good quality example of a lady's chair. Carved decoration on the top rail, hipped seat decoration and a good curve to the jointure of the back and seat, now all one, make this a desirable chair.

1850-1870   *£800 — £1,100*
     Pair £2,250 — £3,000

293 A walnut example but of less quality, the decoration on the over-thick knee is very slight.

1850-1870   *£1,100 — £1,400*
     Pair £2,500 — £3,500

CHESTS AND CHESTS OF DRAWERS

Chests, often referred to as coffers, were very important until the mid-seventeenth century and were still made in quantity throughout the eighteenth century. They were about the only form of storage for most people.

The earliest form of chest was probably a hollowed-out tree trunk with a crude lid. By the thirteenth century, however, simple coffer-like chests with carved decoration and hinged lids, which could be locked, were in use. The solid sides reached the floor to act as feet. By the sixteenth century a joined frame construction with panels was used and the panels, and possibly the lid, were decorated with carving and inlays in the grander examples.

The later part of the seventeenth century saw the introduction of drawers, both in the base of the chest to make what are now called mule chests, and in the top to form a type of half chest and half cabinet construction. There would be one or two drawers in the top half of the piece and doors below enclosed either a cabinet or more drawers.

The drawers were first grooved in the thick sides to run on bearers fixed to the carcase frame inside the piece but after about 1660 the bottom runner, which required a bearer or lining below the drawer, was used.

After the use of carved and inlaid decoration up to about 1650, mitred geometrical mouldings and split balusters were applied to the chest for decoration and this type of chest is characteristic of the period 1650-1680. Sometimes carved decoration and inlays of holly, box, bone, ivory and mother-of-pearl were used, adding to the richness of the piece. It is interesting to note that mother-of-pearl and ivory of this type came to Britain in this period from the Netherlandish craftsmen who emulated their Spanish conquerors. The latter in their turn obtained such decoration from the Moors, who use it to this day.

With the use of walnut from about 1680 onwards, a lighter construction of a pine carcase was used, with pine or oak outer surfaces on which decorative veneers were laid. These chests were very often mounted on stands with twist-turned legs or legs of baluster and inverted cup-turned forms. Whereas earlier chests had carried the frame to the floor to form feet or, after about 1650, had used the turned 'bun' foot, these now started to give way to the bracket foot. The bracket foot is, of course, a design feature, not a constructional one, since the weight of the chest is taken on an inner block on to which the outer bracket-shaped pieces are fixed. It is aesthetically more in sympathy with the square outline of the chest above it and enjoyed successful use on square chests up to the nineteenth century.

After the walnut period of 1680-1740, mahogany was used, in veneered or solid construction. The grander pieces of the famous designers, Adam, Chippendale, Hepplewhite and so on, showed greater varieties of design, with serpentine, bombé, bow and concave drawer fronts. Cabriole legs were used on finer pieces and the bracket foot was curved in serpentine form too. Hepplewhite's designs showed the rather elegant splayed foot with its tapering curves, a most suitable design for serpentine and bow-fronted chests.

It is interesting to note that the fine semi-circular (or *demi-lune,* for Francophiles) satinwood commodes were a later eighteenth century innovation, appearing in Adam and Sheraton designs from about 1780 onwards. Before that the commodes featured by Chippendale and others followed somewhat French designs with scrolled or cabriole legs.

During this mid- and late-eighteenth century period not only mahogany was used for chest exteriors. Oak was used for country or provincial pieces, often cross-banded with mahogany.

From the start of the nineteenth century a gradual change started to take place in which heavier, classical designs came into use with darker decorations such as ebony stringing. Gradually the influence of mass-production began to make itself felt towards the middle of the century, with chests of drawers being turned out in large numbers and varying qualities for the bedrooms of the booming population. The feet became turned and rather bulbous, then gave way to a flat apron around the chest which gives a heavier appearance of a solid base with no feet at all. Nevertheless a variety of woods was used, from mahogany, rosewood and satinwood to burr walnut, maple and much pine or deal.

Oak for drawer linings called wainscot oak was imported from Scandinavia. The grain is even and well suited to making of panelling (hence wainscot) or drawers. One often finds that good quality chests are lined in oak and, moreover, that the better the piece the thinner the linings and the finer the dovetails. Thus a good quality marquetry or walnut chest could have oak linings of about ¼ins. whereas a poor quality country example might have pine linings of double that thickness. Always look at the back of a drawer and the front to make sure that any holes on the inside are accounted for on the outside, i.e. no reveneering has occurred. There is more faked or doctored walnut furniture in existence than almost any other English furniture.

Value Points:
Oak Period (up to 1690)
1973-1977 have seen an enormous boom in oak furniture

and although oak chests have not been in the forefront of it, they have followed it and many of the same value points which apply to other pieces apply also to chests. These are:—

Colour and patination + + +
Originality and lack of restoration + + +
Original handles + +
Original feet +
Carving and decoration of high quality + + + +
Original stand to chest on stand + + +

Walnut Period (1680-1740)
Original stand to chest on stand + + + +
Marquetry or parquetry + + + +
Choice of veneers and figuring + + +
Patination and colour + + +
Original handles and keyplates + + +
Cross-grained mouldings + +
(We have assumed that pieces have an original, veneered top unless a high chest on stand or chest on chest which was above eye level. Beware reveneered tops or 'top halves' with newly veneered tops.)
Veneered and cross-banded sides + +
(Country pieces have plain veneered sides or sides in plain oak or — less quality — plain pine.)
Oak drawer linings +
(Country chests lined in pine.)

Original bracket or bun feet +
Size: 3ft. wide or less + +
        2ft. 9ins. wide or less + + +
        2ft. 6ins. wide or less + + + +
Quartered top + + +
(The best walnut chests have a top veneered with four consecutive veneer sheets set contrapositionally so as to form a symmetrical pattern. Less quality pieces have only two sheets or a plain sheet or sheets not geometrically arranged on the top.)
'Feather' or herring-bone inlay or crossbanding + +

Mahogany Period
Choice of wood and figure + + +
Serpentine or bombé front + + + +
Original handles and keyplates + +
Decorative inlays + + +
Oak linings + +
Colour and patination + + +
Size: as for walnut chests
Brushing slide + + +

Nineteenth Century Chests
Colour and patination + + +
Choice of veneers or figured woods + + +
Size: as for walnut period above
Original handles or knobs + +
Quality of construction + +

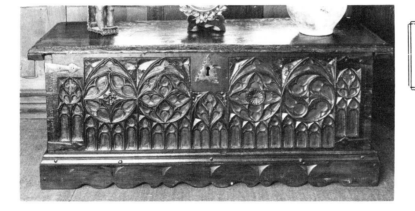

CHESTS

We start this section with two Spanish examples because a large number have been imported over the last ten years and some have been passed off as British.

294 At first sight a Gothic coffer, something that anyone interested in oak would very much like to own. Closer examination would suggest that the age is nearer eighteenth century than pre-1550. It is Spanish, one of a number of these good looking chests that have been imported over the last twenty years.

18th century   *£3,000 — £4,000*

295 Very heavily constructed chest, decorated with stylised geometric carving. The cross in the middle suggests use in a church or private chapel — both sources of many early chests. Country of origin not always easy to determine — possibly Spanish.

Late 16th century   *£1,000 — £1,500*

296 A highly ornate, well-carved and impressive chest. One can see the depth of carving, the assurance of the execution and almost feel the rich quality of what is obviously a fine patination. Inlaid panels and a bold deeply-carved bottom moulding could add substantially to the price.

c.1600 £6,000 — £8,000

297 (above) This small, simple, solidly-made chest has two panels decorated with linenfold panelling. The multiple panel top is typical of the early period.

Late 16th century £2,000 — £3,000

298 By no means a top quality chest, but vigorously and well carved with the traditional arch in the centre panel. Would now be sold as a 'high quality' chest.

c.1640 £1,000 — £1,300

163

299 Although the panels are carved using a simple gouge chisel, the design is vigorous and well drawn and the effect is good. The rails and stiles are decorated with the same repetitive pattern of figures of eight but it, too, is well done.

Mid-17th century   *£1,400 — £1,800*

300 An unusual form of chest in which the front is divided up into a number of small panels both horizontal as well as the normal vertical. The carving is just slightly crude, the serpents being simply gouged out. An interesting piece that will sooner or later be given a location as more research in this field is undertaken.

Mid-17th century   *£900 — £1,200*

301 A fairly common type with lozenge decoration and crudely executed lunettes. It has the advantage of being small.

Late 17th century   *£700 — £900*

302 This is an improved version of the previous example. The same pattern has been employed but the decoration both inside and around the two diamonds is more deeply cut and carefully carved. The line of arcading along the top rail is accurately executed, while the guilloche carving on the middle stile is also of high quality. The top is panelled and the size is small.

Mid-17th century   *£900 — £1,200*

303 A lesser example in which the arches are crudely outlined. Compare, too, the running carving which is of a much more simple form than its equivalent in the previous example. Nevertheless, a piece of considerable charm with a good three-panelled top.

Late 17th century   *£700 — £900*

304 The 'six plank' chest, in which the sides extend to the floor, was made by carvers contemporaneously with the mortise and tenon type made by the joiners. The well-executed arcading and not quite so good half-round decorations, made it an attractive piece.

Late 17th century   *£500 — £650*

305 (below) A much more simple chest and slightly larger than the last example. It is in elm and is later than it looks. The quality of the lunette-type patterns is about average for this type of chest.

Early 18th century   *£300 — £400*

306 (below right) Typical of the large well made but undecorated chests frequently found and harder than usual to date. This is a four-panel version; the majority have only three panels.

Late 17th century   *£250 — £350*

307 Richly decorated with the desirable features of human figures on the stiles and inlaid decoration surrounded by two formal carved arches. The decorative effect is further enhanced by the use of diamond-shaped alternating black and white inlaid wood. Typical of the flamboyant decoration of the period, only the bun feet and the odd-looking moulding along the side (but not the front) seem later additions. One would expect to see the end stiles continued through to make short feet like the third example on this page.

c.1610   £4,000 — £6,000

308 The moulded fronts to the bottom drawers and the use of very fine inlay decorations of ivory and mother-of-pearl suggest a date about the Restoration. It is strictly not a mule chest as the middle now comes out in the form of a drawer, a feature that may have been added later. The broad half-round moulding on top of quite a deep straight bottom edge suggests that the piece once sat on a stand.

c.1665   £2,500 — £3,500

309 A plain mule chest with fielded panels and drawers. A simple oak piece that needs good colour and patination to make it desirable, unless, that is, you go through the following procedure. Remove the lid, turn the chest upside down and reverse the drawers. Cut off the legs and attach to the new base (made from floorboards). Replace the lid which now becomes the top, and make side mouldings in place of the strips which held the lid together. Turn the two end panels into doors. Complete by fitting a dresser rack, ideally with a canopy (see Dressers). Place in a provincial auction or better still a marquee sale and put a reserve of £1,500. Ask the auctioneer to catalogue it for you. Hope nobody notices the wear on the *top side* of the drawer linings on your "fine and unusual small canopy Welsh dresser, early eighteenth century" or best of all can't get near enough to have a proper look.

c.1720   *As mule chest £700 — £900*

310 The ogee-shaped bracket feet, the fielded panels together with the quarter-round reeded pillars set into the end stiles, all point to a date in the third quarter of the eighteenth century.

c.1770   £1,000 — £1,400

166

311 A walnut chest on stand with bracket feet, the chest fitted with carrying handles. The piece features herring-bone inlays, crossbanding and cross-grained mouldings of the period. The price reflects the value of period walnut.

1720-1730   *£4,000 — £6,000*

312 A walnut chest on a more elaborate stand, with cabriole legs incorporating shell motifs and ball-and-claw feet. Carrying handles are again fitted. Legs and stands of this type were extensively reproduced between the wars.

1725-1735   *If stand right £2,000 — £3,000*
                              If stand wrong £800 — £1,000

313 A lacquer chest/trunk on stand with simpler cabriole legs ending in pad feet. Carrying handles are fitted and the top is slightly domed. This shape affects the price, since the domed top does not provide a utilitarian surface. All lacquer should be regarded with profound suspicion.

1720-1740   *If right £4,000 — £5,000*
                                     If wrong £1,000 — £1,500

314 A mahogany domed chest/trunk on a square fluted stand. Again the domed top affects the price as does the size and the stand which, despite the use of fluting to lighten up appearance, does nothing to disguise the bulk of the piece.

1740-1760   *£600 — £800*

CHESTS — early oak with moulded fronts

316 (left) A less decorated example, illustrated with one lower door open to show the three drawers fitted in the lower part. Many of the mouldings and applied split balusters are made of fruit-wood which would originally have been ebonised. The piece is typically Anglo-Dutch and the ivory and pearl inlay, of Flemish-Spanish origin, have been referred to in the introduction to this section. Notice the original iron loop handles on the drawers.

c.1660   *£3,000 — £3,500*

315 (above) A typical early oak example in which the lower drawers are enclosed behind doors whose moulding and decoration matches that of the upper drawer. The piece is in two halves which can be lifted separately, the join being hidden by a case moulding, and the lower half is on bun feet. Note the applied decoration and the receding 'chequer-board' centre panel in the top drawer.

c.1665   *£4,000 — £5,000*

318 (right) A small oak chest on bun feet missing some of its brass drop handles. There is a pleasant split bobbin decoration applied horizontally under the top and between each drawer. The remaining decoration consists of pairs of split balusters applied vertically beside each drawer. The moulding on the drawer fronts is very simple, and the top drawer is simply panelled. Note the thicker top with its simple edge. Later handles.

c.1680   *£800 — £1,200*

317 (above) A small oak chest with fruitwood front, 34ins. wide, made in one carcase piece, with the typical deep top drawer which is left over from the two types above, where the lower drawers were cupboarded. Now, in this piece, the lower drawers have emerged in their own right and are suitably moulded. The decoration of the top drawer is interesting, with four ivory 'buttons' placed around an oval moulding. Note the 'stump' feet, which are formed by a continuation of the vertical carcase frame. Handles missing.

c.1670   *£3,000 — £3,500*

319 (right) The simplest later form of these chests with each drawer divided into two panels by the mouldings. There is a simple half-round moulding applied across the carcase front between each drawer, a precursor of the half-round or D moulding of the walnut period. The bracket feet have been added later. Instead of the simple, thin top of the earlier examples, the top has now become thick enough to have a 'thumb nail' edge moulding around it. Replacement handles.

1700-1720   *£650 — £750*

CHESTS OF DRAWERS — transitional

The increasing use of contrasting wood to add to the decorative quality of geometrically moulded chests might eventually have led to the idea of veneering on flat surfaces. However the Continental influences which flooded into England at the Restoration brought foreign craftsmen as well as foreign ideas, among them veneering, so that the changeover took place quickly. These three examples show interesting transitional pieces.

320 Retains the geometric cushion-shaped mouldings of the previous period but the mouldings are no longer the dominant feature, instead the eye is drawn to the fine burr walnut veneers. In this chest therefore are combined the decorative applied pieces and an almost dentil moulding with the new technique of veneering. The bracket feet are later. The price will very much depend on patina.

c.1680   *£3,000 — £4,000*

321 Veneered in very thick elm with fine bold mouldings not only at top and bottom but where the piece would originally have come in half. The veneers are still arranged on the drawers in two halves as they would have been had they been moulded first. Again, colour most important affect on price.

c.1680   *£3,500 — £4,500*

322 The transformation to all-over walnut veneered carcase is complete, but the maker had still the old designs very much in mind. The geometric design of the fragmented square is used on the veneered top and bottom drawer, while the second drawer continues the familiar cross design, see the bottom drawer of the chest above. Even the broad edges of the front have long thin straight shapes where applied balusters might previously have been situated and the centre of the drawers reflects the traditional division of the design into two. Again the feet have been replaced. Note the half-round cross-grained moulding between the drawers — typical of the walnut period.

c.1700   *£3,000 — £4,000*

Four moulded front and plain oak chests on stands, showing different forms of both drawer mouldings and stand turning.

It is nearly always the stand and rarely the chest which provides the problem of verification. Even in oak the weight of the chest proved too much for many of the relatively thin legs used, even though often the oak stands are more squat in design than the walnut ones. Usually the bottom drawer is genuine, though the legs often need close examination. Replacement buns below the stretcher are quite common and reasonably acceptable, original buns should have some sign of age if not a touch of rot or damage.

323 (above) This chest has brass drop handles, varied drawer mouldings and a half-round moulding to the carcase front. The stand has a single drawer and five robust baluster-turned legs united by a simple curved stretcher above bun feet. The panelled sides also incorporate a variation of moulding between chest and stand. A good example.

1680-1700   *If stand wrong £3,000 — £4,000*
    If legs wrong £1,500 — £1,900

324 (right) The drawer mouldings on the chest are all similar. There is a half-round moulding on the carcase front, which is repeated round the drawers in the stand although the latter are not moulded. A bold top moulding, showing later influences than the simpler design of 323, is echoed round the top of the stand but it is not a mirror image.

The stand is on six rather thin legs with inverted cup-turning and rather elongated buns and thick stretchers, but has a nicely shaped apron with a lip moulding to emphasise the ogee curves. The side of the stand is not panelled, unlike the chest, but this is a common difference as can be seen in the next two examples. Original handles and scutcheon plates are lost. The fact that the drawers in the base are not moulded like those in the top would prompt a close investigation to detect a possible marriage.

1700-1720   *If legs right £3,500 — £4,500*
    If legs wrong £1,500 — £2,000

325 (right) A chest on stand with plain panelled drawers and drop handles. There is a half-round moulding to the carcase front and reasonably bold top and bottom mouldings to the chest, which echo each other in a mirror image. A further moulding decorates the top and bottom edges of the stand. The sides of the chest are panelled and it has been made in two halves for ease of handling (as opposed to being cut at a later date).

The stand is on four rather weak legs joined by turned stretchers using baluster shapes. They and the stretchers are probably not original. The drawer panels in the stand, however, certainly match those in the chest.

1700-1730   *Assume stand right £1,800 — £2,500*

326 (left) A chest on stand with plain early eighteenth century drawers with no crossbanding or decoration, and fitted with later pierced mid-eighteenth century backplates to the handles. There is a double-D (or double half-round) moulding on the carcase edges of the chest which is repeated around the drawer in the stand. The sides of the chest is panelled. The top and bottom mouldings are bold, as is that around the top of the stand, which has a shaped apron like that of 324 but without the lip moulding around the curves.

The six legs are of an unusual shape, with a heavy turned knob at the top repeated on the bun feet, which are linked by a square stretcher with ogee curves shaping its outward edges. The design of these legs does not somehow ring quite true, mainly due to the unimaginative turning of the bulbous knobs. Handles later.

1700-1730   *However assume right £2,500 — £3,500*

327 A very fine oyster veneered chest of drawers on bun feet which are a bit small in proportion. Parquetry work of this kind, involving geometric designs made up from *small* oyster veneers, requires a high degree of skill. Note the 'thumbnail' top edge moulding and deep proportion. Just short of 2ft. in depth.

1690-1710   *£12,000 — £15,000*

328 (above) A marquetry chest of drawers in faded sycamore with panels of sharply contrasting woods. A very striking piece with the typical thumbnail moulding of the period. Marquetry in panels is associated with this earlier period, but perhaps even more desirable are the flower vases and buds in panels with green stained bone pieces inserted. Later the marquetry spread all over and gradually became thinner and rather effete.

c.1685   *£8,000 — £10,000*

329 (left) The classic profile of an early walnut chest — herring-bone crossbanding to the drawers, matched veneers, half-round or D cross-grained mouldings on the edges of the carcase front. The bun feet are replacements but of correct proportions. The top is quartered and cross-banded. Brasses later, keyholes original.

1700-1720   *Assume good rich colour*
and original handles £5,000 — £7,000
If cleaned off, no colour,
and later handles £2,500 — £3,000

172

Plate 49 is of a good oriental lacquer chest. The finely wrought drawing of the scene is skilled and realistic. There is perspective and the artist has created a sense of space by resisting the temptation to crowd the scene. Japanese work is black and of a very high quality; this excellent example is, however, probably Chinese. *Early 18th century*

On the return of Charles II in 1660 lacquer became progressively popular. Imports from the Orient were gradually supplemented by European imitations after Stalker and Parker's treatise published in 1688 by amateurs. The gradations in quality are therefore considerable, but two examples should make the difference clear.

Plate 50 makes a good contrast. This is European work, possibly British. It is carefully executed but lacks the fineness of execution and artistic imagination of the previous example; there is none of the sense of space, even serenity. *Early 18th century*

Plate 51. The warm colour of this William and Mary oyster veneered olivewood small cabinet on stand is typical of this wood which, compared with walnut, has a slightly more 'oily' and often darker appearance. A good decorative effect has been achieved by using oysters (pieces cut across a branch or small tree rather than sliced longways) of varying size.

The stand is interesting; the spiral turnings are bold and the connecting stretchers are thinner than most reproductions (see the next example). The bun feet are a good original shape which relates to the turning of the legs.

Plate 52. Oysters again but this time in walnut, smaller and more tightly arranged, but still with a good sense of design. The spiral turning looks as though somebody had pulled it longways and stretched it out, a feature often found in later spiral turning. The stretchers at the base are on the thick side, too. One would want to have a very careful look at the stand before accepting it as genuine; it looks wrong. *c.1690*

Plate 53. Of the same date as the last example, this cabinet is inlaid with elaborate floral marquetry in the Dutch style. The central vases give a good balance to the design. The long 'cushion' drawer under the top moulding is typical of the period.

The stand was restored — compare the thickness of the first example — and the buns have that 'cannon-ball' look commented on elsewhere. Nevertheless, a decorative and most desirable piece.

c.1690

Plate 54. Late 17th century and great fun. The design is just the same as the previous example but the maker went flat out for effect and succeeded using oysters of lignum vitae. As you can see, the sapwood of yellow provides a startling contrast with the dense black heartwood. It has a curiously timeless look; for example, it would not be out of place in an art deco room. The centre slides and has tortoise-shell drawers and a mirror. Is the stand right? Difficult to tell from a photograph but this day and age does it matter greatly with such a piece, presumably destined to be part of an exciting interior design where effect is more important than originality?

Plate 55. For Queen Anne's reign an unusual design of small walnut chest, only 30ins. wide. Three-quarters of a century later Sheraton published a very similar design and quite a lot were made — see figure 377. The proportion of width to height is excellent and the curve to the front gives it a touch of character that marks it out as exceptional. Apart from the later swan neck handles and, perhaps, the loss of an inch off the bottom of the feet, time has treated it well. There are many shades of colour and what looks like a warm, glowing patination. Notice the darkness of the right-hand side of the bottom drawers melting into the darker moulding of the bottom. Truly a collector's piece

Plate 56. Just as photography can be gratuitously unflattering of people so it can be of furniture. Some pieces look glorious, others are maligned. This well shaped standard small (2ft.8ins.) walnut chest of the 1720s may look fine in the flesh but what is probably a gremlin in the printing provides us with an object lesson in the colour to avoid when buying walnut. It gives the impression of an overcleaned surface — no fading, no tones of colour, no attractive matching of grain, no extra depth of colour caused by wear. One can fantasise that it was french polished by an unskilled hand on a damp evening. A consistent all pervading matt bloom of dull yellow disinterest is all we see from the illustration!

330 A laburnum parquetry veneer chest with inlaid boxwood stringing lines in typical patterns. Even the diamond shape inlaid in the sides is quite usual and is possibly a design left over from oak carving or applied moulding on much earlier chests. Bracket feet and walnut crossbanding are the other principal features. Handles are not original.

1700-1720 £6,000 — £8,000

331 (above) A burr yew chest on bracket feet, with boxwood banding to the drawers. The heavy top moulding is of cross-grained yew, as is the lighter bottom moulding, but the half-round on the edges of the carcase has been cut along the grain. Again, the handles are later. Price high because yew is expensive.

1700-1720 £7,000 — £10,000

332 (left) A country walnut chest with inlaid boxwood and ebony stringing lines in conventional patterns. The straight grained walnut of this more humble piece still matches. Note the original handles which are fixed through the drawer fronts with thin steel wire. The wire has often broken and been replaced by bands, but this is not very important. Buns are replacements.

c.1710 £4,000 — £6,000

CHESTS — on turned stands

The distinction between chests on stands and chests which merely had bun feet to support them is that broadly speaking apart from the round holes for the buns at the four corners of the bottom of the chest, the former did not have veneered tops while the latter did. Our ancestors were shorter and it seems that as long as the chest had a stand which lifted it by about two feet or more there was no need to veneer the top. Chests with newly veneered tops are those which have either lost their stands altogether or have lost their feet (normally replaced by oversize buns) which exposes the top to view. Obviously chests on stands should have no bun holes. Clearly 337 (assuming the stand were original) would be much happier on the type of legs supporting 336. The thin flat stretchers should be veneered on the top and normally on the front edges. The same general rule applies for replacement legs as given for bureaux on stands, viz where stands or legs have been replaced, the value is reduced drastically, if badly done, by over 50%.

333 A marquetry chest on stand incorporating oyster veneers. The design is similar to 334 but the spirally-turned stand of five legs joined by a curved flat stretcher on bun feet is the more usual for this design, which is frequently found in figured walnut. The stand has a single drawer. Very often the turned legs may have been removed due to damage and the chest is modified to sit on bun feet.

1680-1700   *£14,000   £18,000*

334 A similar walnut chest on stand with 'thumb-nail' top edge moulding and rather bulbous turned legs. Again a design frequently found without the turned legs and with the single drawer stand mounted on bun feet due to damage. Stand looks particularly suspect.

1680-1700   *However, assume it is right*
                              £7,000 — £9,000
                          If wrong £4,000 — £6,000
Sometimes one finds top halves of chests on chests which have lost their bases (see 344) and sit on newly made stands; these normally have no drawers and the stands are not very desirable.
                                    £700 — £950

335 (above) A large walnut chest with burr veneer mounted on a shaped stand showing typical ogee curves to the edge of the apron. The faceted legs look a little slender for the size of chest but the robust stretcher of elaborate design is veneered on the top surface with the same walnut burr veneer as the rest of the piece.

1680-1700   *If original £6,000 — £8,000*
                                    If wrong £4,000 — £5,000

336 (above right) A simpler walnut chest on stand with matched veneers on the drawer fronts. There is a diagonal cross-band veneer to the drawers and double-D moulding to the carcase edges. The turned legs are perhaps a trifle heavy, with rather modern-looking tapered central sections.

1680-1700   *With original legs £9,000 — £12,000*
                                    With replacement legs £6,000 — £8,000

337 (right) A walnut chest on a stand which has lost its legs and been resettled on large bun feet. The difference in the figure of the walnut veneer of the chest, which is close-figured with plenty of curl, and the stand, which is straighter grained, leads to the conclusion that the chest and stand did not start out in life together.

Top c.1710   *However stand if original £4,000 — £6,000*
Stand c.1690 and   *if not just a chest see 329*
once with turned legs
broadly like 333

CHESTS — on cabriole leg stands, 1700-1750

The introduction of the cabriole leg meant that stands as well as chairs had to have the new fashion, which was unfortunate for chests are heavy, the cabriole form is not even as strong as turning and walnut is not the strongest of woods. Add to this the addiction of furniture beetles for solid walnut and it is not surprising that after 250 years of varied treatment many legs have broken. All stands should be carefully checked. Note that tops are not veneered.

338 A fine quality walnut veneered chest on cabriole leg stand, the legs have a scroll at the shoulder. The veneers on the drawer fronts are matched and the carcase edges around the drawers have double-D cross-grained mouldings.

c.1720   *£10,000 — £12,000*

339 A quality walnut chest on stand. It appears here with cabriole legs which have rather effete shells on the knee. The contrast between the heavy William and Mary chest and stand and the rather thin legs raises doubts. It would look a great deal happier with a turned leg stand supported by flat stretchers like 336.

c.1715   *Assuming right £7,000 — £9,000*
Assume cabrioles later addition £4,000 — £6,000

340 (above) A fine small solid walnut chest on stand with original brasses and a nicely shaped apron to the stand. The small slightly stumpy cabriole legs and the deep moulding at the join of chest and stand give it a pleasantly robust, country look. The drawer edges have an ovolo lip moulding. The walnut is heavy and dense-grained. Thought to be from the slow growing northern areas, possibly Cumbria.

c.1730   *£6,000 — £8,000*

341 (above right) An oak chest on stand incorporating a secretaire drawer. Note the well-proportioned legs ending in the typically English pad foot, and the elaborately scrolled apron to the stand. The drawers have a lip mould which overlaps the carcase edge and they are cross-banded with walnut. The secretaire interior is a very pleasant design with elegant applied pillars flanking the central door.

1730-1750   *Assume good colour £8,000 — £10,000*

342 (right) A good quality chest of well matched walnut veneers with good grain and pleasant ripple effect. The base is a bit heavy (can one see here the move towards the chest on chest?). The legs are replacements and are of a design sometimes known as Hackney Road after the main area of their production.

c.1725   *As is £5,000 — £7,000*

CHESTS OF DRAWERS, 1710-1760

343 To many collectors not the favourite form of walnut top moulding but at 3ft. wide and with a brushing slide and good colour it can command a very substantial price. Note that the handles are not original for the marks left by the previous late eighteenth century oval plates can still be seen. A small example, say 2ft. 6ins., with glorious golden colour, could be double this price.

c.1730   *£8,000 — £10,000*

344 This is a walnut chest which was originally mounted on a larger chest (see Chests on Chests section). It has all the characteristics of a 'top half', i.e. three small top drawers, canted reeded corners, heavy top moulding, new bracket feet and a new top surface. (The original top would have been left unveneered as it would be above eye level.)

1725-1740   *£1,500 — £2,000*

345 A walnut chest with later walnut period features, i.e. inlaid stringing lines in boxwood, no crossbanding on the drawers, and a small double lip moulding around the drawers. Although there are three small top drawers and the top is not quartered, this is a lower quality chest of the later walnut period. Usually the three top drawers indicate that the piece has been on a stand or lower chest, but in this case the veneered top could be an indication that this was not necessarily so.

1730-1750   *£3,500 — £4,500*

346 The square solid character of the very early eighteenth century chest is well illustrated in this panel sided oak piece with double-D moulding round the drawers and thick top mouldings.

c.1720   £1,000 — £1,400

347 A walnut chest of country make with a higher and narrower proportion than earlier examples. Plain thick veneers with simple half herring-bone crossbanding (or diagonal crossbanding). Made on into the later part of the century.

1740-1760   £2,000 — £2,750

348 Obviously the bottom half of a chest on chest. Tell-tale signs are the sunburst on the bottom drawer, the three long drawers of almost equal depth, the low proportions and the new top.

c.1730   £1,000 — £1,300

349 The end of the walnut era. Broad mouldings which soon refined down to the typical Chippendale type, no crossbanding, just a line of contrasting walnut where the herring-bone would originally have been and a form of cockbeading which, instead of being round the drawers, is on the carcase. A trifle too high

c.1740   £1,400 — £1,800

350 A really fine quality bachelor's chest in veneered walnut with original handles and plates. Not simply content with the folding top which characterises these pieces, the cabinet maker has also fitted a brushing slide under the top. The short cabriole legs are unusual, but original. In short this piece has just about everything needed to give it maximum points for quality.

c.1710   *£35,000 — £45,000*

351 A simpler veneered walnut bachelor's chest, with cock-beaded drawers, on the more standard bracket feet. The handles are not original.

1730-1745   *£8,000 — £11,000*

352 A solid mahogany bachelor's chest with a flush moulding to the top edge. The drawers show the ovolo lip edge moulding; and the handles are probably original. The sides are unusual — going 'straight through' to the ground with no bottom moulding and having feet shaped from the solid side. The front is treated more conventionally, with bracket feet and a moulding. Not a very good example of the specie.

1730-1750   *Restored £5,000 — £7,000*

353 (left) A plain mahogany version with cock-beaded drawers and conventional bracket feet. The top is rather heavy and square and the handles are new.

1730-1750 £7,000 — £9,000

354 (right) An unusual veneered bachelor's chest on cabinet with cupboard doors under the folding top and false drawers down the sides.

Mid-18th century £10,000 — £14,000

355 (left) The later equivalent — an unusual bachelor's (or maiden's) cabinet with folding top, fitted underneath with writing compartments. The false top drawer and real second one have black inlaid stringing lines. The square panelled doors house sliding mahogany tray shelves.

1800-1820 £4,500 — £5,500

CHESTS ON CHESTS

356 (left) The grandest form of walnut chest on chest, incorporating an inlaid 'sunburst' in the bottom drawer, brushing slide and canted corners on the top half, the corners being fluted with cross-grained moulding. The drawers are veneered with finely matched walnut and have herring-bone cross-banding and a walnut cock-bead.

c.1715
£15,000 — £20,000

357 (right) A plainer walnut chest on chest with inlaid herring-bone to cross-banded drawers edged with ovolo lip moulding to cover the carcase edges. No slide, canted corners or sunburst.

c.1735
£7,000 — £9,000

358 (left) A fine quality mahogany chest on chest with cross-banded drawers with cockbeading, mounted on serpentine bracket feet. The top chest features pillared fluted corners with brass mounts and a blind fret beneath the dentil top moulding and the pillars.

c.1765
£7,000 — £9,000

359 (right) A good quality mahogany chest on chest on serpentine bracket feet, with reeded canted corners to the top chest.

c.1770
£3,000 — £4,000

360 A Chippendale mahogany chest on chest, of high quality, with broken pediment, dentil decorated cornice, brushing slide and serpentine bracket feet.

c.1760
£10,000 — £13,000

361 (right) A plain mahogany chest on chest with no decoration, on bracket feet. Also made in oak.

1760-1800   *£1,750 — £2,500*
                               Not very desirable

362 (above) A good quality mahogany chest on chest with reeded canted corners, key pattern to the top moulding and an inlaid ebony and boxwood stringing line round each drawer. Often found in oak as well as mahogany.

1760-1780   *£2,500 — £3,500*

363 (left) A bow-fronted chest on chest with dentil top moulding and splay feet.

1780-1800   *£2,500 — £3,500*

364 (right) An interesting bow-fronted chest on chest on Hepplewhite-style splayed feet. The top shows the black inlaid stringing lines popularised by the revival of classical design. Note, too, how the gradation of the drawers produces a better effect than 363 which is altogether an inferior piece.

1800-1820   *£5,000 — £7,000*

365 (above) A semi-circular satinwood inlaid two door commode on tapering legs.
1780-1790   *£20,000 — £30,000 (right)*
  £4,000 — £6,000 (wrong)

366 A Hepplewhite serpentine-front commode chest of drawers in mahogany. Fitted with slide. The fin-lire projections on the sides and the shaped apron beneath together with shape of moulding all point towards the work of this designer. An elegant piece with fine patination and original handles.

1770-1780   *£8,000 — £11,000*

367 (left) A mahogany serpentine-front chest on heavily carved cabriole legs. The design is similar to Chippendale but shows later influences in the acanthus leaf carving and scrolling of the legs. It is a type often reproduced.

1760-1780   *£40,000+*
1890s   *£6,000 — £8,000*
1920s   *£1,750 — £2,500*

368 An interesting design of Thomas Hope influence, showing Egyptian heads and ebony stringing lines.

1810-1820   *£5,000 — £7,000*

369 A mahogany commode on spirally fluted tapering legs. A more classical design not unlike those illustrated by Sheraton.

1780-1800   *Even though quite large*
  £5,000 — £7,000

188

370 A fine quality serpentine mahogany chest with canted fluted corners, a slide and bracket feet. The handles are possibly original.

1770-1780   *£6,500 — £8,000*

371 A Sheraton design mahogany serpentine chest featuring inlaid shell motifs and boxwood and ebony stringing lines. The plate handles may be original. Note the heavy bracket feet.

1780-1800   *£8,000 — £10,000*

372 A mahogany serpentine chest of drawers without slide and with a narrower corner with fluting, on bracket feet. The drawers are cross-banded and the swan-neck handles are original.

1770-1790   *£5,000 — £7,000*

373 A mahogany serpentine chest on splayed feet with inlaid boxwood stringing lines and mahogany crossbanding. Note how the corners terminate in a sharp edge without a canted surface or decoration. The splayed feet follow the late eighteenth century designs of Hepplewhite.

1780-1800   *£5,000 — £7,000*

374 A late eighteenth century example with brushing slide showing fine use of the mahogany grain to provide the maximum decorative effect. Note the bottom moulding which soon disappeared, and the use of reeded top moulding which started with Sheraton but came into wide use in Regency times. The splayed feet add to the value. Good original handles.

c.1790   *£2,000 — £3,000*

375 A bow-fronted chest with slide, splayed feet and shaped apron. The top is cross-banded in satinwood. A fine quality piece.

1780-1800   *£1,750 — £2,500*

376 Splay feet with apron, good ripple effect on the mahogany and brushing slide — all point towards Georgian quality. Only the flat D-shaped top moulding, which suggests a move towards the Victorian, and the lack of crossbanding detract.

c.1820s   *£1,200 — £1,600*

377 A small chest cross-banded with satinwood on the top and showing the flat fronted form of bow which appeared in Sheraton's design book in 1793. (In another variant of the same form pillars are found superimposed on the ends.) Quite an elegant piece helped by the existence of a brushing slide but odd and untidy in that it lacks cockbeading to the edges of the drawers. Notice that all four examples on this page have long top drawers instead of two short ones.

1795-1810   *£3,000 — £4,000*
But imagine satinwood crossbanding, original shells — writing drawer, good polish etc., etc.   *£6,000 — £8,000*

378 A low bow-fronted chest with splayed feet, veneered in feather figured mahogany. Not a favourite type because it is too squat and out of proportion, almost as though a bottom drawer has been taken out.

1800-1830   *£500 — £700*

379 A fairly plain mahogany veneered example. With splay feet at both front and back. It has a flat top moulding and Bramah locks. Quite elegant in a modest way.

c.1830s   *£650 — £800*

380 A little wooden-knobbed chest on particularly Victorian bun feet with an almost flat moulding, not very exciting perhaps but it has two virtues — it is small and the maker made an effort with the grain of the wood. It will probably end up with a reeded moulding, apron and splay feet and oval brass handles. Why oval? Because the knob holes are too near the drawer ends to put on round or octagonal; oval shaped handles will make them appear better spaced. Could end up looking better than 379.

1840-1860s   *£450 — £600*

381 A feather figured veneered mahogany chest on turned feet of good quality throughout and with good patination. With brass replacements handles could look very handsome, despite its height which traditionally counted against it.

c.1850-1870   *£400 — £600*

382 An early mahogany chest. The top moulding is the simple half-round which together with the bold high bracket feet can be found on later walnut examples. Fine cut-out handles which could be original. With good patination a fine piece.

c. 1740-1750   *£3,000 — £4,000*

383 A good quality mahogany chest with fine faded patination. Signs of quality are the recessed top moulding (made up of the Chippendale moulding with an additional curve below), the chamfered corners with a vertical bead decoration and stop end at the bottom, and the finely moulded ogee feet.

c.1760   *£3,000 — £4,500*

384 Typical of a group of chests with Chippendale moulding, brushing slides and ogee feet of good quality dense grained (though the photograph exaggerates it) mahogany. The best ones have reeded canted corners which help the price. Size of course is critical to price.

c.1750-1760   *2ft. 6ins. £4,000 — £6,000*
                        2ft. 10ins. £2,500 — £3,500

385 The recessed quarter-round fluted pillar, the use of white stringing lines and strange little decorations at the bottom suggest late eighteenth century provincial workmanship.

c.1770s   *£2,500 — £3,500*

Plate 57. A George III commode with panels of Chinese lacquer decorated with figures and pavilions in shades of dark red and gilt. The scenes are more crowded than those of the earlier part of the century, shown as Plates 49 and 50, but the detailing is of good quality and perspective is retained. The panels are set with an English japanned border. Probably the panels were made in England, exported, lacquered and returned. This is a very desirable form of commode and to be so well decorated gives it a considerable premium price.

Two examples of lacquer work from the late 18th century.

Plate 58. This bow-fronted lacquer side cabinet also contains Chinese lacquer panels on coromandel, but as you will notice there is no cohesive design. In fact the flowers on the bottom of the doors have been cut off. This has probably been made up from pieces taken from an imported screen.
c.1780

Plate 59. A superb bombé commode, c.1770. The master cabinet maker has selected consecutive sheets of veneer to give this fountain effect, not just on the drawers but right across the front by taking in the drawer dividers as well. He has repeated this right across the top. The movement in the design of the piece and its balance, elegant height and fine fittings make it a top collector's piece.

Time has enhanced its appearance. Faded down to a rich gold it becomes even more desirable.

Plate 60. A good example of very much the same Hepplewhite design but without the movement on the sides. The fountain effect is there again but not through the drawer dividers. The bottom rail has a slightly too fussy fretted edge and the handles do not have the grand look. It lacks the clever touch of the black line to outline the shape.

It too has faded down well. The elegant moulding looks particularly well in the photograph. The two provide an excellent example of gradations at the very top of the quality scale. When this sold it made four times the auctioneer's estimate of £5,000 — £7,000. Quality, colour and patina together make a superb combination bested only by the additional presence of provenance

Plate 61. The type of good quality serpentine chest made from the 1760s and later in the provinces. The good colour illustration catches the feel of the wood which in these pieces nearly always seems to be of excellent quality. In the unfaded area, particularly, one can see the many vertical burrs sometimes looking like bruises — the so-called 'plum pudding' effect. The blind fret on the side is also typical but more expensive pieces had carved motifs while the cheaper were undecorated.

This piece also illustrates the dealers' dilemma. Some customers, notably the Europeans, like the unfaded dark colour, while others, including some Americans, prefer the faded look. Sadly, until recently, few overseas buyers went for this 'naturally faded look' so if it is not aimed at the UK market it may now either be bleached or repolished.

Plate 62. The classical influence makes itself felt in the pillar sides and gilt metal hairy paw feet which became increasingly fashionable. This chest, c.1800, in mahogany crossbanded with rosewood and with a satinwood stringing line, is attributable to Gillows of Lancaster, a firm renowned for good quality workmanship, but other influences are becoming apparent. At 3ft.6ins. it is no taller than the last example but without a moulding it looks bigger and the fussy inlaid lines, squares and dots detract rather than help the overall design. The 19th century has arrived.

Plate 63. Strictly a side cabinet but in this section by virtue of our definition, this is a deceptively simple rosewood example with pleated silk on panels. The brass diamond stringing lines and the restrained corner decorations on the top make it less exciting from the viewpoint of a decorator but it is, none the less, a good piece of Regency furniture. Judging by the dark grain, it has been repolished this century. *c.1810*

Plate 64. A more exciting example dating from 1810. The painted eagles supporting the top shelf give it more decorative interest, added to which it is made in kingwood veneer, not unlike rosewood but with figuring that can be seen on the curve to the right of the lower drawer.

386 A plain mahogany chest on typical mid-century bracket feet with original swan-neck handles; the drawers have cockbeading. A design which was used for oak and propor- tions. Ivory inlay keyholes usually go with stamped brass plates like 387.

c.1760-1780 £1,400 — £1,800

387 Well figured and with slightly stilted splay feet (compare with 388 below). The apron with the shaping repeated around the sides is a pleasing feature. Overall good quality reflected in the fine section mouldings.

c.1780 £900 — £1,200

388 A simple small well-faded mahogany chest with well- made splay feet and apron and the unusual feature of portrait brasses. The square flat moulding on the top with a simple crossbanding and black stringing line to emphasise it suggests a later date.

c.1800 *Because small £900 — £1,200*

389 As with the bow-fronted chests so here is a small late example which might 'improve'. One can visualise an effort to turn it into 388. Cockbeading, splay feet, apron, and flat moulding. Apart from the pine drawer linings (and maybe even pine sides) what will give it away is the 'flash Alf' use of the matching grain. Look at the preceding three pages and notice that in the rare case where a matched grain is used, as in 374, it is done with restraint. In any event the original buns will have left big round holes which will raise question marks. It really ought to be appreciated in its own right.

Late 19th century *In top showroom condition mahogany*
sides and with brass handles £300 — £400
Rough condition and pine sides £150 — £250

CHESTS — military

The military chest first came into use in the Napoleonic wars. Ideally it has no projections such as handles and is projected by metal fittings at all vulnerable points so that it can be loaded easily — an early appreciation of containerisation. They are found in mahogany, padouk, cedar and camphor woods, i.e. solid strong woods, not pine or veneered as are some of the reproductions now being hugely reproduced as campaign furniture. Clearly the secretaire feature adds considerably to the value.

390 A superb example in which the secretaire folds down to reveal a line of three drawers on top, pigeon-holes with a central drawer below and a lift-up desk for maps and papers. Brass protects the corners and is also used as inlay as well as on the traditional folding handles. The paw feet presumably are easy to screw off — if not this would defeat the whole object of the piece which, of course, comes in half and is provided with carrying handles.

c.1810   *£6,000 — £8,000*

391 Another good example unusually well fitted inside. Made in cedar wood and with the usual brass edges and carrying handles.

c.1810
£3,000 — £4,000

393 (right) A simple military chest in padouk with another style of folding brass handles. Again brass corners and carrying handles but the locks are of the ordinary variety. It now sits on a plinth made later. Perhaps it was brought home and used in retirement. 2ft. 6ins. wide.

Early 19th century
£900 — £1,200
If much wider
£700 — £900

392 Moving down the ranks, this is more typical of the small secretaire type sometimes found in the form of a writing slope which opens out. Made by Day & Sons of The Strand it is very solidly constructed in cedar (?) with utilitarian handles and the minimum of brass work.

Early 19th century
£1,500 — £2,000

The term Wellington chest is applied to those specimen chests having a hinged flap at the side which can be locked over the drawers to prevent them opening. Presumably the inference is that they can be taken on campaigns, but why Wellington, ingenious as he was, should be credited with them is a mystery. Perhaps it is really a generic name stemming from the war period, like Trafalgar and Waterloo.

394 A collector's specimen cabinet in maple, with spiral pillars at the sides, and a glass panelled door enclosing the twelve drawers. The carved decoration has a mask and leaf form over the door. Quite a remarkable specialist piece.

c.1860   *£5,000 — £7,000*

395 An ebonised exhibition-style specimen chest with sophisticated in-laid decoration and a brass gallery round the top. It has ormolu mounts and reflects the rather grand exhibition styles of the mid-nineteenth century influenced by French designers.

c.1850   *£3,000 — £4,000*

396 An Edwardian Wellington chest, made by the celebrated firm of Edwards and Roberts, who have, as usual, used all the decorative motifs associated with Sheraton — satin-wood inlaid shells, ribbons, husks, etc., etc.

c.1900   *£2,000 — £3,000*

397 A walnut veneered Wellington chest with pleasantly curled figure of almost burr type.

c.1855   Walnut £1,000 — £1,400
Bird's eye maple £1,000 — £1,250

398 A plain oak Wellington chest similar to the previous example.

c.1855   *£500 — £700*

CHIFFONIERS

A chiffonier is basically a side cabinet, developed with a shelf or shelves above from the late eighteenth century. The term has come to be used rather loosely but is current in the antique trade to describe small cabinets with shelves for use as a small sideboard, incidental library or drawing room piece. It is really very difficult to be didactic as to where a cabinet and a chiffonier change places, but the examples in the section which follows are those generally described as chiffoniers.

400 (above) A rosewood chiffonier with glazed door panels in gilt Gothic design frames. The shelf above is supported on ormolu pillars and has a gallery rail. There is a mirror at the back.

1810-1830   *£4,500 — £6,000*

399 An elegant chiffonier with shelves above, brass latticed doors and bracket feet.

1810-1830   *£4,000 — £6,000*

401 (right) A mahogany chiffonier with scrolled shelf supports. Several similar types appear in designs of this period.

1820-1830   *£3,000 — £4,000*

402 A rosewood chiffonier with heavy turned and reeded pillars and brass latticed arched doors with silk backing.

1820-1840   *£3,000 — £4,500*

Many chiffoniers of the Victorian period now on sale in the market are in fact small Victorian sideboards with the top rail or back removed and, possibly, a new shelf added. The really frequent 'improvement' of such pieces is to take a Victorian sideboard or cabinet, with its arched panelled doors, and remove the panels. The resulting door frame is then 'squared' at the top to provide a more Georgian design and a brass lattice, with silk behind, is added to produce a 'Regency' piece.

Value Points:
Small size (under 2ft. 9ins.) + + +
Decorative inlays + + +
Brass latticed doors + +
Rosewood +

403 (left) A mahogany chiffonier or sideboard with machine carved top rail and scrolled decoration.

1840-1880
£600 — £800

404 A small mahogany chiffonier with a brass latticed door. The lattice could be a latter addition. The convex drawer design is typical of the period.

1840-1850   *£2,000 — £3,000*

CLOTHES PRESSES — 1700-1800

405 (left) Not strictly a press, but this cabinet on chest shows the early stages of evolution. Typical features of the walnut period include quartering of veneers and lip mouldings on the drawer edges.

1720-1740   £5,000 — £7,000
Assuming it is right and not a bottom half with cabinet, and depending on the interior fitting

406 (right) A later walnut bookcase on chest with inlaid stringing lines.

1730-1750   £4,000 — £6,000

407 (left) A mahogany clothes press on serpentine bracket feet with original swan-neck handles. Finely figured veneers. Hence high value.

1750-1780
£2,000 — £3,000

408 (right) Mahogany clothes press with bracket feet and original handles. The applied mouldings on the doors add to the quality.

1760-1780
£3,000 — £4,000

CLOTHES PRESSES AND WARDROBES — 1750-1820

409 (left) A mahogany clothes press with cupboard beneath, on serpentine bracket feet. Cupboards below are less useful and less popular.

1760-1780   £800 — £1,200

410 (right) A Sheraton style wardrobe with high quality mahogany veneers in oval panels on the doors and two drawers beneath. Inlaid boxwood stringing lines emphasise the design.

If 1790-1800 £2,000 — £3,000
If Edwardian £900 — £1,200

411 (left) An unusual clothes press or wardrobe in which the doors have simulated drawers with black stringing lines let into them. The top moulding is a good example of an arcaded cavetto with dentil above.

1790-1810   £1,200 — £1,600

412 (right) An example of a Gothic design of clothes press door using high quality veneers and beaded mouldings. The drawers have matched quartered veneers — unusual in mahogany.

1820-1840   £900 — £1,200

CORNER CUPBOARDS —
hanging, bow-fronted

The hanging corner cupboard remained in favour throughout the eighteenth century, but as it was not so suitable as the large free standing example for the display of china, it was not in demand by the wealthy, and hence prices have been fairly modest but are now rising as they come into fashion. The bow-fronted are normally preferred and are especially desirable when they have drawers fitted.

413 Veneered in walnut with wide cross-banding and moulding cut along the grain. Well constructed with ovolo mouldings to the doors which gives the piece a more finished appearance.

c.1730   *£1,100 — £1,500*

414 (right) Modest quality lacquered example with the butterfly hinges typical of the period. As with most examples painted dull red (sometimes blue) inside.

c.1730   *£7,000 — £10,000 (red)*
£1,500 — £2,000 (black)
according to the quality and condition of the lacquer but beware modern lacquer

416 (below) A plain mahogany example enlivened by a stronger than usual moulding with dentil decoration. The matched veneers have been carefully chosen to the maximum effect of the grain. Typical H hinges and matching keyplates, one false.

c.1770-1780   *£800 — £1,200*
But with fine matching grain and say a decorative top, etc.
£1,700 — £2,500

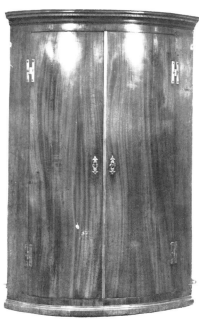

415 In oak with the medullary rays showing and supported on each side by reeded pilasters. Although the top moulding isn't very strong it comes forward at the end, a nice touch.

1770-1790   *£800 — £1,000*

417 The broken pediment doesn't quite succeed but the bold shell and well-thought-out stringing lines make this an attractive piece. The Edwardians occasionally 'improved' these pieces by adding inlays and a cornice or pediment. This does not help value!

c.1800   *£1,000 — £1,400*

CORNER CUPBOARDS — hanging, straight-fronted

419 (left) In plain Cuban mahogany, with decoration in the straight broken pediment with dentil moulding.

c.1750
£1,500 — £2,500

420 (right) A simple glazed oak corner cupboard. The moulding has been brought forward at top and bottom to give a balanced finish.

c.1780-1810
£750 — £1,000

418 This well veneered walnut example with arched broken pediment and shaped top to the door is ideally suited for focusing attention on its contents. Note the clever use of the half-round beading line for this purpose.

c.1730   *Assume glazing original*
£4,000 — £5,000

421 (right) Typical of the little oak cupboards with a moulding round the edge which were set into walls.

Early 19th century   *£300 — £400*

422 Inlays of white wood make this an impressive example, fine figure in the centre oval.

c.1800   *£2,000 — £3,000*

423 A simple country cherrywood example with a boldly executed fielded panel. Here colour and patination are all important to the price.

1740-1770   *£900 — £1,200*

424 (right) With the frieze veneered in mahogany and three small drawers beneath, this is a little above the run of country pieces. Note wide price bracket.

c.1780-1810   *£700 — £900*

CORNER CUPBOARDS —
free standing

This type of corner cupboard is much in demand and the supply of the better quality examples has never been plentiful. Prices are therefore constantly increasing. Beware of 'marriages' like 431.

425 (left) A fine large architectural corner cupboard of a type that would have been built into the corners of large panelled rooms, often in pairs. The heavy moulding, pilasters and glazed windows make it a desirable piece. A shell carved in the back would help the price considerably. It happens to be American in tulipwood and is thus more expensive than the British equivalent.

c.1780   *£8,000 — £10,000*

426 (above right) A poor photograph of a deeply patinated built-in corner cupboard in oak with a large number of fielded panels cross-banded in yew. The candle slide in fact supports a triangular fold out section. Removed from Tideswell, Derbyshire.

c.1750   *£4,500 — £6,000*

427 (left) Being much the same idea as the previous example but later and less well designed. The oak has been cut to produce decorative grain and the sides are reeded.

c.1780   *£2,000 — £3,000*

428 (right) A satinwood and marquetry corner cupboard typical of the well reproduced Victorian copies of earlier designs. The type of elegant furniture now much sought after for decorative effect.

1860s   *£3,000 — £4,000*

429 (left) Pine is often seen at its best in corner cupboards. Perhaps this is because pine panelling was extensively used in the early eighteenth century in even the best houses and corner cupboards were built-in. This has the attractive feature of the rounded barrel back coming forward at the top. Sometimes this is carved into a shell, a most desirable feature. Fine fretwork adds to the overall effect of quality. Well-waxed eighteenth century pine has a fine faded patination. This is a good example.

c.1760   *£3,500 — £4,500*

430 (right) A good quality mahogany example, it is relatively thin and elegant. The matched mahogany panels in the two base doors and the bracket feet with the outward kick all indicate quality.

c.1820   *£2,250 — £3,000*

431 (left) A more typical mahogany example of the late eighteenth century, decorated with very refined dentil moulding and thin layer of yellow stringing lines in unimaginative geometric patterns. Note the stringing line on the edge of the top half: there is no decoration at all on the bottom half, which looks cruder. Examination of the back boards would probably prove the misalliance conclusively. Was the top originally a hanging corner cupboard?

c.1780   *As married £800 — £1,000*

432 (right) Plain oak with mahogany cross-banding and undersize shell decorations inset into the doors which have conventional corner pieces as well. If it has an attractive inside, which is unlikely in view of its plain exterior, the doors might be removed.

c.1810   *£900 — £1,200*

Nomenclature in antiques is as much subject to confusion as it is to snobbery. The word 'buffet', which has connotations of sideboards loaded with cold sandwiches or of damp railway stations, is not used by the cognoscenti to describe those open-shelved, bulbously supported pieces shown in this section. They are called court cupboards. There the matter does not rest, however, for the term court cupboard is itself something of a misnomer. So, as simply as possible:—

1 The term cup-board was applied to an open shelved side table (or sideboard) used to display plate (cups) and for the serving of food or the 'dressing' of it (hence the term 'dresser').

2 The open cup-board had one, two or three boards or tiers and sometimes had a drawer fitted to it.

3 The word 'court' in French means 'short'. It is possible that this is the origin of the term 'court cupboard' since these pieces are usually low, i.e. below eye level. This seems reasonable when one thinks of the gigantic size of Continental cupboards.

4 The word cupboard gradually came to mean a closed piece of furniture, with doors below, i.e. a two-stage closed version of the court cupboard. This, in Wales, was called a cupboard deudarn, i.e. a two-stage cupboard. It should really be called a hall or parlour cupboard but, since the modern words hall and parlour no longer mean the principal living room, the word court has been used as a substitute.

5 In the seventeenth and eighteenth centuries the cupboard deudarn was so popular in Wales that they developed a three-decker version of it, called a tridarn. This piece of furniture is virtually unique to Wales.

The author is indebted to Messrs. Thomas Crispin and Victor Chinnery for the above excursion into the clarification of semantics and humbly hopes he has done them justice. Now read on.

433 This quite exceptional piece was rightly described by the auctioneer who sold it as a 'parlour cupboard' but court cupboard suits it admirably. Noble heraldic lions support the superbly decorated top. The whole piece is so finely and crisply carved that the often misused word 'important' could fairly be applied. The melons with their cotton reels at the top and bottom, even the decorated shapes below, are precisely spaced and exactly executed.

c. 1570(?)   *£15,000 — £18,000*

434 (left) Copiously inlaid with box and holly, and ebony on the base. The maker has indulged in the love of playing with perspective that haunts European furniture of this, and slightly later, periods. Technically well carved but perhaps a little fussy without the overall panache of the first example. Note the absence of a top moulding. The top boards are simply nailed onto the frieze — a fairly common feature around this period.

c. 1590   *£6,000 — £8,000*

435 Well-turned and carved melons (cup and cover). Again, note that the pattern does not need to match, also the box or holly and ebony inlay on the base appears in a mild form on the top of the two drawers. These were used as Tudor status symbols which could be employed to display the family silver when a show of wealth was required.

c. 1600   *£4,000 — £6,000*

436 Good strong gadrooning on the middle drawer and the linked rectangular pattern on top and bottom. The disappointments are the turned supports which are very modest in terms of the preceding examples but still retain the proper classical form at the top. Notice how wrong they look if you turn the page upside down, but how much better the strong bottom moulding would look at the top.

1625-1650   *£2,000 — £3,000*

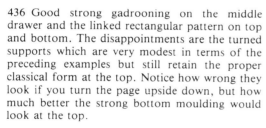

437 The end of the road for the court cupboard (which incidentally haunts British furniture in the form of huge mahogany trolleys — 'Buffets' — still to be seen in old hotels). The carving is weak and stylised, the turned supports a shadow of their former selves. Could even be a fake, and frankly, on an aesthetic level, if the colour of the original has gone there is a surprisingly small difference between them.

Mid-17th century   *If right £1,000 — £1,400*
                              If wrong £300 — £400

Most furniture of any height has a moulding round the top. Many court cupboards do not, or just very shallow ones. This seems to have caused a degree of embarrassment to generations of connoisseurs and dealers with the result that many now appear to have 'later top moulding'. One should not be unduly worried by these additions. From the number of later enclosed types one assumes that they gradually superseded the open variety. This subject is dealt with in detail in Chinnery.

438 As it was meant to be, a very impressive piece with inlay of strongly contrasting coloured woods of simple bird and foliage design and stringing lines of equally arresting formation. Every flat inch of the front is covered in finely executed carving. One wonders how the carver managed to keep his chisel off the bulbous turnings — yet there are others equally heavily decorated with the same simple deep centre grooved turning.

If c.1610
But in fact made in the north 1665
(see Chinnery)

£5,000 — £7,000
£2,500 — £3,250

440 Unusual in being small, this court cupboard has finely carved repetitive decoration on the frieze, while the doors have the usual heavy well-moulded frame. The panels appear to be beautifully carved with crisp stylised plants and flowers. The lower doors too, are well moulded. The big change is that the bulbous supports have contracted to emasculated stalactites — in this case so small they lack full form and may even have been cut off slightly. Expensive because 'small is beautful'. 3ft. 9ins. wide.

c.1640

£2,500 — £3,000

439 A later, simpler version in which the inlay, which appears to be of much better quality than the previous example, is reserved for the important arched centre panel. The doors either side are inlaid with broad geometric patterns which are also used for the decorations on the lower doors. The top decoration is confined to a line of dentil mouldings. Frankly, for the money, an uneven and not wildly exciting piece.

c.1630

£2,750 — £3,500

441 Of more normal size and proportions and typical in that the doors and centre panel are the focus of attention. The bottom doors are also carved but with a more formalised repetitive pattern. The pendants are of bold form. The feet are a simple continuation of the outer stiles, the identical form to that used in the chests of the period.

c.1650   *£1,800 — £2,500*

442 An interesting piece. The liberal application of well-formed split baluster turnings and sprinkling of cabochon cut pieces, together with the geometrically applied cushion moulding to the central panel, argues a date of at least 1680. This is supported by the large ogee top moulding. On the other hand, the double arch and the two turned supports look back to an earlier date. A Low Countries craftsman working to a basic English style? A very interesting piece especially if a good colour with fruitwood incorporated and plenty of contrasts of light and shade.

c.1680   *£5,000 — £7,000*

444 A late example of the type. The top section has grown in size at the expense of the lower portion. The piece is panelled with a very poor arch on the top door and a wide frieze. If the bracket feet are original, they confirm the late dating. The pendants have become inverted finials. With its inability to provide display, it would be easy to see here the end of the road for such a design.

c.1770   *£900 — £1,200*

443 Interesting because dated 1744. Fielded panels with the middle centre panel holding prominence purely on size. As one would expect by this date a broad moulding, but the construction still the same with an extension of the stiles forming the feet.

c.1744   *£1,500 — £2,000*

DAVENPORTS

The name davenport is assumed to have arisen from an entry in Gillow's Cost Books in the 1790s: for "Captain Davenport, a desk" written alongside this design. The sloping lid and the gallery — brass or wood — around the top, are characteristic, as are the real drawers on one side and the false ones on the other. Another feature is the rising compartment at the top released by a spring, containing drawers and pigeon-holes. Inventiveness of design was a feature of this type of furniture. *The Pictorial Dictionary of 19th Century Furniture Design* shows some 45 different designs.

445 A satinwood davenport of the very early nineteenth century showing the restrained early design, a brushing slide at the top of the drawers.

c. 1820   *£6,000 — £8,000*

446 Rosewood, with elegant Regency decorations, showing the unusual feature of a towing handle.

1810-1820   *£4,000 — £6,000*

448 A burr walnut, fine quality davenport with inlaid stringing lines and brass gallery rail. The flap folds over and is supported by two lopers, a more comfortable arrangement than most.

1820-1840   *£5,000 — £6,500*

447 Made in rosewood, with an arched door, flat Corinthian pillars. A restrained and elegant piece not unlike a design shown for 1835.

1830-1840   *£2,500 — £3,500*

449 In mahogany, with an elegantly turned wooden gallery. Looks like half a pedestal desk perhaps because of the broad plain plank at the bottom.

1830-1840   *£2,000 — £2,750*

Plate 65. A flamboyant late Elizabethan court cupboard (livery cupboard) combining many of the favourite motifs of this type of cupboard — floral inlay and perspective architecture, probably using holly or box for its light colour, masks, carved arches, pillars, etc., etc. Yet for all its dramatic qualities modern taste does not value it very highly compared with 18th century furniture. *c.1600*

Plate 66. By comparison a later restrained example, c.1620, which relies for its decorative effect on carving, most of which is in fairly low relief except for the gadrooning on the pillars and along the top of the doors. A restrained piece with good colour.

Plate 67. A grand George II mahogany pedestal desk of the finest quality. The pedestals are shaped at the sides (bombé) and have well carved naturalistic decoration at the angles. The top is carved with a flower head pattern, repeated in minor key below the top line of drawers and the plinth base. The wood and colour are good quality and a similar model is in the *Dictionary of English Furniture*. Style, quality, colour, utility and provenance — what more can one look for?
c.1740

Plate 68. A good standard model from the 1770s made in the form of a partners' desk, i.e. with identical fittings on both sides so that it can stand in the centre of the room. The joins where the doors and sides are panelled are covered by a standard form of moulding, curved at the end (re-entrant corners) to soften the line. Solid and unpretentious but of sound quality and reasonable colour, these pieces are in strong demand for the office, where they are tax deductible, and hence expensive.

Plate 69. This illustration gives a good idea of the colour and texture of Victorian burr walnut.
In design and date quite similar to figure 461. However, this example uses the old method of
rounding corners — a piece of solid wood to form the round — whereas 461 has veneer rounded
corners. Another old feature, the use of panelling, is still used here as against the flush sides of
the black and white example. Altogether this is a more attractive piece.
c.1850

Plate 70. As it made a 'sensible' price of £15,000 in 1989 this 1930s mahogany pedestal desk in
the George II style makes an instructive comparison with Plate 2. It is beautifully made, of fine
figured Cuban(?) mahogany. There is plenty of movement in the outline of the top and the masks
are pleasing. Only in the feet does it feel unhappy. Surely in original work the carving on the
bottom rail would not just stop at the feet but would be continued round. The feet themselves lack
the boldness to give a proper sense of support. Still, a pleasing confection at little more than the
reproduction price.

Plate 71. An East Anglian sideboard, c.1665. This is a delightful piece of furniture under 5ft. wide. The unusual form of baluster legs balance well with the bun feet and give it boldness. The drawer front arrangement, though conventional, is strong and the fine details of the angle curves and detailing of the bottom rail provide the subtle touches. It has a good dark patination. At £10,000 in 1986 undervalued, perhaps because of unusual form.

Plate 72. A good Charles II oak low dresser, c.1680. What look like original hinges hold the two central doors, decorated with arches and centred with applied mouldings. These, together with the moulded fronts of the doors, indicate the relative lateness of the piece. The top is well supported by dentil moulding and traditionally shaped angles. The long deeply curved bottom moulding gives it a well finished look.

It appears to be in original condition. Look at the number of shades of colour from warm red to black. As one would expect, there is wear too on the bottom of the doors where boots closed them.

216

450 Regency elegance gives away to Victorian opulence in this piano fall piece, with pull-out front.

c.1850 £2,000 — £3,000

451 By contrast a slightly earlier restrained design; note the small side drawer in which the ink was kept. As usual drawer fronts each side but one side false.

c.1830 £1,500 — £2,000

452 The all conquering cabriole leg, so typical of the 1850s, seen here supporting a fine walnut example with pop-up gallery decorated with fret. It has a piano front and is almost identical to an example in W. Smee & Son's 1850 catalogue. Increasingly in demand with these features.

c.1850 £3,500 — £4,500

453 Yew, inlaid ivory, Irish harp, views of ruins, a product of the Muckross Abbey School, who made a wide variety of highly decorated pieces using yew. The foliage is typical.

1840-1860 £5,000 — £7,000

454 The grapes carved on the knee of the cabriole and brass gallery give this a touch of quality.

c.1860 £2,000 — £2,750

455 The crude carving on the knees of the cabrioles, the lack of gallery and inlay all indicate a step down in quality.

c.1860 £1,500 — £2,000

Pedestal desks for study, library and office use do not really stem from the same origin as the kneehole dressing table. They come from another branch of the furniture tree — those grand library and writing tables of the mid-eighteenth century which the great cabinet makers, including Chippendale, made for wealthy clients. This has some bearing on style, for these grand tables did not have bracket feet, like kneeholes, but had a flat plinth base right around. Pedestal desks tend to follow this design, with a solid base, rather than bracket, splay or later forms of turned foot. As a broad rule 'the higher the leg the lower the price'.

456 (above) A fairly grand mahogany library or writing table, with a leather inlaid top, blind-fretted frieze and carved decoration on the angled corners and kneehole section.

1750-1770 £60,000+

457 (right) A mahogany pedestal desk with leather top and a typical arrangement of cock-beaded drawers. A type illustrated by Hepplewhite.

1770-1800 £14,000 — £20,000

458 The kidney-shaped writing table or desk was very popular in the nineteenth century but is originally an eighteenth century form, being illustrated by Sheraton in his design books (and in his early nineteenth century books on paw feet). This is a mahogany example with cross-banded drawers and leather top.

1800-1820 £8,000 — £12,000
If good later reproduction £5,000 — £7,000

459 A burr yew pedestal desk on paw feet in the early nineteenth century manner. Being large and with drawers both sides, it is termed a partners' desk. There is a possibility that this could be early eighteenth century, with later feet and top, in which case the price would be much greater.

Early 19th century £14,000 — £16,000

460 A nineteenth century mahogany pedestal desk of a type made throughout the century for office use. This has a bit of extra quality in the fluting on the front carcase edges and features a lip moulding to the drawers.

Early 19th century £5,000 — £7,000
Late 19th century £3,500 — £4,500

461 A burr walnut pedestal desk with ring handles which gives the piece an attractive appearance.
1840-1860 £7,000 — £10,000

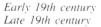

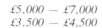

462 (left) A typical nineteenth century standard quality pedestal desk. Made in mahogany, oak and pine throughout the period and understandably popular due to its utilitarian value. Any small feature of interest adds to its value almost disproportionately.

Early 19th century Large partners' £3,000 — £5,000
Late 19th/early 20th century £2,000 — £3,000

463 An almost exhibition piece in the Talbert-Eastlake-Seddon-Burges manner. All these mid-nineteenth century designers reverted to 'medieval' designs and revealed construction in some degree. This piece is made of oak and is considerably decorated with inlays. No longer underestimated.

£50,000+
Wide gap because of specialist interest

464 A kidney-shaped desk of Sheraton design, made by Edwards and Roberts, a nineteenth century firm who specialised in reproductions of eighteenth century designs. This is a Sheraton design, made in plum-pudding mahogany with inlaid satinwood banding and with stringing.
1860-1880 £4,000 — £6,000

465 (left) An oak dresser of the second half of the seventeenth century, showing very thick boldly turned front legs and square back legs. Each of the four drawers is divided into two panels and the side is panelled as well. The top edge is heavily moulded and another moulding has been fixed along the front edge under the drawers. The square endings to the front feet might suggest the use of stretchers but was normally a design feature. A large heavy bold piece.

1650-1670   £9,000 — £12,000

466 (right) A slightly later oak dresser with plain plank ends and moulded fronts to the three drawers with attractively applied split balusters between them. The turning on the legs is a slightly more refined version of the first example. Also it *looks* old. It has sagged slightly towards the middle; the two planks which make the top have parted slightly. The dresser appears to have a very good colour. A thoroughly desirable piece.

c 1670-1680   £7,000 — £9,000

467 (above) In contrast to the previous example this piece looks a little thin. The applied mouldings lack imagination, the rail rebated into the middle leg looks thoroughly unworkman-like (see example 469 where the rail is mortised and joined on each leg). The late handles do not help and the piece looks a little dull.

c 1700   £3,000 — £4,000

468 (right) A late seventeenth century dresser base with moulded fronts to the drawers and legs of typically turned form for the period, supporting a superstructure which looks of much later date. Dressers of this early form did not have racks on them though there may have been shelves above them secured to the wall. The top moulding here looks much too thin compared with the bottom. It would be interesting to look at the back to see if the age of the unpolished woods matches up.

1700-1750   £3,000 — £4,000

469 (left) A very fine example from the first years of the eighteenth century. The basic form remains, but a decorative under-rail has been added and emphasised by the use of cockbeading; there is also the unusual feature of a stretcher. The drawers have been cross-banded in a contrasting wood. The effect is very successful

c.1710 £10,000 £14,000

470 (right) At first glance this cherrywood dresser might be placed in the seventeenth century. The fairly bold turned stretcherless legs, the double moulding supporting the top and the heavy equivalent beneath the deep drawers together with panelled ends all point to an early date. The handles are later. The whole piece has the look of the seventeenth century except the drawer fronts which give the game away by having an ovolo moulding round the edges which fits over the front of the carcase. This feature must place the piece post 1720.

c.1730 £5,000 £7,500

471 (right) More sophistication — this time on cabriole legs of good quality and an elaborately scrolled frieze. The drawers have a simple scratch-moulded line around the edge to emulate a cockbead.

1740-1750 £6,000 £8,000

472 (left) A later development of the dresser; still the large top moulding but the legs are now Chippendale, even though the two decorations on the bottom of the front rail suggest an earlier date. There is a groove line round the drawers to suggest cockbeading. Quite a successful piece if the colour is good.

c.1760-1770 £2,000 £2,750

473 A dramatic piece with the moulded three-drawer form we saw in the previous section plus two extra cupboards below. The heavy top moulding, the geometric moulding on the cushion-shaped drawer fronts and the applied split baluster pieces on the cleverly arranged centre panel suggest an early date.

c.1680 £7,000 — £9,000

474 A typical dresser from the West Midlands made over a long period of time in the country and therefore hard to date. The side is panelled and decorated with scratch moulding, and the feet are formed as a simple continuation of the end stiles. The doors have arched shaped panels constructed in the traditional manner. There is a scratch moulding round the frames into which the drawers fit — a simulation of cockbeading.

c.1750 £2,250 — £3,000

475 A fruitwood example dated towards the end of the eighteenth century though it exhibits many early features. The two end drawers are false, no doubt a concession to the view that a dresser should have a row of drawers in line under the top board. There is still the feeling that a good bold moulding is needed and two appear at the top and bottom. The ends are panelled and the feet are simply an extension of the side stiles. Most significant is the fact that the drawers are formed with mouldings round. The area of manufacture is ascribed to Yorkshire, where this type of dresser was made over a considerable period.

c.1770-1780 £4,000 — £5,000

476 Unlike 474, the joiner, using framed panels, has made a conscious effort to imitate the smooth flat expanses of the finer cabinet maker's work, clearly seen in the careful flush fitting of the end panels, thus avoiding the archaic effect of the sides of example 474. The feet were originally bracket. The ogee headed fielded panel stands out from the door as in mahogany work, whereas in 474 the rails and stiles are at the same level as the panel — an earlier feature. This is the last stage in the development of the joiner's art. A good colour helps the price.

c.1780 £2,500 — £3,500

477 It looks like a dresser base so it comes into this section, but in fact what on the face of it could be rechristened a 'dresser of drawers' is in fact a chest because all the drawers are false! Each has two handles, a keyhole and is cross-banded in mahogany. The keyhole for the lifting top is under the top moulding. The give-away as to date is the reeded quarter pillars.

c.1780 £1,500 — £2,000

DRESSERS — with shelves, and tridarns

It may seem odd to start a section on dressers with shelves by discussing tridarns, but they are closely linked both in their Welsh origin and in the possibility that the court (short) cupboard had a third layer superimposed on top purely for display and that this proved so popular that the middle was turned over to display rather than storage which resulted in the dresser. This subject is fully explored in Chinnery, *Oak Furniture,* his earliest date for tridarns, incidentally, being 1685, the latest in the nineteenth century.

478 (right) The tridarns are surprisingly similar in design but in details there is a wide variation. This one has solid sides to the top level instead of parallel straight or wavy slats. It is decorated with contrasting woods and has a well-designed central panel. The back also is closely panelled. It probably dates from the first few years of the eighteenth century. It is at the top end of the quality scale.

c.1710 £3,000 — £4,000

479 The arched fielded panels of this tridarn suggest a later date for this piece. The top third seems to be gaining in importance at the expense of the middle section.

c.1735 £3,500 — £4,500

480 (right) An early dresser. The overhang and the pendants result in it being described as a canopy dresser. Cupboards on either side in the middle section are all that remain of the tridarn design. Probably from Denbighshire in North Wales. A good piece with panelling throughout except on the back-boards which is normal.

c.1720s £11,000 — £14,000

481 An enclosed oak canopy dresser. It has the moulded edges to the drawers that one associates with a country chest of drawers 1700-1720, and a heavy moulding beneath the drawers which is also to be seen on pieces of that period (see 319). The top has shaped sides at top and bottom as does the previous example, also the same bold pendants or terminals and good depth to moulding. The backboards are, however, thinner. A north Welsh origin seems reasonable. The iron wing hinges are later, internal pin hinges being normal. A superb dresser of a type that is being increasingly appreciated.

1700-1710   *£6,000 — £8,000*

DRESSERS — enclosed front

It is hard to recollect in 1982 that until ten or fifteen years ago dressers hardly occupied a place in the furniture collecting world. Indeed, there are many books on antique furniture, some of them by famous authors, which hardly mention the dresser at all; it was a kitchen piece, not worthy of comment. Now like the clothes press it is an acceptable piece in the sitting room.

Yet dressers have been so central to the core of antique furniture trading in the last ten to fifteen years, so spectacular in their increase in price, that they must now occupy an important place in any book on furniture. What may have started as a fashion is now an established segment of the market. The dresser incorporates so many of the features which the market demands now: styles of the centuries, decorative value, utilitarian appeal for dining room or kitchen and — so important — it *looks old*.

It has another feature which is also likely to make it increasingly sought after. Because it was a country piece there is a great deal of individuality to be found in the design and, indeed, many can be identified as coming from a particular area. So much of British furniture is anonymous that to find an attractive piece that can be identified to an area, and may even eventually be tracked down to a family of craftsmen, makes it even more interesting. Thomas Crispin the well-known St. Albans oak and country furniture dealer, wrote the first detailed article on this topic in *Antique Collecting* Vol. 7, No. 8 and Vol. 8, No 1. I am grateful for permission to draw on this information for the descriptions of most of the better quality pieces illustrated. Valuing furniture is always difficult but good quality dressers present even more problems than usual for some of them are almost unique. As a broad generalisation dressers with drawers below came first from north Wales and spread into northern England where they acquired regional differences, whereas pot board dressers (i.e. with an open space below) came from mid and south Wales. Montgomeryshire produced a particularly high quality example of the latter type.

482 Another transitional dresser. The base containing five drawers and three cupboards, the panels to the doors being fielded with top ogee moulding. The superstructure of shelves having the shelves tenoned and pegged through the sides. The canopy not so pronounced with shaped and cusped frieze between the two end terminals or droppers.

c.1730   *£10,000 — £14,000*
            A good marriage £4,000 — £6,000

483 (left) A magnificent example of an English oak enclosed dresser of architectural proportions, containing two cupboards and three drawers. The doors with shaped fielded panels, and these, together with the drawer fronts, being cross-banded and inlaid. The sides to the base with shaped canted corners and applied pilasters. The superstructure of shelves, unbacked, with central figure compartments, the top finely shaped and pierced frieze under the cornice supported at the sides by applied pilaster supports.
1750   *£11,000   £16,000*

484 (right) Northern Welsh oak enclosed dresser of six drawers and two cupboards, the door panels shaped and fielded. The superstructure of shelves, with shaped sides, the frieze shaped and cusped.

c.1730
£6,000 — £7,000

486 (right) An Anglesey, oak, enclosed break-front dresser of six drawers and two cupboards, the doors to which have applied shaped panels, the break-front with reeded column. The superstructure of shelves has shaped sides, better quality examples have been seen with reeded columns on the ends and the frieze.

c.1780
£5,000 — £6,500

485 Northern Welsh oak enclosed dresser of six drawers and two cupboards. The drawers cross-banded with mahogany, the plain panelled doors with mahogany inlaid line to the framing. The superstructure of shelves with pine back-boards containing two cupboards, the doors cross-banded with mahogany. The frieze of simple shaping and centrally pierced with heart motif.

c.1780   *£4,500 — £5,500*

487 A Lancashire dresser with applied raised moulding and the drawer fronts cross-banded in mahogany. The superstructure of shelves containing nests of drawers with figure compartment above. The frieze under the dentil cornice with applied pierced banding.

c.1800   £14,000   £18,000

488 Northern Welsh oak enclosed dresser. The front is inlaid with mahogany forms and ivory escutcheons. The superstructure of shelves is very simple.

c.1850   £4,000 — £5,000

490 (below) Anglesey, oak, enclosed break-front dresser. The corner of the break-front has applied quarter turning which any longcase clock collector will recognise. Other examples have split applied double columns at the ends as well as the break-fronts, and are inlaid with mahogany stars.

c.1850   £3,500 — £4,500

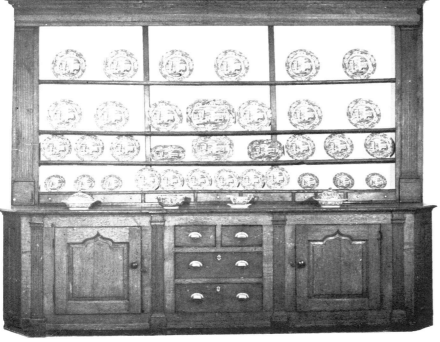

489 A large Cumberland oak enclosed dresser. The framed doors to the cupboards with ogee fielded panel doors. The applied pilasters to the front giving the whole architectural proportions. The superstructure of shelves, containing at the base a row of spice drawers.

Early 19th century   £10,000 — £15,000

226

491 An English dresser, which makes an interesting comparison with 487. The rack arrangement, the reeded canted column supports at the ends, and the applied raised moulding round the door all suggest that it too comes from Lancashire.

c.1790(?)   *£5,500 — £7,500*

492 A plain example, the decoration is supplied by the reeded support, shelves and top moulding.

Early 19th century   *£2,500   £3,500*

493 A slightly unusual oak example because of the use made of the fielded panels at the ends of the base and the architectural moulding on the supports, as well as the very wide space between the shelves. The use of mahogany crossbanding on the drawers indicates a late date.

Late 18th century   *Assuming right £6,000 — £8,000*

494 A very simple dresser with panelled doors and the traditional six drawer arrangement. The ivory key surrounds are typical of late production.

Early 19th century   *£2,500   £3,500*

495 A magnificent and large example of an English oak dresser of four drawers, raised upon three frontal cabriole legs, united by finely pierced and shaped apron. The superstructure of shelves, containing two cupboards with fluted frontal stiles, containing doors with square fielded panels. The frontal edges to the shelves and the upright supporters finely shaped. The frieze under the cornice, finely pierced and shaped, carrying out the design of the apron. Shropshire.

c.1750 £27,000 – £35,000

496 Southern Welsh pot boarded dresser of two drawers. The legs to the base being square, the apron with ogee shaping. The superstructure of shelves being unbacked, and with finely shaped sides. The frieze of simple shaping.

c.1740 £3,500 £4,500

497 There are clear similarities between this piece and 495. The clever use of a similar pattern of decorative frieze on the top and bottom give it a feeling of lightness. The use of cabriole legs and the two side doors suggest that this also may come from Shropshire, certainly the West Midlands. The only slight quibble is that the cabrioles are cut straight down one side and do not look as good as 495.

c.1770 £6,500 £8,500

498 Mid-Welsh or Montgomeryshire pot boarded dresser of four drawers. The legs to the base being of baluster turning, with a shaped apron of ogee form between the legs. The apron and the drawer fronts being cock-beaded. Between each apron and drawer an applied reeded moulding. The super-structure of shelves, with horizontal back-boards, supported by cupboarded sides, the small base cupboards of plain panelled doors, the tall narrow cupboards above, with reeded panel doors. The shaped frieze having an applied pierced tracing above the shaping.

c.1750   *£13,000 — £16,000*

499 An English chestnut dresser of three drawers raised upon square tapered legs, united by a finely pierced and shaped apron. The superstructure of shelves, unbacked, with finely shaped sides, and shelf edgings with figure compartments at the sides. The top frieze, under the cornice, finely pierced and shaped, carrying out the design in the apron.

c.1780   *£3,500 — £5,000*

500 Mid-Welsh or Montgomeryshire pot boarded dresser of three drawers. The legs to the base being square, and reeded upon the frontal surfaces. This reeding carried on between the drawers. The apron shaped with ogee moulding between the legs. The superstructure of shelves containing two cupboards with 'Gothic' shaped doors. The frieze to the superstructure with fretting and scalloping. Initialled and dated inside the right-hand shelf cupboard 'W. G. 1801'.

Early 19th century   *£3,000 — £4,000*

502 A Welsh open-based dresser, the top board raised upon three silhouette baluster-shaped legs. The moulding around the base, forming a simple bracket foot, is of later addition. The sides with two upright rails in the framing. The superstructure of shelves, with shaped sides and plain frieze to the top.

c.1720   *£5,000 — £6,000*

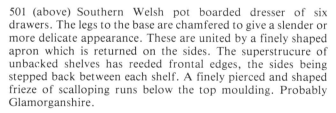

501 (above) Southern Welsh pot boarded dresser of six drawers. The legs to the base are chamfered to give a slender or more delicate appearance. These are united by a finely shaped apron which is returned on the sides. The superstrucure of unbacked shelves has reeded frontal edges, the sides being stepped back between each shelf. A finely pierced and shaped frieze of scalloping runs below the top moulding. Probably Glamorganshire.

c.1780   *£5,000 — £7,000*

503 (right) A mid-19th century version of the South Welsh oak pot board dresser, of five drawers, all cock-beaded with small twin domed arch aprons simply inlaid as sunbursts in mahogany, between the two outside drawers. The drawers, all with their original wooden knobs with mother-of-pearl inlay. The whole is supported on three turned balusters, terminated upon the pot board surmounting bracket feet. The very simple superstructure of shelves is backed by wide pine back-boards which is typical of the period.

c.1840   *£3,000 — £4,000*

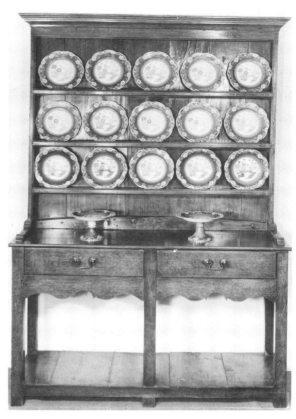

504 An oak pot board dresser with a pair of well-turned legs and bun feet, which give it the 'lift' necessary to avoid the rather square appearance of the other dressers on this page.

Late 18th century   £4,000 — £5,000

505 A cottage oak dresser with pot board and simple square legs. The design is helped slightly by the shaped fret to the underside of the base. It is however small and desirable where space is limited.

Early 19th century   £2,250 — £3,000

506 (left) A tiny little dresser in oak with a pot board base. Short of decoration but desirable because small.

Early 19th century
£1,200 — £1,600

507 (right) A very simple square legged dresser with drawers, cock-beaded and cross-banded in mahogany. Very basic in design with only Regency type flat reeded moulding to give it a more finished appearance.

c.1820 £1,200 — £1,800

The pine dresser seems to be almost exclusively a Welsh product. Up to about 1840 the shelves were open, after that some parts were glazed until 1870, when totally glazed racks appeared. Pine became scarcer towards the end of the century so that back-boards became narrow; by the 1890s plywood panels came into use and bun feet appeared. Like most items in Victorian Britain decoration became increasingly important as the century progressed.

Particularly since oak dressers have escalated in price pine dressers have become more popular, though early well-patinated pine (as opposed to pieces originally painted and recently stripped in a large acid bath) has always had its keen admirers. Well-polished stripped pine fits well into kitchens both modern and old and, like the dressers on the previous pages, are find their way into the living room. For more information see the article by John Creed-Miles of John Creed of Camden Passage, London, who wrote on this subject in *Antique Collecting*, Vol. ll, No. 12 and from which the information in this section is largely drawn.

508 A North Wales pot board dresser. The main body and pot board are in pine, the legs fruitwood, and the shelves and side elm-faced with pine strips. The dowelled construction is evident from the photograph. The reeded feet are a rare feature not seen on late pieces. The shaping on the sides of the rack add greatly to the attractiveness as do the good patination and original handles.

c 1750   *£1,750   £2,500*

509 An exceptional pine North Welsh dresser with three drawers, two cupboard doors and three false drawers in the base, as does 510. The excellent rack above has two cupboards with drawers underneath and a remarkably moulded top cornice with an unusually complex dentil frieze. Comes from the North Wales coast.

1800   *£2,500   £3,500*

510 A North Welsh pine cupboard dresser base with three drawers across the top, a plain panelled door on each side, and three false drawer fronts down the middle. The space behind the false drawers is reached via the cupboard doors. The handles are replacements for the original wooden knobs but the ivory key escutcheons are original. Originally this dresser would have had a shelved rack above it.

1800-1820   *£1,000 — £1,500*

232

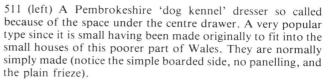

511 (left) A Pembrokeshire 'dog kennel' dresser so called because of the space under the centre drawer. A very popular type since it is small having been made originally to fit into the small houses of this poorer part of Wales. They are normally simply made (notice the simple boarded side, no panelling, and the plain frieze).

c.1830   *£1,500 — £2,000*

512 A later development of the 'dog kennel'. It is better made than the previous example with panelled sides and bracket feet.

1840s   *£2,500 — £3,000*

513 (left) A simply con-
structed piece with cham-
fered edges to the doors in
place of applied mould-
ings. All the doors open.

c.1840s *£1,100 — £1,500*

514 (right) A larger more
sophisticated design of
open based dresser. Good
bold mouldings and a
well-executed dentil frieze,
attractively shaped sides
and good broad back
boards. A fine example.

1770-1780 *£1,400 — £1,800*

DRESSING
TABLES

515 (left) Georgian enclosed mahogany on tapering fluted legs with a slide.

1760-1780
£3,000 — £4,000

516 (above) Mahogany, shown open with mirror resting on the rack. A fairly simple piece with none too elegant legs.

1760-1780   *£2,500 — £3,500*

517 (right) A very fine harlequin dressing and writing table in fiddle figured mahogany cross-banded in tulipwood. The back section pushes down against a spring. A tambour concave cupboard beneath, tapered legs and original small leather castors.

1780-1800   £6,000 — £8,000
more if it can be attributed
to a known designer

518 (below) A mahogany dressing table of Chippendale style, with fretted brackets, slide and tray beneath.

1750-1800   £2,250 — £3,000

519 (below) An interesting enclosed dressing table/chest with concave tambour doors and drawers beneath.

1780-1800   £2,500 — £3,500

520 A painted satinwood dressing table/chest, with Adam-style neo-classical decoration. This type of decoration was much copied in Edwardian furniture.

1780-1800   *£20,000+*
          Good Edwardian copy £4,000 — £6,000

521 A fine mahogany dressing table of enclosed type, shown open and closed, with cupboard below and a crossed flat stretcher with rimmed chamber platform.

1790-1810   *£2,000 — £2,750*

522 An interesting mahogany dressing table shown closed and open with hinged top which lifts to reveal its fitments. The oval handles are a replacement.

1790-1810   £1,500 — £2,000

523 (above) Late eighteenth century Sheraton type dressing table with the usual fittings. Decorated with shells and using stringing lines to vary the veneered decoration.

Early 19th century
£2,000 — £3,000

There seems little doubt that this piece of furniture was evolved for bedroom or dressing room use; it has subsequently been found extremely useful as a desk. People did write in their bedrooms, of course, and we happily illustrate, in the mahogany examples, a piece fitted with both mirror accoutrements and writing paraphernalia. This is just to show that we are not prepared to be didactic; the concensus is that this is, generally speaking, an 'upstairs' piece, but there is no reason why it should not have been found useful downstairs as well.

Value Points: as for Chests, also if centre section pulls forwards + + +

524 (above) A walnut kneehole of high quality on replacement bracket feet. The pillars in the recessed corners are fluted and the top is quarter veneered and cross-banded. The drawers have a simple, straight crossbanding, with a lip edge moulding. North country with new heavy feet.

1730-1740   *£9,000 — £12,000*

525 A simpler walnut kneehole with herring-bone banding to the drawers. The top is quartered and cross-banded. Note that the shaped section over the kneehole space is, in fact, another drawer. Original handles.

1720-1740
£5,000 — £7,000

526 A solid yew wood kneehole with lip-moulded drawers. A fairly simple piece which will depend largely for its value on the colour and patination. A faded nut brown colour being much more valuable than a reddish tinge. Hence the wide price range.

1720-1740
£6,000 — £8,000

527 A high quality 'Chippendale' kneehole with canted corner decorated with a blind fret. There is a slide under the top and the piece has single serpentine bracket feet. The three previous examples all have 'double' bracket feet, i.e. a foot under each front corner — both forms are found in this period.

1740-1760
£5,000 — £7,000

528 Another mahogany kneehole, with fluted canted corners and a slide. Original handles. The photograph and lack of polish do not do it justice. Price assumes a deep rich colour.

1740-1760
£5,000 — £7,000

529 (left) Here we are — an unusual but genuine fit-up under a hinged top and a false front top drawer. This mahogany piece is fitted both for dressing and titivation purposes as well as with ink-holding drawer and letter/envelope rack inside. The drawers are cock-beaded.

1740-1760
£6,000 — £7,500

530 A high quality veneered mahogany kneehole with slightly serpentine front, canted fluted corners and fluted central arch.

1750-1770   *£4,000 — £5,000*

531 (left) A solid mahogany serpentine-front kneehole on ogee bracket feet. Note that the foot has an extra facet to match the squared corner. There are in fact three main shapes of ogee feet, the most simple curves out where it meets the floor, the second is squared off just at that point (see 528) but this one, the best type, has a more pronounced curve over the foot as well as the squaring off where it meets the floor.

c.1760   £5,000 — £7,000

532 (above) A very decoratively veneered mahogany serpentine-front kneehole. One often sees early 20th century reproductions made broadly to this design.

1750-1770   £4,000 — £5,000

533 An American block-front mahogany kneehole with characteristic 'shell' carving over the central door.

1750-1770
£18,000+

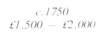

535 (right) An unusual oak kneehole fitted with a secretaire drawer (see below) — clearly a 'writing' piece.

c.1750
£1,500 — £2,000

534 A simple but very pleasant solid mahogany kneehole on bracket feet, with cockbeaded drawers.

1750-1770　　　　*£3,000 — £4,000*

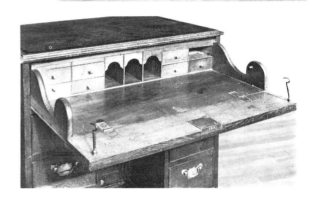

536 A late nineteenth century mahogany kneehole in the Sheraton manner, with quarter-fan inlaid satinwood decoration in the corners of the door. There is also a slide.

1860-1880　　　　*£3,000 — £4,000*

537 A late nineteenth century carved kneehole desk in mahogany with a gadrooned edge to the top.

1890-1920　　　　*£2,500 — £3,000*

DUMB WAITERS

Dumb waiters were used in the eighteenth century as an adjunct to the dining table. They were placed near the table so that the diners could help themselves to extra dishes and implements without the need for servants ("I wish to God you wouldn't keep rubbing your great greasy belly against the back of my chair", comment by Great Whig Duchess to the footman standing behind her at dinner, quoted by Frank Muir in *The Frank Muir Book*). In this case they were rather like the Canterbury in its supper form. Sheraton includes them in his *Cabinet Dictionary* but the designs are rather complicated and include drawers and plate buckets. Others are to be found equipped with a wine cooler and box.

One has to be very careful when making generalised statements about English furniture; but a useful rule of thumb for the beginner is that where the pattern of turning on a three-tier example does not correspond between the tiers, it should be regarded with grave suspicion — it may very well be married.

538 (left) A mid-eighteenth century three-tier dumb waiter on a bold tripod base, in mahogany. The turning of the central column is crisp and the tiers are well dished.

1750-1770   *£3,000 — £4,000*

539 (right) A later Georgian dumb waiter on castors, with folding flaps to the tiers, like a drop-flap table.

1790-1800   *£1,750 — £2,250*

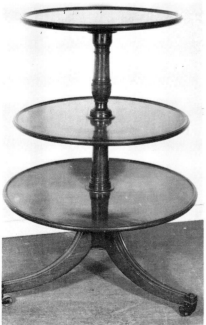

540 (left) A mahogany three-tier dumb waiter on reeded tripod legs and with dished tiers.

1790-1800   *Assuming wrong*
                     £1,200 — £1,800

541 (right) A variation on the centre column type — a two-tier dumb waiter on which the upper tier is supported by three turned columns fixed to the lower tier. The reeding of the centre column and legs, which are starting to 'knee', indicate the early nineteenth century.

1810-1830   *£2,000 — £3,000*

KNIFE BOXES

Adam's pedestal urn design (see Sideboard section) appears to have been used not only for storing iced and hot water but also, rather ingeniously, to be capable of adaptation as a knife box. His second design, for a sideboard table, shows two knife boxes of the more conventional design we expect but the use of an urn-shaped box appears to have been not uncommon.

There is no doubt of the superb elegance of these urn-shaped knife boxes and the workmanship in them. They were usually produced in pairs and were a specialist item, not being made by regular cabinet makers.

Value Points:
It is very important that the interior fittings remain intact. A knife box of any type which has had the interior stripped out for conversion to a letter box is not nearly in the same price range as one with its original fittings. A 30-50 per cent price differential exists between them as a minimum. Prices given assume internal fittings.

542 A knife box shown on its original pedestal. It would have been one of a pair, flanking the centre section of a sideboard as envisaged by Adam.

1780-1790   *£3,000 — £4,000*
                   pair £6,000 — £9,000

545 (below) A yew wood knife box with satinwood banding. Fine quality, using rare woods.

1800-1820   *£1,000 — £1,500*

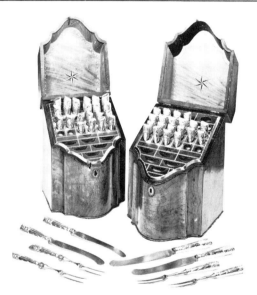

546 (right) A mahogany knife box of Sheraton design with an inlaid patera in the lid. The lock has been broken off at some stage. The inlaid edge stringing made of boxwood and ebony (yellow and black) is typical of the period.

1790-1810
        With original cutlery divisions £600 — £800
        "Now fitted for stationery" £250 — £350

543 A similar fine quality mahogany knife box with original lock and inlaid stringing lines.

1790-1800   *£1,800 — £2,200*

544 (left) A pair of mahogany knife boxes shown open to demonstrate the cutlery fittings.

1790-1810 £2,000 — £2,500 (pair)
                without cutlery

MIRRORS — cheval

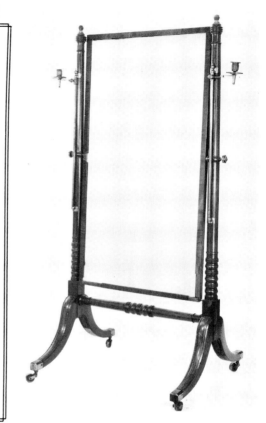

These date from the start of the eighteenth century when it became possible to make a sheet of glass large enough. They are known as 'horse dressing glasses' or chevals because of the frame or horse (cf. clothes horse) on which they are suspended, not because of their use by sartorially conscious cavalry officers. *The Pictorial Dictionary of 19th Century Furniture Design* illustrates a number of examples all with the decoration appropriate to the date. They were still being illustrated in catalogues in 1910.

Value Points:
Fine decoration and turning + + +
Original glass in reasonable condition + + +
Candleholders + +

547 (above) An unusual example with small glass area. On very fine carved tripod base and three pillar support. A good provenance would raise the price considerably.

c.1790   *£2,000 — £3,000*

548 (above right) A mahogany cheval dressing glass with candleholders and turned frame.

1800-1830   *£2,000 — £3,000*

549 (near right) A mahogany cheval glass with square reeded uprights and two drawers in the base, on curved feet. The top of the mirror is of ogee form.

1800-1820   *£900 — £1,100*

550 (far right) Typical of the Sheraton type, which was also produced in the later nineteenth century. With the exception of the oval inlay the piece is utilitarian rather than decorative.

1820   *£500 — £700*

This form of mirror was introduced into Britain from the Low Countries in Queen Anne's reign. The lower section was a miniature replica of a bureau. The mirror which was often of cushion shape was supported between two uprights. Usually in walnut or japanned.

Value Points:
Complexity of bureau part + + + +
Shaped fronts + + +
Figured woods and inlays
Original glass with bevelled edge + + +

551 A walnut toilet mirror with deep cross-grained moulding supporting the glass. A pretty little interior with stepped drawers (see Bureaux section). By no means the most complicated fittings but a good piece.

c.1710   *£1,500 — £2,000*

552 (below left) A walnut toilet mirror with concave-fronted drawers and inlaid stringing lines. The tapering supports are veneered and have acorn finials. The handles and keyplates are original.

c.1715   *£1,000 — £1,500*

553 (below) A serpentine-fronted walnut mirror with bevelled glass and one replacement (Victorian) finial on the upright. The drawers have an inlaid ebony and boxwood stringing line.

1730-1740   *£800 — £1,200*

554 A mahogany toilet mirror, missing one finial, with a gilt surround. The top corners of the moulding have inward points. The handles and keyplates are replacements. The key serves as the pull for the centre drawer.

1745-1760 £600 — £800

555 A 'Hepplewhite' toilet mirror with oval glass, edged in ebony and boxwood stringing. The front is serpentine, and the outer drawers have replacement pulls, but the centre drawer still has inset brass keyhole and key.

1770-1800 £450 — £600

556 A Sheraton bow fronted example. White inlay on the edges of the drawers and top, the supports reeded. The ivory keyplate is missing. The small bracket feet are a pleasant minor detail.

c. 1800 £250 — £350

557 The paws, the heavy decoration on the uprights and the top scroll all point to late Regency. The mirror is landscape shape rather than the portrait shape of Queen Anne's days.

c. 1820 £200 — £300

MIRRORS — wall, and pier glasses

The wall mirrors of the walnut period were mounted in a rectangular frame of deal, with a convex section which was veneered in walnut and embellished with parquetry or marquetry if required.

With the influence of architects (and particularly William Kent) on furnishings in the 1715-1740 period, the wall mirror became the object of architectural treatment. There were essentially two sorts of mirrors in a room — an overmantel mirror above the fireplace, and pier glasses on the pier walls between windows, hung over pier tables. The overmantels tended to be given the full treatment — pediments, etc. etc., and are rather outside the scope of the normal collector. However the narrow pier glasses can be used in the modern house and are quite charming.

The original Vauxhall glass was rather thin and had a very shallow bevel. Where the glass was very long it had to be made in two pieces. Gesso was often used for the gilt versions and was useful for less important frames where the cost of carving was high.

From about 1745 a lighter form was used in rather rococo style and the Adam and Chippendale designs reflect this. Later on the convex mirror became popular with its gilt balls and surmounting eagle.

At the turn of the eighteenth century mirror decoration was rather French Empire in style — neo-classical. As the century progressed, manufacturers made large overmantels and smaller girandoles in plaster which emulated rococo or exuberant French styles.

Value Points:
Carved wood frame + + + +
Original glass in good/fair condition + + +
Original gilding + + +
Condition of plaster or gesso + + + — frames are expensive to repair.

558 (above) A walnut 'cushion' mirror with convex frame inlaid with seaweed marquetry. The mouldings are in cross-grained walnut and there is a large cresting with a fret-cut border of seaweed type enclosing a panel of more marquetry. The glass looks like a replacement. The cresting is often missing, in which case the price is less than half.

1680-1700   *£9,000 — £12,000*

559 (right) A pier glass in gilt with the shallow bevel of the original Vauxhall glass clearly evident.

1700-1720   *£6,000 — £8,000*

560 (far right) More architectural pier glass with broken pediment, made in two pieces of bevelled glass. The frame is gilt.

1700-1720   *£5,000 — £6,000*

561 (left) Heavy architectural pier glass in the William Kent manner.

562 (right) A carved and gilt gesso glass with Prince of Wales feathers decoration above and shell below.

1725-1745   *£8,000 — £10,000*

1720-1730   *£2,500 — £3,500*

563 (left) A wall mirror in a carved gilt frame, in the rococo style.

564 (right) Still very architectural — gilt frame similar to designs of William Jones in 1739.
1740-1750 £3,000 — £4,000

1735-1745 £12,000 — £16,000

565 A mahogany and gilt frame with carved pediments.

1740-1750   *£6,000 — £8,000*

567 A mahogany framed mirror with fret-cut cresting and baseboards.

1745-1755   *£500 — £650*

566 (above) A mahogany and gilt mirror which shows the transition from the grandness of 565 to the relative simplicity of 567. The carved and gilded basket of flowers, together with flower and leaf down the sides, add to value.

c.1745   *£3,000 — £4,000*

568 (left) A Chinese rococo mirror in the Chippendale manner. The larger sizes are more valuable.

1750-1760   *£7,000 — £9,000*

569 (right) A rococo Chippendale oval giltwood mirror with foliage, C scrolls and urns. Again size important.

1755-1770   *£9,000 — £12,000*

571 (below) A convex gilt mirror surmounted by an eagle, of a type reproduced for over one hundred years.

1790-1820   £2,500 — £4,000

570 (above) An unusual mantel mirror in the Chinese rococo manner with scroll, leaf, branch and ornithological decoration — birds were always popular.

c.1760   *£6,000 — £8,000*

572 (left) An oval gilt wall mirror surmounted by a vase and scroll pediment.

c.1780   *£1,500 — £2,000*

573 (right) A nineteenth century pier glass with an eagle surmounting it and copious decoration — two female busts, two birds, flowers, scrolls and acanthus leaves. In the style of Thomas Johnson (1760) but a later reproduction.

Mid-19th century   *£3,000 — £4,000*

574 A nineteenth century mirror with pillar decoration.

Early 19th century   *£300 — £500*

SCREENS — cheval

Cheval screens are basically intended to be put in front of an empty fire-place, either to disguise the fact that the maid has not yet cleared the ashes or, in summer, to shield the eye from the offensive sight of an empty grate.

575 (left) A late Georgian satinwood cheval screen, shown open, with writing fall. The interior fabric is decorated with floral designs.

c.1790   *£1,200 — £1,600*

576 (above) A rosewood firescreen elaborately carved with scroll and leaf forms. This and the following example are very similar to designs from Henry Wood's design book of mid-nineteenth century date.

c.1850   *£600 — £800*

577 (above) A walnut cheval firescreen of more 'naturalistic' design with an elaborate wool tapestry screen of heraldic design. The frame is carved with leaf and floral forms. The cabriole type feet end in scrolls and the whole effect is altogether simpler and freer than that of the previous example, which retains a certain formality in the restraint of the turned uprights but which has come only halfway towards the freedom of this one.

c.1850   *£600 — £800*

SCREENS — pole

A pole screen was designed to shield the delicate physiognomy of those wishing to enjoy the heat of a fire without suffering a scorching on the exposed skin. It is thus a commentary on the prevailing system of heating rooms and on the genteel nature of some of their inhabitants. High quality original embroidery will enhance the value considerably but the main consideration is the quality of workmanship in the tripod.

578 (left) A George III mahogany screen with a crisply carved tripod base, the screen decorated with birds and flowers. Note the spiral carving on the stem, usually a sign of some quality.

c.1770   *£1,400 — £1,700*

Plate 73. A very attractive mahogany kneehole desk or writing table of the mid-18th century. It is well designed — the corners, for example, are pleasantly rounded and stop chamfered at the bottom, it has a well placed brushing slide and a good moulding round the top where the corners have been cut at the front to lighten the appearance of the piece.

Made of good quality mahogany, it has fared well over the years and developed a rich colour, fading on the top and on the bottom drawers. There is perhaps for modern taste too much dirt where it has been handled, but that only adds to its totally genuine and pleasing appearance. Only because they are awkward to use are they so cheap.

Plate 74. A kneehole dressing table made by George Bullock (see page 37) for Napoleon on St. Helena. It was the Prince Regent's wish 'that B should be furnished in his banishment with every possible gratification and comfort. . .' This can therefore be taken as the ultimate in fashionable taste in 1815-1817, just before Bullock's death and the sale of his business.

The difficulty of obtaining mahogany during the Napoleonic wars started a nationalistic fashion for British woods. This piece is in brown oak sparingly adorned with ebony — an irony Napoleon may not have appreciated. The designer was an architect, William Atkins, and the square neo-classical taste is obvious in this square, sober piece which is now very much back in fashion. Fashion and provenance being so important, the price was of course huge.

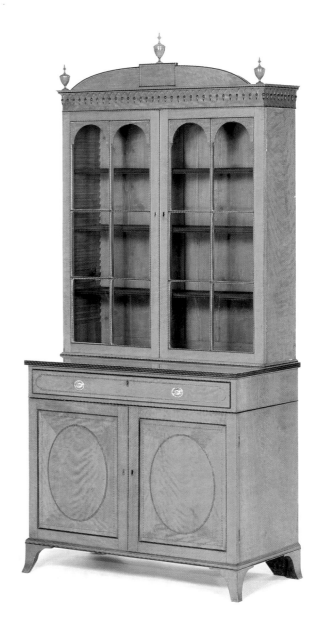

Plate 75. A mahogany secretaire bookcase, c.1770, in the manner of Thomas Chippendale. A well made piece with an unusual glazing pattern which matches the design on an important breakfront bookcase known to have been commissioned from Chippendale. Apart from that the design is absolutely standard for the period with the typical mouldings to hide the join on the panel. The idea of repeating the device of the glazing pattern was a good one but doesn't mean that Chippendale himself was involved. There were plenty of cabinet makers around with a good eye.

The colour is a warm glowing red with a good range of faded tones. A good piece.

Plate 76. Much the same quality as figure 592, a fine satinwood secretaire, c.1785. It is very much the standard form except that the top appears slightly larger than normal and the splayed feet are not connected with the usual curved section along the front of the base, the glazing is a bit restrained. Could this be because it is a slightly early example? Certainly the quality of the finials, inlay and decoration of the cornice point to it being the product of a top rate workshop.

Plate 77. Typical of the form of secretaire found in the closing years of the 18th century, especially the glazing arrangement and the panels of figured veneer. However, the curved pediment, boxwood decoration of Greek key motifs and allusions to triglyphs (the stylised beam ends in a Doric frieze) and metopes (the square spaces between) are too crowded. There is something about the thinness of pediment that is reminiscent of north country longcase clocks. Is this a well made provincial piece?

Plate 78. Unmistakably a secretaire from the first decade of the 19th century. The classic influence is restrained and the satinwood, ebony and brass inlay give it a sophisticated look while still retaining the traditional shape. A popular and useful piece.

251

Plate 79. A walnut and beechwood settee from the first years of the 18th century, covered in *petit* and *gros point* floral needlework. The date is apparent from the legs and stretchers which, like so many settees from the early 18th century, are built up rather like a series of chairs.

Just over 5ft. long, it sits very well and the walnut has taken a good rich patination. The main attraction, of course, is the wonderfully vivid needlework which is probably very like the original and adds greatly to its desirability. Furniture collectors tend to underestimate the value of good needlework. It made £40,000 in November 1986.

Plate 80. When this piece came up for auction the auctioneers gave no date. Like so many top reproductions, it is more heavily decorated and probably better made than the original. The form of back is typical of the Chippendale period sofas but the heavily carved mask and hairy feet indicate that the man who made it, perhaps in the early years of this century, had in mind the heavily decorated furniture of George II's reign.

Such pieces often make little more than the current cost of reproducing, polishing and upholstering them. This made £8,000 in November 1985.

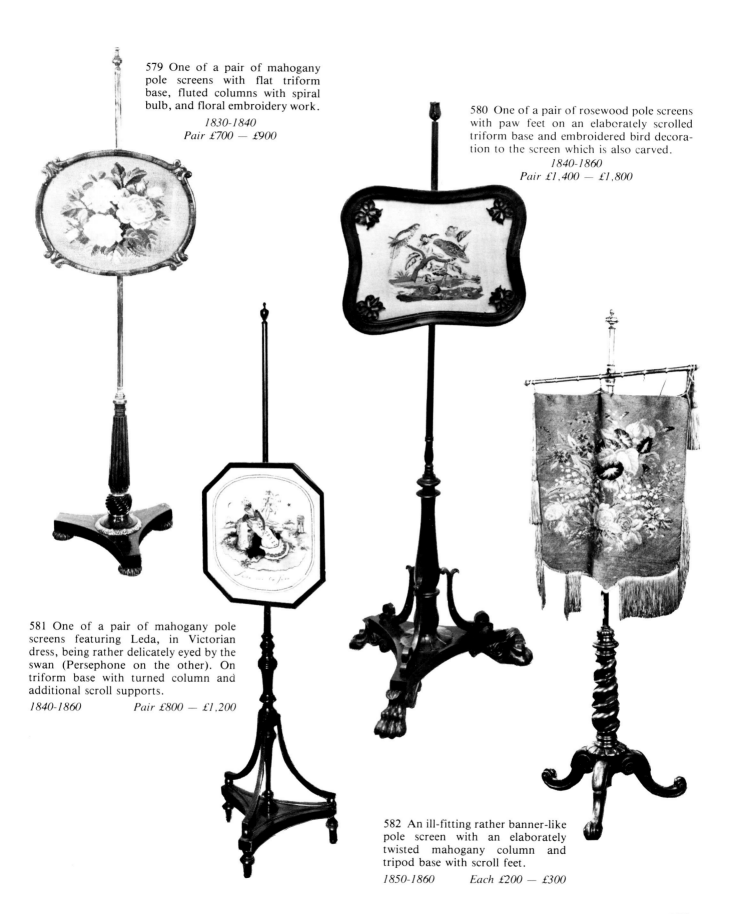

579 One of a pair of mahogany pole screens with flat triform base, fluted columns with spiral bulb, and floral embroidery work.
1830-1840
Pair £700 — £900

580 One of a pair of rosewood pole screens with paw feet on an elaborately scrolled triform base and embroidered bird decoration to the screen which is also carved.
1840-1860
Pair £1,400 — £1,800

581 One of a pair of mahogany pole screens featuring Leda, in Victorian dress, being rather delicately eyed by the swan (Persephone on the other). On triform base with turned column and additional scroll supports.
1840-1860   *Pair £800 — £1,200*

582 An ill-fitting rather banner-like pole screen with an elaborately twisted mahogany column and tripod base with scroll feet.
1850-1860   *Each £200 — £300*

SECRETAIRES

The term secretaire is a kind of catch-all word for writing furniture other than out-and-out bureaux, davenports, bonheurs-du-jour, pedestal desks and other specific items. It is used for fall-front walnut pieces, often described in their original papers as scrutoires (or escritoires) and for later pieces of a writing nature.

583 A walnut secretaire chest on chest with an unusual design of recessed sunburst in the bottom drawer, indicating quality. The quality of the interior of the secretaire drawer is quite exceptional, with concave curved drawers and pigeon-holes. Note that the drawers have a lip moulding and herring-bone inlaid lines inside the crossbanding. A fine piece with superb patination.

1710-1730   *£25,000 — £35,000*
Wide range because colour and patination very important

584 A high quality mahogany secretaire chest on chest with a broken pediment with dentil frieze. The corners of the upper chest are chamfered and have a blind fret. It is the right height to sit at and therefore desirable.

1740-1760   *£15,000 — £20,000*

585 A rather uninspired oak secretaire chest on chest with slide and pillared corners to the upper chest. The top moulding is arcaded in the cavetto and has a dentil frieze above in the top moulding. The interior is a little crude and either the drawer runners are worn or the drawers don't fit, but above all it is too high to sit at, which renders it unusable, hence undesirable.

1740-1760
£1,500 — £2,000
but not a good buy

254

587 A plain but well-bred mahogany secretaire chest on Hepplewhite splayed feet with shaped apron. A neat interior fit-up in satin-finish wood and original handles to the drawers. It will end up married to a bookcase top, trying to look like an impoverished cousin of 590.

1780-1800   *£2,500 — £3,000*

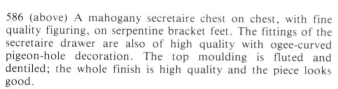

586 (above) A mahogany secretaire chest on chest, with fine quality figuring, on serpentine bracket feet. The fittings of the secretaire drawer are also of high quality with ogee-curved pigeon-hole decoration. The top moulding is fluted and dentiled; the whole finish is high quality and the piece looks good.

1750-1770   *£5,500 — £7,500*

588 (right) A good quality mahogany secretaire chest of slightly later date with boxwood stringing and ivory inlaid keyholes. Note that instead of the top moulding of the previous example, there is a flush top raised above the secretaire drawer, with inlaid stringing lines in a pattern. The use of light coloured wood to imitate swags of drapery over the pigeon-holes is particularly imaginative — a good crisp piece, which will be hard to marry. If attempts are made, the satinwood stringing line design will be repeated on the frieze of the bookcase but the grain of the wood is likely to give the game away.

1790-1810   *£3,500 — £4,500*

SECRETAIRES — bookcase

> The late eighteenth century saw something of a flowering of secretaire-drawer bookcases and some of the finest cabinet makers worked on this form.

589 (left) Mahogany secretaire bookcase on bracket feet. The rather square design of glazing bar is typical of the third and last quarters of the century.

1760-1780   *Assuming it is as good as it looks £8,000 — £10,000*
Well married £3,500 — £4,500

590 (below left) A mahogany secretaire bookcase on splayed feet of 'Hepplewhite' type. The veneers on the drawer fronts are perfectly matched and there are two oval panels of veneer, edged with inlaid stringing lines on the secretaire drawers.

1780-1800   *Right £6,000 — £8,000*
Well married £2,500 — £3,500

591 (below right) Another splay-footed secretaire bookcase with oval panels to the drawers, this time repeated in circular panels in the doors beneath. The top has an arcaded cavetto moulding. Top price for 3ft. 3ins. wide and smaller.

1780-1800   *Right £5,000 — £6,000*
Wrong £2,500 — £3,250

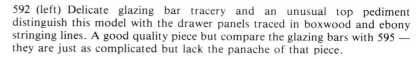

592 (left) Delicate glazing bar tracery and an unusual top pediment distinguish this model with the drawer panels traced in boxwood and ebony stringing lines. A good quality piece but compare the glazing bars with 595 — they are just as complicated but lack the panache of that piece.

18th century   *£18,000 — £24,000*
19th century   *£6,000 — £8,000*

593 (below left) A secretaire bookcase on bracket feet, with doors beneath the secretaire drawer which is open to show a quality arrangement with satinwood central door with an oval panel of mahogany. But the satinwood circles lack inspiration and do not work as well as those on 591.

1800-1820   *£6,000 — £8,000*

594 (below right) A Gothic arch to the glazing pattern and satinwood inside drawer facings distinguish this Regency model. The stars in the frieze take up the Gothic motif in restrained form.

1810-1830   *£8,000 — £10,000*

595 (right) A High Regency model with the highly successful effect of the circular glazing bars enclosing two small central mirrors. Vase-shaped finials to the top; gilt decoration; gilt paw feet; key pattern brass stringing à la Thomas Hope; ebony inlaid vase-shaped keyhole decoration; illustrated in *Regency Furniture* by Margaret Jourdain, revised by Ralph Fastnedge; what more do you want? These superb and documented pieces are difficult to value.

1805   *£40,000 — £50,000*

596 A rosewood secretaire cabinet with two tiers of brass shelves above and brass and gilt decoration. A delicate and beautifully balanced piece. Although the woods on the doors match outside, the grain within the ovals doesn't — unusual in a piece of this quality.

1820-1830   *£18,000 — £25,000*

597 (right) The kneehole variety, though few knees would fit it — a secretaire bookcase with a pedestal style lower half with panelled doors. Not a successful design, and a shattering comparison to place so near the other two pieces on this page.

1790-1810   *£3,000 — £4,000*

SECRETAIRES — fall-front

598 (left) A walnut fall-front secretaire on stand. Under the top moulding there is a 'cushion drawer' with its characteristic convex surface veneered in cross-grained walnut. The fall is quartered with matched veneers and inlaid with geometric circles of sycamore. There is a single drawer in the stand which has typical Charles II spiral twist legs and single drawer base. The baluster shape near the flat veneered stretcher is a good touch. Inside, the fittings include drawers and pigeon-holes and the writing surface is hinged, with a rack beneath, to enable it to be raised at an angle for reading a heavy book or ledger. There is a similar piece at Ham House.

c.1675   *Original legs £6,000 — £8,000*
                            Later legs £3,000 — £4,000

599 A secretaire on chest with a fine bold top moulding and cushion drawer. The fall is below two more shallow drawers, which are herring-bone banded like the fall and other drawers. The fall is quartered in matching sheets of veneers and has another, inner banding of herring-bone with keyed corner design. The arched base is original and very unusual. The interior has a conventional fitting of drawers and pigeon-holes. There are more veneered drawers behind the door.

1680-1700   £6,000 — £9,000

600 A walnut fall-front secretaire, with cushion drawer and typical inside fittings, on bracket feet. The handles to the lower chest are Victorian replacements. The drawers are herring-bone banded.

1690-1710   £5,000 — £7,000

SETTEES — sofas, day-beds and couches

The earliest forms of settee were simply extended versions of the armchairs of the period, whether upholstered or, like Chippendale's examples, with backs that were a two-, three- or four-fold repeat of the single chair back with which the settee went *en suite*. These are, understandably, not very popular and it is not until the return of the fully upholstered back that any great enthusiasm emerges amongst general collectors.

From about 1770 onwards the fully upholstered settee, then the couch or day-bed of Regency times and the exuberantly carved Victorian chaise-longues and couches, the Chesterfield and all the other forms made their appearance in sequence. These are now part of the general antique collecting scene, whereas the upholstered late seventeenth century pieces and hard-backed Chippendale versions are a specialist taste.

The price is obviously greatly influenced by the condition of the upholstery, and unless otherwise stated values are based on the piece being covered in good quality modern upholstery.

601 (above) A George I walnut settee with shepherd's crook arms. The cabriole legs have thread and scroll decoration and end in pad feet. The fabric is not contemporary, which would increase the price considerably.

1715-1725   *£6,000 — £9,000*

602 (centre) A Chippendale mahogany settee showing the double back design taken from a single chair.

1750-1770   *£5,000 — £7,000*

603 (left) A Hepplewhite mahogany upholstered settee on slightly splayed legs. Note that the hessian below the seat has been ripped out. At this price one needs to check that the *frame* is period as well, as it appears somebody has done by the torn canvas at the bottom of the seat.

1780-1800   *£5,000 — £7,000*

604 A Hepplewhite button upholstered settee on tapering legs. An elegant serviceable piece.

1780-1800 £5,000 — £7,000

605 A superb Adam sofa or window seat. The workmanship is of the highest quality. A very elegant piece.

c.1775   £8,000 — £10,000

Bear in mind that the prices which follow take account of the cost of new upholstery, which they are assumed to have.

606 (left) A four-seat Sheraton settee on turned and fluted legs.

1790-1810   £2,000 — £3,000

607 A Regency mahogany chaise-longue with carved decoration on the front.

1810-1830   £2,500 — £3,500

608 A Regency mahogany chaise-longue on paw feet.

1810-1825   £4,000 — £6,000

609 (left) A Regency mahogany chaise-longue with metal decoration and heavy rounded padded ends.

1810-1830   *£3,000 — £4,000*

610 (above) A Victorian double-ended settee with flowing scrolled lines and considerable carving, offered over a wide range of time.

1850-1880   *£1,800 — £2,500*

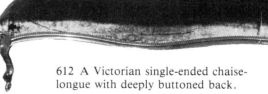

611 A William IV mahogany sofa, with rather bulbous reeded legs, showing the doubleended design favoured by several designers.

c. 1825-1850   *£2,000 — £3,000*

612 A Victorian single-ended chaise-longue with deeply buttoned back.

1850-1865   *£1,200 — £1,800*

613 A Victorian walnut richly carved settee.

1850-1865   *£2,000 — £3,000*

614 A walnut Victorian double spoon-backed settee with leaf carving and fretted scrolls.

1850-1870   *£1,800 — £2,500*

615 A mahogany Victorian settee with French influence in the back design. The legs are the same as the chairs of this date.

1850-1870   *£1,500 — £2,000*

616 An unusual Victorian button backed Chesterfield with scrolled arms and turned legs.

1860-1880   *£1,200 — £1,500*

617 A Victorian Chesterfield with typical button upholstery. Now very often recovered in leather.

1860-1900   *£1,200 — £1,500*

SETTLES — and similar furniture

The earliest settles were probably fixed close to the fire-place as a piece of built-in furniture. They were high and box-like to exclude draughts. By the end of the seventeenth century the settle was a popular piece of furniture and it was made throughout the eighteenth century and into the nineteenth century, particularly in country districts. Dating is thus only approximate, as with other country furniture. Prices vary fairly widely as this is very much a specialist market.

618 A very fine North Country settle. Good vigorous carving on the back, the lines of lunettes on the top rail are highly accomplished. Note the side pieces on the ends — rather like wainscot chairs. Moulded seat rail and good bobbin turns. A very desirable piece and not expensive, despite its high quality, as settles are not in great demand.

1670-1680   *£4,000 — £6,000*

619 A good quality piece showing real wear on the front rail. It has curved terminations at the top of the side rails which suggest North Country design and bobbin turnings on the legs and baluster supports to the arms which give the date. The additional back legs are sensible later additions. A box seat is dearer.

Late 17th century   *£1,400 — £1,800*

620 Much more modest and indeed typical example of a well-made seventeenth century panelled settle. Bobbin turned supports to the arms and the less usual lift-up seat. This is one of those pieces that look old.

Late 17th century   *£900 — £1,200*

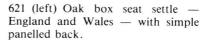
621 (left) Oak box seat settle —
England and Wales — with simple
panelled back.

Mid-18th century
£700 — £900

622 (right) A simple three panelled back
eighteenth century example with rather thin
arms and thick seat rail.
Late 18th century   *£600 — £800*

623 (left) A box seat table settle. Pegs at
either end enable the table to swing back and
form the back of the settle. There are two lids
to the box underneath. The sledge feet point to
a Welsh origin. Although the table is incon-
venient to use, such settles have been seen at
nearly twice the prices quoted below, which is
rather too much for the workmanship
involved.

Late 17th century   *£3,000 — £4,000*

624 Elm bacon settle. Welsh. The box seat has two drawers beneath, while the back, stepped out at the top, contains cupboards in which to hang bacon. Found in oak, ash, elm and pine.

Early 19th century   *£4,000 — £5,000*

625 Bacon settle in elm. The lack of stops at the back of the drawers has broken off the projecting ovolo moulding on two of the drawers.

c.1740   *When restored £3,000 — £4,000*

626 Welsh pine box settle with sledge feet and panelled front.

If late 18th century   *£400 — £600*
If 19th century   *£250 — £350*

627 A settle in mahogany with well-panelled back and Sheraton decorative inlay. Something of a mixture but typical of how country designs persist and adopt new decoration, and the result of a long-lived design. Still to be seen in old pubs.

1780-1790   *£600 — £800*

628 A Sheraton design mahogany sideboard with serpentine front. This high quality piece incorporates inlaid shell motifs and boxwood stringing decoration, even on the square tapering legs. 4ft. 6ins. wide.

1780-1800   *£11,000 — £14,000*

629 Another Sheraton design with the same motifs but illustrating the inlaid circular panel on the deep drawers which is often found in quality pieces of the period. The square tapering legs end in a thicker foot. 4ft. 6ins. wide.

1780-1800   *£12,000 — £15,000*

630 (right) A plain mahogany serpentine-fronted sideboard with a brass back rail on square tapering legs. Quite apart from the lack of decoration, perhaps missing the elegant compactness of the previous example.

1790-1800   *£3,500 — £4,500*

SIDEBOARDS

The sideboard, as distinct from the side table or sideboard table, is generally attributed to Robert Adam, who showed his first designs some time after 1760. The original design contains within it, when the side pedestals are removed, the nucleus of the eighteenth century sideboard and its later developments.

The Adam brothers were dedicated to Roman and Greek classical forms. The pedestals at each side of the piece had vase-shaped urns which were for iced water for drinking and hot water for washing silver. The pedestals were used as a plate warmer and cellaret (wine store) respectively. The central section, without the pedestals, is the form we generally associate with later Georgian sideboards, with or without the brass gallery at the back. Shearer and Hepplewhite illustrated pedestal types and so did Sheraton.

In later designs, like Gillows, the side cupboards of the central section became drawers and later still, in the Regency period, the side sections were extended downwards to form cupboards. The proportions of these later sideboards became heavier as a result.

From the mid-nineteenth century onwards the sideboard became either a solid-doored cabinet of long proportions with or without carved decoration, or in emulation of the famous 'Chevy Chase' exhibition piece of 1857-1863, highly carved in oak or mahogany with fruit, deer, rabbits, birds and other game.

At the end of the nineteenth century the return to eighteenth century designs produced some rather good quality reproductions in mahogany, satinwood and satin maple.

Value points:
Colour and patination + + +
Carved and inlaid decorations + + +
Figured woods and satinwood + + +
Width under 4ft. + + + +
Width under 5ft. + + +
Tambour shutter to eighteenth century types + +

631 A mahogany break-front sideboard with inlaid ebony stringing lines in key-type patterns of Egyptian influence. Square tapering legs also inlaid with the black stringing line. The handles are probably replacements of a standard modern reproduction type with stamped urns. The originals would probably have been lion mask types, like those on 632.

1800-1810   *£3,000 — £4,000*

632 A break-front mahogany sideboard with a sliding door, also with inlaid black stringing lines in key patterns, but this time on turned legs and with a reeded lower section repeated around the top edge. Lion mask brass handles.

1810-1830   *£2,250 — £3,000*

633 A large bow-fronted sideboard with brass back rail and turned and reeded legs with carved leaf decoration at the top. Still an elegant piece.

1820-1840   *£3,500 — £4,500*

634 A small compact example with well-selected veneers. The decoration is handled with restraint and the piece is a desirable one. Nevertheless one can see in it the ancestor of well-made but unsaleable larger ugly pedestal sideboards made from 1850 onwards.

1835-1845   *5ft or under £1,400 — £1,800*
                 If much over 5ft £800 — £1,100

Plate 81. The popularity of the classical images and current fashion for marble have combined to make this a desirable piece. Such was not the case in the 1970s and it is hard to be enthusiastic about a set of feet whose one virtue is their realism — one feels that at the correct command they would march off.
c. 1850

Plate 82. Four leopard monopodia with the inevitable hairy paw feet balance unsurely on their heads a heavily carved serving table, c.1830, which retains the corner 'ears' that became the hallmark of classicism at a commercial level (look round memorials in any church). The carving is robust, and the coat of arms carefully included in the centre, together with the rich colour, give this at least a valuable furnishing function.

Plate 83. Sideboards take a great many shapes. One we left out of the last edition of the *Price Guide* was the semicircular or demi-lune. Here is a good example from the late 1780s with its super-structure and the original large brass stamped handles. The mahogany veneer is well chosen and has acquired a good colour.

The only problem with these is that because they are half circles they can be very deep and consequently come a long way into a small room. For this reason the trade sometimes used to take a few inches off the back and call them 'D-shaped'. No longer — they are appreciated in their own right.

In 1988 fetched £20,000

Plate 84. Here is a second sideboard of roughly the same shape. They make a good comparison. This example lacks what can only be called the grandeur of the first. The veneers have not been so carefully chosen, nor do they seem to be of the same quality. The use of the white wood and the metalwork decoration is less successful than on the previous example. The colour of the mahogany in the centre arch seems to have gone an unfortunate yellow. Even the little oval stars can't compete with the ovals set out on the first.

1790s   *In 1988 fetched £4,100*

Plate 85. Although small sideboards are appreciated, length without reason is not a disadvantage. This is a very smart Regency 7ft.6ins. example with well chosen good mahogany veneers — see, for example, how the grain on the centre drawer is balanced with a great deal of movement. The brass decoration has been effectively used, particularly in emphasising the change in level. Perhaps the only weakness is the rather insignficant brass paw feet, but then fashion has now changed so we find these acceptable.

c.1805   *This made £13,000 in 1986*

Plate 86. Another large double bow-fronted 18th century mahogany sideboard but of slightly earlier date. Fifteen years ago its classic designs and tapering legs would have made it a more desirable piece than the last example, but now we see it as lacking colour, a less interesting grain. The tiny quarter circle decorations under the middle drawer are not attractive. We have got used to bolder statements and this piece is now viewed as lacking 'zap'.

1790s   *Made £3,200 in 1989*

Plate 87. Here is a side cabinet, nicely faded and with a marble top, which has the huge accolade of being in the manner of George Bullock. It has the requisite Egyptian caryatids on the hugely fashionable scrolled foliate feet. They are pure Thomas Hope and the rest of the applied metalwork conforms to this taste which is now very much in.
c.1815

Plate 88. A Regency date, even when a piece is useful and by a named maker (James Newton) and blessed with provenance, is no guarantee of high value. This piece lacks the square chic look with heavily articulated references to Thomas Hope; only the heavy pillars emerging from lotus flowers give nodding acknowledgement to formal classicism. Heaviness is the problem and is there not a 'Victorian' feel to the cresting rail?

635 (left) The final Regency development — the deep drawers have reached the floor and the lion masks and hairy paw feet of classical design are incorporated. The choice of veneers is still very good.

1820-1840   *£3,000 — £4,000*

636 Another late Regency or early Victorian version, with spirally turned columns of purely decorative function and turned bulbous feet. High quality veneers.

1830-1850   *Under £1,200 — £1,600*
                            Much over £900 — £1,200

637 Break-front example with turned legs and ornate gallery. The end of the road for this elegant design. What will probably happen is that the gallery will be cut down (as it cannot be removed without leaving marks) unless cross-banded, and brass handles will replace the buns. If it had really good veneer, tapering legs would be a possibility.

1830   *£1,500 — £2,000*

639 A 'Chevy Chase' type sideboard with highly carved decoration. The type of piece made for exhibitions to demonstrate the technical ability of the manufacturer. Normally of such huge proportions that it is inconceivable in the normal domestic environment, quite apart from the off-putting subject matter, but it appeals to certain European taste, for example Bavarian.

638 A simple mahogany side cabinet incorporating the flattened arch design very popular from the 1840s. One has only to remove the middle section to drop the price to £60 — £90 and still hard to sell.

1840-1880   *£500 — £700*   *1850-1870*   *£7,000 — £9,000*

Strictly speaking, all the following should fall under side cabinets, but the term credenza is generally used for a highly decorated, shaped piece, so it seems sensible to use it as well. A cynic might think that in designing a credenza the object was to strap, glue, carve, bolt, screw or paint as much decoration on the front as possible, bearing in mind that colour and texture contrast might be as loud as could be managed and that there should be as few straight lines as the ingenuity of the designer could contrive. This is clearly an exaggeration but in any event the market is more discriminating and the quality of workmanship has a strong influence on the price. Good quality metal work and a serpentine shape to the side doors are also important to value. They start in the late 1850s and continue into the Edwardian period; fortunately however we stop at about 1880 so that the final designs do not concern us.

First, however we continue the development of the Regency cabinet, then move to the straight-fronted pieces before discussing the curved-end variety.

640 A Sheraton rosewood cabinet, only 3ft. high, with gilt enrichments to the pillars and mouldings and with a white marble top. The short tapered feet *(en toupie)* are of French origin and one can clearly see that in the 1820s the collar widened and the rest withered to give the familiar bun effect. A very rich piece in which the credenza shape is apparent.

c.1800   £7,000 — £9,000

641 A mahogany break-front side cabinet decorated with inlaid satinwood stringing and rosewood crossbanding. The front has a brass grill, decorated with small flowers at the intersections, backed by silk. Again pillars are used and the effect is very elegant.

c.1810   £10,000 — £15,000

642 A rosewood side cabinet with a brass gallery to the marble top and delicately arched brass lattice work to the doors with a backing of silk. The decoration is restrained but the tight, well-carved scrolls and the fine oval beading are forms which coarsen with the following twenty years.

c.1815   £6,000 — £7,000

643 (left) An exceptional break-front cabinet in the French taste, decorated with ceramic plaques and very fine quality marquetry in a variety of exotic woods. Just look at the decoration of the turned pillars — the whole piece oozes quality. If it carries the label of Wright and Mansfield, as it might well do, the price would be up to, or even over, the range shown. Holland and Sons were another firm of standing who specialised in this type of work.

c.1865   *£8,000 — £10,000*

644 (right) A good boulle cabinet in which this very high quality work produces a rich red and gold colour. The use of a vaguely Eastern shape gives definite form and is more desirable than the usual oval design.

c.1850   *£5,000 — £7,000*

645 A more common oval design but of high quality workmanship. Notice for example the well-finished ormolu faces. Not unlike a Lawford design of 1867.

c.1870   *£3,000 — £4,000*

646 A fine marquetry example richly decorated and well carved wherever possible. Plenty of good quality ormolu. The pillar effects also add to the feeling of opulence.

c.1855   *£6,000 — £8,000*

647 (left) Decorated with boulle work and *pietre dure* (a mosaic made up principally of hard stones inlaid, worked and polished) floral marquetry. It lacks serpentine sides and better quality decoration to get it right to the top, but it is nevertheless very desirable.

c.1860   *£2.500   £3.500*

648 (right) A satinwood example with serpentine ends. The decoration on the pillars harks back to Regency. Satinwood finely inlaid on the door and the frieze. Not in the main line of credenza design.

c.1870   *£2.500   £3.500*

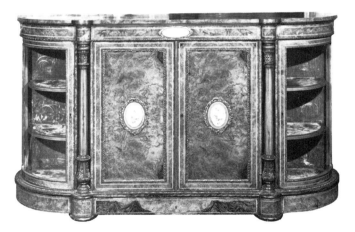

649 Floral painted Sèvres panels certainly help to relieve the relatively simple decoration of this walnut credenza with tulipwood crossbanding and satinwood stringing, but they are perhaps a little too restrained for this type of object.

c.1870   *£3.000 — £4.500*

650 Typical of the type advertised by Shoolbred at the time. The flecked satinwood and the Wedgwood plaque surrounded by delicate marquetry give this piece some style. Notice the widely spaced fluting on the pillars — a later sign.

c.1875   *£2.500 — £3.500*

651 (right) A fairly typical simple floral marquetry and well-framed walnut piece. Brass mounts are kept to a minimum, workmanship is excellent.

c.1850   *£3,000 — £4,000*

652 (left) A simpler example than the last. The metal work is down to four pieces (two in the middle and two at the sides). The decoration here relies entirely on a dark grained streak of burr walnut, carefully quartered, on the door and the Greek key on the frieze.

c.1850   *£2,000 — £2,500*

653 (right) Large Wedgwood plaques and much metal work cannot compensate for the fact that this piece is ebonised. The market does not like black.

c.1870   *£1,000 — £1,400*

654 (left) The marquetry has now shrunk to the frieze and two pillars. The metal work is poor and the door fretted — a sort of poor man's marquetry, satinwood however helps and the top is marble.

c.1880   *£1,500 — £2,000*

STANDS

This one word covers a large number of different types. Most supported some sort of lighting equipment or enabled some work of art to be seen from the right angle. They are popular today because they help to vary the levels in a room and often find employment for vases of flowers.

655 (left) One of a pair of eighteenth century walnut *torchères* with moulded serpentine top. The stem of baluster form on the top half with hexagonal shape below. The (literally) tripod base carved to resemble three buckled shoes with knees and decoration of stylised acanthus leaf. The William and Mary stem with early eighteenth century feet looks a little strange — probably Dutch.

c.1720   *Pair £3,500 — £5,000*
                                      Each £1,400 — £1,800

656 (right) A Chippendale rococo mahogany *torchère* with three pillar column and a hexagonal moulded edge top. An elegant piece that could easily be mistaken for Edwardian.

c.1760   *Pair £4,000 — £6,000*
                                      Each £1,500 — £2,000

657 (left) A set of very elegant moulded mahogany legs supports this small Hepplewhite urn stand with small slide. Although it is slightly damaged there is no disguising the quality. To make an elegant cabriole as long as this takes real skill.

c.1760
Restored £4,000 — £5,000

658 (right) A very striking mahogany urn stand, again with small slide or candle-stand. The elegant curved cross stretcher support with a vase-shaped finial in the centre is a very good touch.

c.1770
£2,500 — £3,000

659 (left) One of a pair of oval classical marquetry *torchères* or lamp stands. The Greek motifs of honeysuckle, continuous C-scroll and square key are all present. The platform and hairy feet are a later addition.

c.1800
Pair £8,000 — £12,000
Each £4,000 — £5,000

660 (right) One of a Regency pair of *torchères* with gilt birds' heads. One can see in the base the same triangular form that appears on card tables of the period.

c.1820
Pair £4,000 — £5,000
Each £1,500 — £2,200

661 A George IV hat stand. Surprisingly elegant turnings, though the overall effect is not exciting.

c.1830
because elegant £800 — £1,000

662 Typical rather late, rather nasty Victorian jardinière. The marquetry adds to value, but otherwise it is useful rather than quality.

c.1880   *£400 — £600*

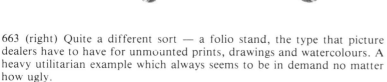

663 (right) Quite a different sort — a folio stand, the type that picture dealers have to have for unmounted prints, drawings and watercolours. A heavy utilitarian example which always seems to be in demand no matter how ugly.

Late 18th century   *£2,000 — £3,000*

As we have mentioned elsewhere, unless you were fairly important, until the end of the seventeenth century, there wasn't much else to sit on other than stools (apart, of course, from benches). The joint or 'coffin' stool was obviously quite plentiful and could at times be superbly carved and decorated. Because of the enormous numbers of fakes and reproductions of joint stools which have been made (and as coffin stools they still appeared in church furnishers' catalogues late in the last century), general collectors are often a little unsure of them, while the real oak enthusiast is always aquiver for a genuine period joint stool. In recent years even fakes are in demand if they look old enough.

As chairs became more plentiful, the stool moved off to other incidental uses but it remained a piece of household furniture and incorporated the design features of the passing fashions — cross-stretchers, cabriole legs, Chippendale legs, and so on. In fact stools follow chair design unless they are for special use, like piano stools.

As a working rule stools with S shaped holes in the top are not British.

664 A fine quality James I oak stool. The frieze carved with a continuous band of deeply carved linked strapwork, the legs well turned and fluted. Note the irregular wear applied across the deeply moulded stretcher, not the smooth 'chamfering' of the faker. A most desirable piece.

c.1620   £5,000 — £7,000

665 Very early form of stool in oak with late Elizabethan-type fluted baluster legs. If it has a good colour and an original top, a good example.

c.1620   £2,500 — £3,500

666 A good example in yew wood. The baluster and suggestion of cotton reel on the legs are robustly turned. Being yew and of good colour, the price is high.

c.1650   because yew £4,000 — £6,000

STOOLS — the walnut period, 1670-1740

> This period produced some extremely fine furniture which attracts a very dedicated collectors' market. The stools present a fascinating cross-section of designs, some highly individual, some common to chairs.

667 Another late type with shaping on the underside of the frieze and moulding on the stretchers. The turning is not over-imaginative (compare with the previous example).

1660-1690

Right £1,200 — £1,500
Wrong £250 — £350

668 Although the top looks convincingly wormy, the underview showing the age of the wood will be much more informative. If it is right, it is still an unimaginative turning. This is typical of a wide range of late and nasty, or simply wrong, joint stools.

Late 17th century

Right £800 — £1,100
Wrong £200 — £300

669 An extremely decorative late seventeenth century walnut stool with gilt decoration. The highly carved scrolled legs and cross-stretchers show very interesting variations on a very sophisticated design. An example of the influx of Continental fashion after the Restoration.

1670-1700

£3,500 — £4,500

670 An excellent William and Mary period stool with cross-stretchers, made from walnut. The octagonal legs with their bun feet and echoing cups, and the curved sweep of the stretchers are beautiful examples of a style found on stands, tables and other pieces of the period.

1680-1700

£3,500 — £4,500

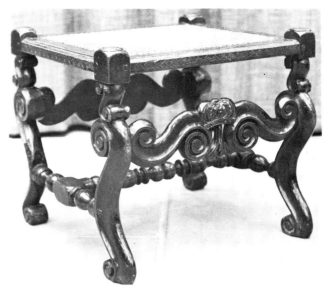

671 An exciting 'one off' walnut William and Mary stool. To make the mortise hole for the top cross-stretcher, one needs a thickened section of the leg. This has been made in an interestingly circular form — a feature which has been repeated on the top stretchers themselves. Early eighteenth century needlework. Knarred or Spanish feet.

c. 1690   *£6,000 — £8,000*

672 No difficulty in dating this stool because of its strong similarity to the well-executed chairs produced during the reign of Charles II. The successful use of the S-scroll is well demonstrated here.

c. 1690   *£1,700 — £2,200*

673 (left) A walnut stool with slight cabriole legs and the interesting feature of turned pieces on the inside top of the legs. The finial rising from the turned joined stretchers is a good touch.

c. 1700   *£900 — £1,200*

674 An elegant walnut stool of the early eighteenth century with an interesting stretcher design. The nicely shaped pad feet are typically English and there is a nice fold at the top of the leg.

1710-1730   *£3,000 — £4,000*

STOOLS — mainly mahogany, 1740-1850

Since stools mainly followed the prevailing fashion in chairs, they are fairly easy to date.

The answer to the conundrum 'when is a stool not a stool?' is 'when it is a broken chair'. Fortunately most chairs are not square or rectangular whereas stools are, so that some cabinet work is necessary to get the opposite sides up to the same length.

675 (left) A walnut stool with drop-in seat on cabriole legs. The stretcher is typical of the early eighteenth century.

1700-1725   *£2,500 — £3,500*

676 (above) A walnut stool on cabriole legs, without stretchers, with pad feet and curved inside knee. The drop-in seat has a period design tapestry covering.

1720-1740 £2,000 — £3,000

677 A superb Chippendale mahogany stool in the Gothic taste given the full treatment in terms of carving, pierced carved legs and upholstering in tent stitch tapestry.

c.1760   *£6,000 — £8,000*

678 A mahogany stool showing the French influence in the scrolled foot on the legs and with high quality carving. Hipped at the leg into the seat. Tapestry seat, this time upholstered right over.

1740-1760   *£4,000 — £6,000*

679 The drop in quality is rather steep. This stool purports to date from mid-eighteenth century and indeed the cabriole legs are of reasonable quality. But the seat rail looks a bit thin and the pegs are too near the edge of the upholstered section.

If mid-18th century £800 — £1,200
If not £150 — £250

680 A mahogany stool with drop-in seat on splayed Chippendale moulded legs, i.e. moulded and tapering square section legs.

1760-1780 £200 £300

681 A mahogany square-legged Chippendale stool with a drop-in seat. No decoration and in need of cleaning and polishing.

1760-1780 £175 £250

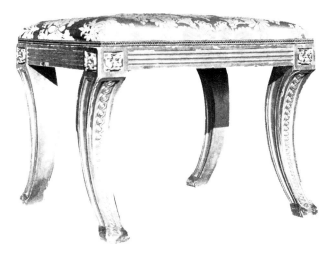

682 (above) A gilt stool on sabre legs with reeded and floral decoration. The legs have an inset panel with tapering guilloche decoration.

c.1820 £1,000 £1,500

683 A mahogany music stool of the adjustable type with a back and the needlework covering to the seat associated with such pieces. The reeded legs end in a tapering section which curves outwards — a Regency touch. By 1834 Thomas King was illustrating similar stools with straight, turned legs. Often broken or badly repaired perhaps because it is structurally a bad design.

c.1820 £1,400 £1,800

684 (left) A mahogany music stool like the previous example but without a back. The turning at the top of the legs has become more fussy and the outward curve less evident — tending more towards early Victorian.

1830-1840 £1,000 £1,300

685 (right) A simple stool with needlework covering on four turned mahogany legs with carved embellishment.

c.1840 £150 £200

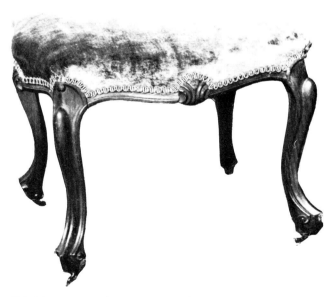

686 (above) A walnut stool of the Victorian scroll design found in balloon-back chairs of the period and derived from France.

c.1850 £300 — £400

687 (right) A classic Victorian music stool of the same period showing the return to the 'cabriole' form of leg, scrolled carving and fruity centre column.

c.1850 £400 — £550

These rather specialised pieces were produced for professional use and seem to have been very solidly constructed perhaps, as Cescinsky suggests, because the ledgers architects used were so heavy and it was useful to have a means of inclining them to a more convenient position.

689 This mahogany architect's table with candlestands and on square legs makes an interesting comparison with the previous example. The inner legs show the columns inside with castors which are said to give greater stablility. The side drawer is missing.

1750-1770   *When restored £4,000 — £5,500*

688 This well-fitted architect's table is in mahogany. It has castors on all six turned legs which, as can be seen, are masked by rather ugly straight false legs. It has brass candlestands and a side drawer. The front pulls out to form a convenient writing table. The date is suggested by the indented corner mouldings.

c 1740s   *£4,500 — £6,500*

690 A lighter architect's table in mahogany, without pillars, shown with the front open.

1750-1770   *£2,500 — £3,500*

691 Another type of architect's table, with fitted drawers, on castors.

1750-1770   *£3,000 — £4,500*

It is perhaps ironic that the design of early games tables can be traced back to sacred and ecclesiastical pieces. Furniture from one period borrows from another in ways which can be surprising. Card playing and gaming once occupied a place which has since been replaced by other forms of gambling and much care was lavished on the instruments used.

692 (above left) An oak folding-top table with a back gateleg to support the flap when open. It is a type known as a credence table, used in churches on which the bread, wine and water were placed before consecration. The block-like feet are clearly not original and must be ignored, but above the stretchers all is original, including the drawer. The column turned legs, with rims at top and bottom, taper almost imperceptibly at the top. The bold curve below the stylised arcaded moulding shows the maker was aware of the need to avoid a straight line.

c.1630   *When sensibly restored £2,500 — £3,500*

693 (above right) A development of the previous design. The main difference lies not in the legs, which have overall retained their simple cannon turning and only acquired decoration at the base, but in the rounded top frame. It is still a credence and very overpriced for what it is.

Late 17th century   *£2,000 — £2,750*

694 (above) The Continental influences which arrived with the Restoration, 1660, and the coronation of William of Orange and Mary, 1689, are described in every textbook on furniture but the progression from the previous table to this example provides a dramatic demonstration of the effect on British furniture design. Techinically it can hardly be improved upon: splayed feet, shaped stretcher, finials, turned hexagonal legs, ogee frieze with cock-beaded edges, veneered frieze, double-D drawer edgings, herring-bone crossbanding to the drawers, double-D moulding to the top and Italian figured veneers, but even that had to be touched up with black to show more contrast. Within a few years craftsmen had adopted the techniques to produce some of the most elegant furniture ever made in Britain.

c.1700   If walnut as shown £10,000 — £14,000
If burr walnut or burr elm £12,000 — £16,000

695 The shape has changed to the rectangular form, which is more familiar, but the arrangement of the legs remains the same. Although there are formal contrasting inlays on the top, it is the turning on the legs which attracts attention — sharp rims and baluster forms and, at the top, flat bobbins are mixed to provide a decorative arrangement. A feature of this type is that the tops of the legs are veneered and fit flush into the carcase.

c.1690 £10,000 — £14,000

TABLES — folding card, 1720-1750

On the previous page we show how, from early sacred examples, tables could be adapted for profane purposes. The move from turned or turned and faceted leg to a cabriole form followed quite simply the general furniture pattern (see Chairs). The fold-over as opposed to hanging flap type was ideal for the card-cum-side table. While the gateleg method of support was still used a new method was also evolved. 'Concertina action' as it has come to be known, enabled the two back legs to be folded out and stand square, giving a more stable and attractive appearance to the table which in this position could be used as a centre table and looked the same from every angle. A photograph of this mechanism half extended is seen in 708.

The pad foot coexisted with the cabriole leg but seems in general to have been used for the more humble pieces. However, as can be seen, some very attractive early pad foot examples exist.

Another variation which one meets is the three-top table in which there is merely an additional flap to provide an alternative top. This is sometimes inset with contrasting woods to provide a games top, e.g. a chess board. The value of these pieces is greater than their two-top equivalent by about fifteen to twenty per cent. They are found mainly from the second quarter of the eighteenth century.

The fold-over action requires hinges to be placed on the side. This is a perfectly sound method, but abuse over the years can lead to ugly or ineffective repairs having been made which will, of course, reduce value.

696 Shows a fine quality walnut example, the cabriole legs having shell decoration carved on the knee and being 'hipped' at the top to flow into the veneered frieze surface in the same way as the chairs of this quality of that period. The legs end in ball-and-claw feet. The only features of quality lacking in this table are, on the top playing surface, the candlestands and scoops for gaming counters which can be seen in the next example.

c. 1720   £14,000 — £18,000

697 A mahogany example with a baize top surface highlighting the corner candlestands and the inset scoops. This table also has cabriole legs ending in ball-and-claw feet, but the knee is carved with leaf and scroll forms. The flap is supported by a leg which pivots on a gate.

c.1735   £7,000 — £10,000

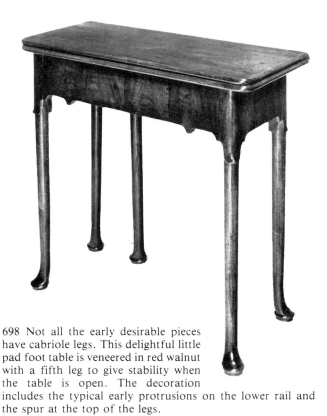

698 Not all the early desirable pieces have cabriole legs. This delightful little pad foot table is veneered in red walnut with a fifth leg to give stability when the table is open. The decoration includes the typical early protrusions on the lower rail and the spur at the top of the legs.

c.1720   £3,000 — £4,000

Plate 89. An opulent walnut card table from the 1730s of a type that was hugely popular and occasionally reproduced in between the wars. Eagles' heads, acanthus leaf carving and rings on the cabrioles, it has all the conventional motifs of a top quality example. It works on 'concertina' action so that it unfolds to form a rectangular table supporting the top on *both* legs when open (see figure 696). Unlike that example, however, it does not make a central table as it is only decorated on one side which is rather odd. It looks from the photograph to have been heavily cleaned.

Plate 90. A classic form of card table (see figure 702) of the simple straight leg pad foot form, but made more interesting by being veneered with laburnum wood set at an angle. By using the yellow sapwood the maker has achieved a striking effect without too much effort. This example has faded down a little. They used to be very popular with collectors but while they still make good money the taste that wants dramatic effect has rightly found more excitement in pieces from the nineteenth century.
1720

Plate 91. Deceptively simple this is a well made mahogany D-shaped card table of the late 1760s. The legs may lack the tapering elegance of later examples but the quality of wood, the use of box stringing throughout and the shells at the top acting as spandrels, together with the box and ebony collars at the bottom of the legs, have a touch of restrained luxury and quiet appeal

Plate 92. An elegant serpentine shape mahogany card table of 1770. The cabrioles are beautifully made and achieve a good balance in size with the bulk they have to support. Decoration is kept to a minimum and so does not detract from the excellent line the maker has achieved.

Plate 93. This calamander wood card table made in London c.1820 is an upmarket version of figure 722 though the brass feet and casters may be the same pattern, as is the thinking on the location of areas of decoration (one at each end of the frieze balanced by another on the platform). However, this example uses an exotic wood whose dark colour fits in well with the classical ideal, as does the formalised golden lotus leaf. The stringing lines are in satinwood which tones in well with the calamander and puts this piece at the top end of the price range even though the colour is a bit brash.

Plate 94. By contrast a well made but modestly decorated mahogany example which relies for its appeal on well shaped legs of an earlier pattern, a vase shaped turning and a modest line of small round notches. It pays no homage to the neo-classical movement. This lot made more money than the previous example which sounds odd. The answer is that there were a pair. Remember, it is not just in chairs that two lesser examples are worth more than the single better one.

Where two flaps sit on top of one another make sure that they meet cleanly and that no gap appears due to the distortion of one of them. This can be difficult to put right and detracts significantly from the value. 'Grinners' are not appreciated

1790s

Plate 95. An unusual example dating from the last decade of the 17th century. The oak top is ordinary enough but the turner has combined with the carver to produce a base that is almost certainly unique. There is almost too much going on here — scrolls, cross supports, panelled sections and a multitude of turned shapes. It lacks a strong cohesive design but its almost fussy decorative appearance makes it valuable.

Plate 96. An attractive bold red walnut gateleg table of the mid-1730s. The idea of reeding the legs has produced an interesting effect, well defined by the restrained turned rings. The pad feet are placed on discs, an idea Chippendale used later when he put feet on simulated rocks. The base of the gates is in a simple but unusual form designed so that when the gates are closed the exposed under-rail will appear as a solid member. If it has a good colour, this would be a very pleasant table, but not to popular dining taste as there are too many legs to be negotiated.

699 In this example the decoration is confined to ball-and-claw feet and shaped apron to the frieze which is constructed as a drawer. It has, however, the desirable feature of concertina action. Fitted with candlestands and inset scoops.

c.1745   £5,000 — £6,000

700 A simpler but good quality table with legs ending in pad feet. The cabriole form is used only on the front legs, while the back ones are straight. In this table the top, when folded open, is supported by one of the back legs swinging open on a gate, as is also the case in 701.

c.1750   £2,750 — £3,750

701 A George II folding top table in heavy mahogany. The straight legs ending in pad feet are a modification of earlier cabriole legs in that the earlier exuberance has been curbed and the leg is now much more restrained. These tables were probably multipurpose, being used for both games and for refreshments such as tea.

c.1740   £2,000 — £2,750

702 A more simple gateleg type with pad feet and fold-over top. It still, however, retains the spurs at the top of the legs. Although they are straight, the legs are canted out very slightly and give an impression of foursquareness lacking in later pieces.

c.1740   £1,200 — £1,600

The fashion for taking tea and other refreshments such as chocolate undoubtedly led to more occasional use of folding side tables, some even being made in pairs, one with baize interior covering for games and one with a polished surface for use when entertaining. These latter are often referred to as tea tables although multipurpose use must have been frequent.

As in the last section we see the shape of the leg altered in sympathy with those of chairs. If you have read the chair section, it hardly needs to be pointed out that variations increased considerably during this period as did the decoration on fine examples. Rococo carving was back in fashion again and the solid, even grain of mahogany made it an ideal medium for the carver, who apart from a few acanthus leaves and some restrained husks and flowers, had been largely unemployed since the excesses of the Restoration.

703 A high quality mahogany Chippendale treatment with clustered column legs in the 'Gothic taste', carved edges and figured veneer on the frieze. The square bases to the legs are scooped underneath so that the fitted castors are not too prominent. Although not clearly discernible in this photograph, the edges of the table are decorated with two motifs, a simple four petal flower and a rounded oblong projection (cabochon) which are used alternately. A typical Chippendale style decoration.

1755   *£6,500 — £8,000*

704 This table also exhibits decorative treatment associated with Chippendale: bas-relief carving (or blind-fretting) in the 'Chinese' taste on all surfaces except the figured top. The castors are more prominent and the convex treatment of the frieze is perhaps a bit heavy. But then the table itself is very foursquare and lacks the grace of the earlier designs. Notice that here too a number of standard devices are repeated to decorate the edge of the table.

c.1760   *£4,500 — £6,500*

705 This is a much more restrained example with blind-fretting to the front edges of all four legs and fretting to the brackets. This piece looks lighter than the previous example because the insides of the legs are chamfered.

c.1760   *£1,500 — £2,000*

706 Carving appears on the top edges, the delicately gadrooned edge to the frieze, a pattern that last appeared in the early seventeenth century, and a beaded edge to the simple legs — a nice touch, this. Note the lightening effect of chamfering on the square leg. The carving applied to the frieze is light and rococo.

c.1760   *£3,000 — £4,000*

707 This is another good mahogany example with just a remnant of the candlestand in the shaping of the corners. The serpentine top is echoed in the shaped frieze. The legs are chamfered and moulded on the front surfaces.

c.1770   *£2,000 — £2,500*

708 In this table the concertina action for moving the back legs to support the open top is clearly visible on a simple straight-leg mahogany table. Normally one associates this mechanism with earlier examples but, clearly, individual cabinet makers continued to please themselves. The top surface is decorated with an inlaid boxwood and ebony stringing line and star.

1760-1770   *£1,400 — £1,800*

709 A serpentine three-flap example of a games-cum-tea table. The legs are moulded in typical Chippendale manner. Interestingly, the leg which moves out to support the table when open is slightly out of place. This suggests that the hinge on which the leg moves is probably loose.

c.1760   *£1,200 — £1,600*

710 A Sheraton form of the highest quality, in satinwood with inlaid 'fan' decoration on the top and legs, which are of tapering square section with reeded and fluted front surfaces ending in spade feet. There is a crossbanding of kingwood on the top and the frieze.

c.1790   £5,000 — £7,000

As we have seen, the half-round (or 'demi-lune') table, opening to a circular form, has a very early provenance, which continued in the early Georgian period and lent itself to taper- or turned-leg form as fashion progressed. It is commercially important that there is no warping of the top. See 723.

711 The form is more oval, the satinwood inlaid more simply, but the quality is evident. The inlaid stringing lines and the inlaid black line around the edge of the legs all point to quality.

c.1790   £4,000 — £5,500

712 Another late eighteenth century table, made in solid mahogany, with a concave moulded edge to the top. The legs are thicker and less finely tapered.

c.1795   £1,400 — £2,000

713 A veneered mahogany serpentine-fronted table of fine quality, showing the shaping that related back to earlier forms and allied with an inlaid Sheraton shell and satinwood crossbanding.

c.1790   £2,500 — £3,500

714 A table of satinwood with kingwood crossbanding but the chamfered corners are not very successful despite the evident quality of the piece. The small square sections near the bottom of the legs are to balance the proportions.

c.1800   £1,500 — £2,000

715 One meets this type of simple D-end card table frequently. Any inlay or stringing lines help the price, whereas warping or an awkward angle to the legs send the price down.

c.1810   £900 — £1,200

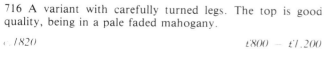

716 A variant with carefully turned legs. The top is good quality, being in a pale faded mahogany.

c.1820   £800 — £1,200

717 The maker has tried to introduce more fashionable Regency forms of post-1820, with 'sabre' legs, paw feet and lion masks, all made in rosewood but although, again, the quality of execution is high, the design is not of universal appeal. Still, it is highly decorative and that commands a good price.

c.1810   £3,000 — £4,000

The centre pedestal applied to side and card tables is a late Georgian or early Regency form.

718 This table is in rosewood, with elegant curved legs ending in brass paw castors. The top is cross-banded in satinwood and the octagonal centre column has an inlaid boxwood line at the edge of each vertical surface.

c.1800   *£3,000 — £4,000*

719 A slightly later form in which the top has similar treatment but the centre column has been embellished with a turned base. This stands on a flat platform instead of flowing into the four legs which support the platform, shaped to give a 'knee' at the top of each leg.

c.1810   *£1,500 — £2,250*

720 A similar base platform but the reeded legs are simpler. The column has been replaced by four curving supports with carved floral forms on the ends of the scrolls. This piece is in mahogany with a refined bead mould around the edges of the top and frieze.

c.1810   *£2,000 — £3,000*

721 A table in which can be seen the curving arc support, much valued by the antique trade as a cabinet maker's sleight-of-hand.

c.1810   *£2,000 — £3,000*

722 A simpler form with a rather bulbously-turned centre support. Figured mahogany veneer and applied mouldings of the split-turned type.

c.1820   *£1,100 — £1,500*

723 A high quality mahogany type with a four-column support and metal embellishments. An opening (i.e warped) top like this seriously reduces the value.

c.1820   *sound top £2,000 — £3,000*

724 (left) Classically Regency; the rosewood is profusely inlaid with brass decoration and the centre column terminates in a flat base supported on four scrolled feet carved with leaf decoration.
c.1820   *£2,000 — £2,750*

725 (right) The top is relatively simple but the spiral column with heavy foliage decoration sits on a heavy circular gadrooned base supported by heavy Thomas Hope-type paws.

c.1830   *£900 — £1,400*

726 (left) A simpler variant of the previous example and on the type of rectangular base with hollowed-out sides that one associates with this period.

c.1835   *£600 — £800*

727 (right) Straight out of W. Smee and Sons' 1850 Catalogue and C. and R. Light's for 1881. It was a popular and long-lasting design. A good example of the Victorian obsession with curves commented on elsewhere. A superb piece of decoration.

1850s plain top £1,000 — £1,500
good marquetry top
£2,500 — £3,500

TABLES — dining, refectory

Oak tables of the seventeenth century, with their rectangular boarded tops, are now generically referred to by their Victorian title of refectory tables. They evolved from trestle-supported boards, and developed into more sophisticated bulbous-legged tables and draw tables (tables with second leaves under, which pulled out to extend the table) in the sixteenth and seventeenth centuries. These bulbous-legged tables became more refined as the seventeenth century wore on and from about 1650 onwards more types of table became available, starting with the gateleg.

There are two schools of thought about the smaller type one commonly sees today. The first says that they were side tables, hence the decoration on the frieze is seen on one side only. The second suggests that they were on a raised dais with the decoration and the V.I.Ps who dined at the table facing those at lower tables. When one thinks back to the wainscot chair section and the throne concept, the second line of thinking rings true. For practical entertaining purposes tables less than 2ft.6ins. wide should be avoided as they break up even the smallest dinner party.

Refectory tables sometimes acquire new tops and it is essential to check for signs of age on each, though new end cleats are perfectly acceptable. The bases should be slightly stained or a little rotted, where damp and stone floors have taken their toll. Refectory tables have been widely faked and reproduced.

The original gateleg tables were fairly crude and simple, with column turning of the legs. Later ones developed more elaborate and decorative turning, including the stretchers. The gateleg form continued to be used with variation, through the eighteenth and nineteenth centuries, incorporating the stylistic features of the oak, walnut, mahogany and other periods. Early oak gateleg tables had the top held on by wooden pegs, but in later tables the top is screwed on from underneath.

The disadvantage of the gateleg is that its legs tend to be in the way of those seated at it and in the Georgian period a popular table was the D-end, connected by essentially one or more drop-flap tables which could be used to lengthen it. This, however, had the same disadvantage as the gateleg table, in that there were still a lot of legs to avoid and so the centre pedestal table, with one or more pedestals, came into being. These pedestal dining tables have remained popular ever since, for they can accommodate varying numbers of people without legs getting in the way.

728 Refectory tables are now really rather a rich man's affair, which is not surprising if you look at this example, which is mid-seventeenth century with elaborately carved bulbous legs and massive construction, needing the right type of room to set it off. It has a good old-looking top. As always there should be plenty of patination — caused by greasy fingers — on the underside stopping sharply where the frame meets the top. Stretchers open to doubt because they should come flush with legs, not be inset as here.

c.1620

8 seater
Right £12,000 — £15,000
Wrong £2,500 — £3,500
New £1,500 — £2,000

729 A good 9ft. oak example with six-column cannon (or sometimes gun barrel) turnings to the legs. Carving of lunettes along the frieze. The stretchers look a trifle thin compared with other examples shown. The fewer planks used to make up the top of a refectory table, the better. If in walnut with a good colour, add about £3,000.

c.1640   *10 seater £8,000 — £10,000*

730 The vase-shaped turning suggests a date in the very early eighteenth century. Just under 6ft long, this is a very pretty little oak table in which you can see the age on the stretchers, a mixture of rot and wear showing an irregular effect, not the smooth simulated wear of the fake.

c.1720   *£3,500 — £4,500*

731 Not really a refectory table at all — it is a farm table of a type which has become very popular for country kitchens and dining rooms, but its provenance is clear from the previous illustrations. These tables were made in oak, elm, pine and country woods throughout the eighteenth and into the nineteenth centuries until the turned leg was imposed on them. When buying, do make sure that your favourite dining chair will allow you to sit at the table as the frieze is sometimes too low. Price will be increased by fruitwood with a good glowing colour, hence the wide price range.

Late 18th century   *£1,400 — £1,800*

TABLES — dining, early gateleg

Examples exist from the early part of the seventeenth century but they did not come into general use until the middle of the century, when dining at small tables became common, not only in the homes of the middle classes, but even the large houses.

The value of a gateleg today is greatly influenced by the number of people it can seat; the quality of the turnings and the type of wood being the other factors. To seat a large number of people, the middle section has to be wide as well as long, as the height of the table limits the drop of the flaps. Apart from new tops, these tables sometimes suffer damage to the ends of the flaps and have to be retipped. This used to be unacceptable to purists but now only affects the price very marginally.

Square gateleg tables also exist, but since they are harder to sell the prices are lower.

732 An early oak gateleg table with good patination. Note the very thick top and the fact that all the underneath members (except the top of the gates which have to fit flush) are turned with a superb bold extended bobbin and rim. Probably a ten seater. Walnut more valuable.

c.1650
price for oak £12,000 — £15,000

733 This table shows two gates to each side, which is an attractive method of supporting large flaps. The arrangement of two centre stretchers giving support for the four legs is a good feature, as is the fact that all the members are spirally turned with thick bold turnings. Has the left-hand flap been cut down? -the leg looks too near the edge, see previous example. Could have had rectangular flaps cut to the more popular oval shap. The price is based on the assumption that the flap has not been cut and that the table is an eight seater.

1670-1680   £9,000 — £12,000
wrong top £3,000 — £4,000

734 Again double gates and the turning all over and of good quality, but the table is smaller and does not have the style of the previous example.

Late 17th century £3,000 — £4,000

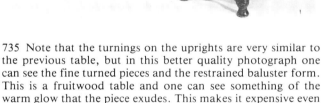

735 Note that the turnings on the uprights are very similar to the previous table, but in this better quality photograph one can see the fine turned pieces and the restrained baluster form. This is a fruitwood table and one can see something of the warm glow that the piece exudes. This makes it expensive even though single gate and seating six.

Late 17th century   *£3,000 — £4,000*

736 The type of table one sees regularly. The classic early eighteenth century single gateleg table in elm. Despite the number of legs, immensely useful as it occupies so little space when not in use.

c.1720   *8 seater £3,000 — £4,000*

737 A simple four seater gateleg table with quite good if uninspired turnings. Too many planks make up the top and too many nail holes in the middle section, which should in any event be pegged. Could the top be newly made out of old floor boards? Despite this, quite a pleasant table. Note the circular white marks on the underside of the far flap where the leg has scraped it. One of the signs that the top could be original.

c.1730   *£1,200 — £1,600*

Just as the stretchers disappeared from chairs in the early part of the eighteenth century, so mahogany dining tables rid themselves of stretchers at much the same time. Perhaps it was the strength of mahogany or simply the desire to refine. Whatever the reason, some superb tables emerged. Good quality examples are perhaps currently undervalued.

742 (left) With gently curved cabrioles, which like the previous example have a simple C scroll at the top, this table could be walnut period but is in fact mahogany. The moulding is slightly unusual with only a very shallow depression and a very wide flat curve almost like a Victorian slope. Rectangular flaps are not as popular as oval.

c.1750   *£2,000 — £3,000*

743 (below, centre) The more simple pad foot version on a straight leg of tapering circular section which, in comparison with 741, gives the unfortunate impression that the weight of the flap is proving exhausting. Nevertheless, very English in concept and clearly related to its country cousin in oak (744).

c.1750s   *4 seater £1,500 — £2,000*
         6 seater £4,000 — £5,000
         8 seater £7,000 — £9,000

744 (below, bottom) Quite literally the oak version of 743. Interesting to see the heavy structure beneath as though the maker would have preferred the old oak method.

c.1760   *8 seater £2,500 — £3,500*

738 (opposite page, top left) Elegant use of the *pied-de-biche* foot from which the cabriole originated, decorated with the ram's head. The cabriole is beautifully executed. The top pieces, each of one plank, are without warp or twist. The rule joints are in immaculate condition. Heavy Cuban mahogany at its best.

1735-1740   *8 seater £15,000 — £20,000*

739 (opposite page, centre left) Another example with *pied-de-biche* foot and the little projection behind it, but with a simple decoration on the knee and a small scroll either side. The top has the same thumb-nail mould but each flap is made up of two planks. All features which, together with smaller size, reduce the price.

c.1740   *6 seater £4,000 — £6,000*
        8 seater £7,000 — £9,000

740 (opposite page, centre right) Conventional cabrioles with ball-and-claw again. Well executed but looking almost clumsy against 738. In fact by itself an elegant table. A walnut style carried on into mahogany.

1730-1740   *£4,000 — £5,000*

741 (opposite page, bottom) Without the panache of 738, but undeniably elegant in dark, almost figureless Cuban or Spanish mahogany. These pieces are enduringly made and, when this book was first written in 1978, were undervalued, but the price has since doubled. Shown both closed and open to make the point that such a table fulfils the dual purpose of elegant side table and comfortable dining table for four to six people. Appears to have glorious patination.

1740-1750   *6 seater £5,000 — £7,000*
        8 seater £12,000 — £15,000

When one considers the revolution in design of chairs associated with the name of Chippendale, it is amazing that he never mentioned dining tables in his trade catalogues. His firm made gatelegs with D-ends among other complicated tables discussed in the next section but, perhaps justifiably, his name must be linked with the low point of eighteenth century dining table design.

745 (left) A small rectangular mahogany table with standard pad feet. A more modest example of the product in mahogany. Made well into the Chippendale period and so included here.

c.1760   *£700 — £900*

746 (right) Shows a good quality example of a large double-gateleg mahogany table with moulded square section legs. Although somewhat severe by earlier standards, it is still a fine piece of dark Cuban wood. Colour very important.

c.1765   *8 seater £6,000 — £8,000*

747 What is known as a 'wakes' table due to its long thin shape on which, by legend, the coffin was rested before the funeral service and on which, after the interment, the festivities took place. As our social customs no longer work in this manner, it is perhaps odd that they are hugely reproduced and faked. This example shows the figure in the rich dark wood.

c.1770   *8-10 seater £6,000 — £9,000*

748 (below) A much simpler, straightforward George III square-leg rectangular table. It looks very similar to the centre-gateleg table in the gateleg and two D-ends combination, see next section. It is interesting that this design, with the ends just slightly rounded, was still available from W. Smee & Sons in 1850.

1800-1820   *£600 — £800*

There were, however, some interesting country pieces which can be very attractive and two variations are shown below.

749 A faithful country copy in burr elm which, as can be seen in 750, can, with good patination, be almost as fine as any wood. Small, so not expensive.

c.1760   *Four seater as shown £1,200 — £1,600*
However, if eight seater and glorious colour £8,000 — £10,000

750 A small square single flap dining table in solid burr elm with very fine patination and superb grain. Top quality veneers were cut from such wood.

c.1765   *£1,200 — £1,600*

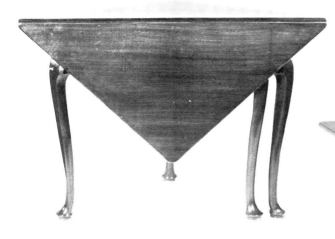

751 (above) Slightly out of the mainstream, a corner or, in American, handkerchief table which opens up to form a square. They are rather unbalanced if the wood is heavy because of the weight of the front flap and, perhaps because of this, are not popular unless a lot smaller than this one.

c.1740   *£3,000 — £4,000*

752 (right) A small George III mahogany spider-leg table, suitable for less important meals like breakfast. They can be extremely elegant and because of this were reproduced extensively in Edwardian times and some can now look convincingly old.

c.1760   *£2,000 — £3,000*

TABLES — dining, Georgian extending

753 Shows two half-circular tables joined together. The legs are reeded overall and fluted for the top one-third, ending in well-shaped blocks. The two inner legs on each half move into the centre to support additional leaves when required. The price will depend on the number that can be seated.

c.1780   Assuming 8 seater with extra leaf £8,000 — £10,000

754 (below) Not as good as the previous example and in need of repolishing. Here the four legs of the D-ends are fixed but the single centre leaf is easily supported by them.

c.1770   In good condition £3,000 — £4,500

755 (below) More ingenious. The D-ends have between them a rectangular gateleg table which can be closed or progressively opened to provide two D-end tables, which either can be separately set against a wall or used together to make an oval table and, at the same time, a gateleg table. With the two flaps down a slightly longer oval table can be made, which in turn can be progressively increased to the full width shown. A good quality piece with stringing lines and double gates to the drop-leaf table.

c.1780   If with good colour £8,000 — £10,000

Plate 97. The Regency date for this piece comes from the frieze which was not used until the very end of the 18th century. This type of table works on a scissor action by which two series of supports running at right angles to one another expand as required to accommodate the extra leaves. The legs, though high swept as was the fashion, show no sign of what used to be the dreaded 'Regency knee' (see figure 771) but which is now quite acceptable.

This mahogany is known as 'plum pudding'. The two centre leaves have not been used much so they have the very dark colour typical of this wood. The ends show the typical flecks.

When fully extended this 'model' looks unbalanced and is sometimes less firm than is desirable. Hence it does not always excite the same degree of enthusiasm as other forms of pedestal tables.

Plate 98. The Georgians who lived in relatively small rooms were keen on the gateleg table which takes up so little space when not in use. Why the Victorians virtually abandoned such a useful idea is odd. A late example, made at any time between 1800 and 1840, this has Regency reeding on the legs and edges. The double gate is a good design, giving firmness and a sense of balance. At 6ft. long it would seat a comfortable six or intimate eight.

This piece is of good quality; the decoration is restrained and well balanced. The cotton reel top to the legs and the gentle terminating of the reeding below are nice touches. It was a good idea to set in the middle legs. The mahogany has a dark burr, usually a sign of quality, and it has some colour. A pleasant object.

Plate 99. A Jupes circular table, c.1830, named after the inventor. It can be used either as a small table or, as shown in the photograph, made larger by the insertion of eight pieces of wood pointed at one end for which space is created by an ingenious mechanism. Used as a dining table, a comfortable four seater converts to a generous eight. The baluster centre support is well turned and restrained, as is the conventional arrangement of the paws.

This has been used in the smaller size over a long period for the eight inserts are noticeably darker – in fact they produce a decorative effect. A deservedly popular design.

£20,000 – £30,000

Plate 100. A typical flamboyant rosewood table of the 1820s. The consecutive sheets of veneer have been carefully arranged to produce a dramatic effect. The scroll feet are quite well detailed and their gilding gives the piece a touch of quality. The work on the Holland piece in Plate 101 is much more subtle.

Repolishing, probably in the last few years, has given the grain a loud dramatic effect — compare with the rosewood Carlton House table in Plate 121 — but the cracking across the top where the boards meet will diminish the value.

Plate 101 A Victorian walnut table, c.1850, by Holland and Son. The top has marquetry foliage and flowers surrounded by segments of walnut, olive wood and mulberry (the dark one on the outside). Round the edge there is a kingwood cross-banding finished off with well carved gadrooning

The base is equally exotic; a spitting serpent twists round a spiral stem decorated in black and gold, the feet with eagle claw feet and ball

The purist may shudder and claim that the feet look as though something too heavy had been put on top, but rude things were said about the neo-classical a few years ago. Perhaps Victorian rococo of this quality is due for reassessment

About £15,000

Plate 102. An elegant luxuriously fitted burr ash library table, c.1815. The crossbanding is in calamander wood and the black stringing line is ebony, an arrangement reflected in the elegant arrangement of the base, which is fitted with brass vitruvian scrolls between the gilt brass feet, well balanced with scroll-work. The gilt brass moulded border is of acorns and oak leaves. A good example of the fashion for British woods (forgetting the calamander).

The ash has faded down well but the black knots remain and work well with the ebony. From the photograph it appears that the gilt has largely gone from the brass but again this contributes to the pleasing harmony of soft tones that add greatly to the charm of this fine piece.

311

Plate 103. A decorative Pembroke table from the 1790s with the usual ovals of satinwood. The simulated flutes are a good idea and give the piece a lift. Compare the tapered legs with those in figures 808 and 809. Perhaps this one has slightly thick tops; the blocks at the bottom are not an exciting feature.

The mahogany has gone down to a lovely golden colour and the satinwood flutes echo the shades so that it has an attractive colour. The escutcheon keyhole must surely have been added. A thread key guard, as on the examples in black and white, would be appropriate.

Plate 104. Again the neo-classical taste finds expression in this c.1800 Pembroke table made in satinwood and banded in burr ash. The squat square uncompromising lines of this piece are typical, only the top fails to conform.

This photograph looks as if it has an extra degree of red or else the piece has been cleaned and curiously repolished. Note that by this date the wheels on the castors are losing the width which gives the earlier examples such character

756 A large table which shows the back legs of the D-ends moved out to their support positions when opened. The reeded legs are of late Georgian design and the reeding round the end is typical. A good, solid table.

c.1810   *£8,000 — £10,000*

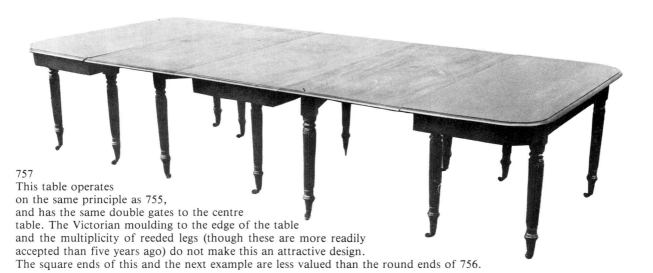

757
This table operates
on the same principle as 755,
and has the same double gates to the centre
table. The Victorian moulding to the edge of the table
and the multiplicity of reeded legs (though these are more readily
accepted than five years ago) do not make this an attractive design.
The square ends of this and the next example are less valued than the round ends of 756.

c.1820s   *£6,000 — £7,000*

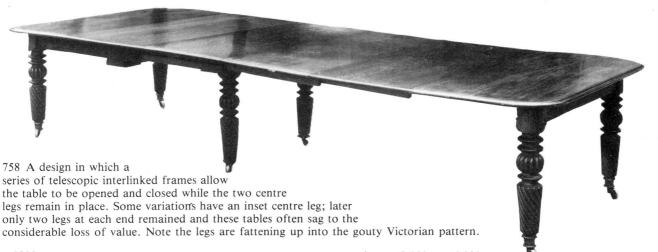

758 A design in which a
series of telescopic interlinked frames allow
the table to be opened and closed while the two centre
legs remain in place. Some variations have an inset centre leg; later
only two legs at each end remained and these tables often sag to the
considerable loss of value. Note the legs are fattening up into the gouty Victorian pattern.

c.1830   *very large £5,000 — £6,000*
                                      6 seater £1,200 — £1,800

The limitations of both gateleg and D-end tables are overcome to a large extent by the multi-pedestal dining table which made its appearance in the later Georgian period. The result is that one rarely sees a fake double D-end table but plenty of wrong pedestal tables. What else does one do with heavy tripod tables or broken breakfast tables? The only real snag is the favourable leverage which a heavy leaner can exert on the edge when determined to spring the join of pedestal and table top centrally; but then, in one's own polite circle, no one puts his elbows on the table, do they?

Extra leaves may not have been used a great deal, so their colour may be darker. Check that the side moulding matches and that there are no new square pieces let in below near the edges where the hinges used to be when it was a gateleg table, or indeed any other unaccountable screw holes or glue blocks.

759 (above) A two pedestal table with column supports and curving legs having a dark inlaid stringing line. The centre leaf is supported by strong metal catches. Note that the tripods are not evenly spaced so that when the flap is taken out they can come together without clashing.

c.1790   £15,000   £20,000

760 Similar to the first example but more the type traditionally found with quatrepod bases. Reeding on the feet and the edges of the table suggests the date. An elegant table in a fine dark mahogany, vastly reproduced often with aestheti-cally disastrous results.

c.1790   £14,000 — £18,000

761 (left) An interesting cross-breed between a pedestal type table and a D-end using a gateleg central section for extension. The overall effect is not very coherent.

c.1780   £9,000 — £12,000

762 (right) A table which succeeds in supporting three leaves between its ends. Three high curving legs typical of the period, in which the 'knee' at the top of the curve is starting to appear.

c.1800-1810   £9,000 — £12,000

763 (right) An example with Regency 'knee' developing that is almost a spur on the legs and spirally reeded columns. The table edges are also reeded.

c.1820   *£9,000 — £12,000*

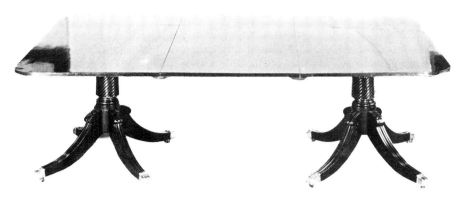

764 (left) The legs have been curled into scrolls that are almost Victorian, but the effect is light and elegant.

c.1830   *£6,000   £8,000*

765 (below) This table is solidly William IV, showing the heavy influence of 'classical' design promoted by Thomas Hope and with gadrooned edges as well as leaf carving. It has been fitted with modern multi-directional ball castors for ease of transit.

c.1830   *£7,000   £10,000*

766 (right) A much-seen design of its period, with enormous paw feet à la Thomas Hope combined with octagonal pumpkin-like centre columns.

1830-1840
£7,000 — £9,000

767 A fine quality elegant mahogany table with a broad band of satinwood near the edge. The turned centre column support with its small rounded section is supported on four elegant curved legs which have ebony stringing lines on top and sides to emphasise their clean lines.

c.1800 £8,000 — £10,000

But assume faded, richly grained top with more cross banding
£11,000 — £15,000

Fashion at the end of the eighteenth century moved away from the long table, with its implications of seniority, towards the round table where such distinctions were less marked. In addition the use of a separate small comfortable room (the breakfast room) for family meals or intimate dinner parties, led to a requirement for a six/eight seater.

Here, and on the following pages, we show two types. Firstly, the simple central pillar with four legs discussed here. Secondly, the newly introduced type with a platform which in turn divides into two. Firstly, those with a central column — the standard Regency type which continues with the platform near the ground. Thousands were made and these appear in the next section. Secondly, the multiple legs which came into favour in the 1850s and, as small loo tables, were prolific from that date until almost the end of the century, and are discussed in the section on Victorian pedestal tables.

768 (right) A simpler circular mahogany example with reeded edges to the table and moulded edges to the legs which are becoming higher, and the first hint of 'Regency knee'.

c.1805 6 seater £4,000 — £6,000
8 seater £7,000 — £9,000

769 (left) A high quality rectangular rosewood breakfast table cross-banded in amboyna with curious half rounds to the corners (compare the shape of the Sheraton chest No. 377). The legs are superb: the high stepping, 'Regency knee' is there but the design makes it a virtue not a disease. White edges to the legs serve to highlight the superb effect.

c.1810 6 seater £7,000 — £10,000

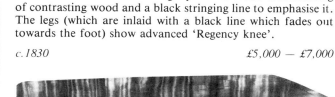

770 A circular table in mahogany with a broad crossbanding of contrasting wood and a black stringing line to emphasise it. The legs (which are inlaid with a black line which fades out towards the foot) show advanced 'Regency knee'.

c.1830   *£5,000 — £7,000*

771 (above) A terminal case of 'Regency knee'. Heavy reeding and circular decoration serve to make it the highlight of an otherwise simple, if slightly heavy, but very useful mahogany breakfast table.

c.1830   *£3,500 — £5,000*

772 (left) The platform design is seen here in Georgian form. The legs have a moulded edge and the high knee referred to earlier and the four supports are plainly turned. (Look at the large space between the legs, on the empty platform. The Victorians would *have* to put a large finial in the middle!) The top is cross-banded, the platform has stringing lines. It is all very restrained.

c.1800   *6 seater £1,400 — £1,600*
                                   8 seater £3,500 — £4,500

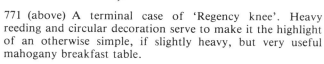

773 (above) Platform and pedestal combine to form a peculiarly Regency type table. Brass inlay on the top, platform and pedestal combine well with the rosewood veneer. More showy but still not obsessively decorative.

c.1810   *£6,000 — £8,000*

774 The same basic design but the pillar has been shaped and more brass applied in what seems an attempt at a more showy quality. Not entirely successful.

c.1820   *£5,000 — £6,000*

The fashion for round tables which could be used as dining tables, loo (a game which enjoyed much popularity well on into the nineteenth century) tables or occasional tables increased considerably in the first years of the nineteenth century. One readily identifiable type of table which was made between about 1820 and 1880 was the triangular base with hollowed sides, more correctly a hyperboloid base. The examples in this section are of this type and make an interesting gradation of quality.

775 (above) A superb example in rosewood with inlay on the top. D-moulding round the top and on the three-sided column, all in brass as well as other fine decoration. The winged feet are typical for the period. Really fine articles like this are very difficult to value.

c.1820   £20,000 — £25,000

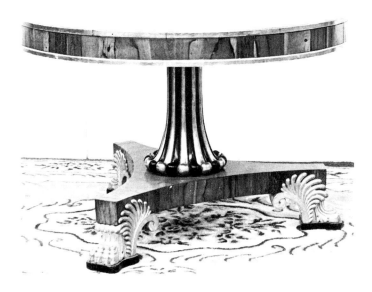

776 (above) A bold rosewood Regency example in which the alternating black and gilt rounded sections are impressive as are the feet with their 'lobed spurs' looking like some Grecian helmet decoration. A pity the bold inspiration ran out when the top was being designed.

c.1825   £20,000 — £25,000

777 (left) A fine, rich pedestal table very similar to a design in Brown's *Rudiments,* 1822. This heavy form of pedestal has been well executed so that it fits in well with the base. Brass inlay and well matched flame flecked mahogany veneers. Only the gadrooning is a trifle heavy.

c.1825   £7,000 — £9,000

778 A rosewood example in which the decoration is centred on the curved petal formation of the base. The stem is thickening and the 'hairy feet' persist.

c.1835   *Because rosewood £3,500 — £4,500*

779 More great 'hairy feet' and a complicated parquetry top, but the octagonal stem has only a disappointing series of half round decoration. Interesting to note that in 1881 C. & R Light were still offering this basic type.

c.1825   *£6,000 — £8,000*

780 (left) The simple carved buns and the plain platform are not exciting. However, the carved decoration to the round base and the high quality top with clever use of heartwood and sapwood rosewood makes it a good table.

c.1830   *£1,800 — £2,500*

781 The use of maplewood and contrasting ebonised moulding and feet, together with faceted sides to the three pillar stem, lift this form from being a very simple table. See next example.

c.1830   *£2,500 — £3,500*

782 (left) It would be interesting to know just how many of these simple tables were made, probably thousands. This is the cheapest type with round flat buns and no ornamentation. Next in the range would be the carved buns, more expensive would be scrolls and on up to hairy feet. This is mahogany; rosewood would be a little extra. Good value as a first dining table for a new family.

c.1835   *6/8 seater mahogany £1,000 — £1,500*

As might be expected the range of pedestal tables was large and the following selection shows the range. Value is affected by decorative potential as well as quality of workmanship.

783 Superb quality in exotic woods, these 'saloon tables' were very much in the grand manner. They were made by firms like Holland & Sons and advertised in Warings catalogue, 1862. When stamped or provenance can be established the value can be appropriately high.

c.1870   *£35,000+*

784 Highly flamboyant in yew wood of the type associated with Muckross Abbey School in Ireland. The pedestal which is not shown is bulbous and covered in bits and pieces of marquetry.

c.1860   *£7,000 — £9,000*

785 Again a bulbous stem, not visible, but this time in walnut with a most attractive walnut top with subtle marquetry inset round the sides and on top.

c.1860   *£3,000 — £4,000*

786 The heavily carved scroll feet, which are set at this angle, but above all the bulbous turning of the mahogany pedestal, all suggest the date when this form was popular. Note that if a marquetry top in exotic woods is by a known maker and invoices, etc. are available, then the price can go up considerably.

c.1850s   *£1,800 — £3,000*

787 (left) Although this type of outward curving foot and the straight three-sided column were first used around the early 1830s, the typical Victorian marquetry top suggests a later date. Smee shows almost this type of foot in 1850. Note the crudeness of the marquetry compared with 785, both now being reproduced with an unabashed newness of finish.

c.1840

£2,000 — £3,000

788 (above) More marquetry of good quality. Note the height of the knee on the cabrioles. This example in C. & R. Light's Catalogue of 1881 shows this characteristic. The faceted pedestal is also found in some later furniture.

c.1870

£2,500 — £3,500

789 The four pedestal straight leg type which was popular from the 1870s onwards. It first came in about 1850s when needless to say the entire structure was curved. Plenty of inlay in ivory with turned centre finial.

c.1870

If no ivory inlay £1,000 — £1,500
8 seater, no ivory £2,500 — £3,500

790 An altogether heavier and coarser design. The finial is gadrooned and the supports are similarly shaped. Along the lines of C. & R. Light.

c.1880

4 seater £800 — £1,200
8 seater £1,500 — £2,000

Nests of tables are illustrated by Sheraton in his *Cabinet Directory* of 1803 and have been much reproduced since then. They were described as 'quartetto' tables and, while Sheraton envisaged them as useful for needlework, George Smith in his *Household Furniture* of 1808 saw them in their more modernly accepted role — for refreshments.

792 (right) A rosewood set with the collared embellishment shown by Sheraton in his design. The feet are curved over in ogee form.

c.1810
£5,000 — £6,000

791 An unusual design similar to a set illustrated by Edwards as coming from Leighton Hall, Lancashire, a house owned by Robert Gillow. It has satinwood and walnut veneer on the table tops and a chequer board inlaid on the smallest table. The nicely-turned legs are ebonised and have three tiers of stretchers. The smallest table also has a scooped tray between the bottom stretchers, perhaps for games pieces.

c.1810   *Forgetting the provenance*
                              £4,500 — £5,500

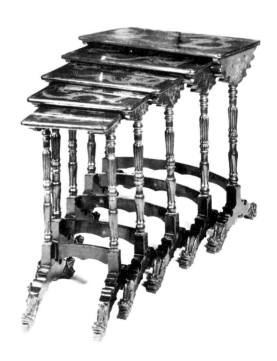

793 A papier mâche set with varied top decoration including an inlaid and painted landscape as well as a chequer board.

c.1850
£2,250 — £2,750

794 (right) A 'quintetto', with dragons decorating the japanned top surfaces and carved heads on the feet. The uprights are turned and reeded but the stretchers are heavy.

c.1830
£2,500 — £3,000

795 A Georgian mahogany night table of serpentine front with a good shaped tray top with hand holes for carrying.

1750-1770   *£1,750*   *£2,250*

In the second half of the eighteenth century the night table was of quite sophisticated design and was included in Chippendale, Ince and Mayhew, and Sheraton's repertoire. Variously disguised as a small chest of drawers or in a more distinct tray-top form, these pieces display considerable ingenuity of craftsmanship. Later on the chest form was still used though the more obvious pot holder also made its appearance. As they are now technically obsolete, they have been adapted to a variety of modern uses according to the shape — drink cupboards, and hi-fi units for instance. If this has been done intelligently and the visible surfaces (when closed) have not been damaged, the value is enhanced rather than diminished — an almost unique situation in the antique furniture world.

796 A mahogany night table with matched figured veneers. Very typical of the type which have split front legs to give support when the lower half is pulled forward for use

1760-1780   *£1,000*   *£1,500*

797 A good quality mahogany night table with tambour shutter which slides horizontally across the front, and tray top with handles fretted into the rim. The tambour shutter, when opened, slides round the inside edge of the cupboard space. The pot holding drawer front has been simulated to look like two cock-beaded and veneered drawers. Often these have been fitted with linings and made to work.

1780-1800   *£1,000*   *£1,500*

798 A simple night table with fretted handles, cupboard and crossed flat stretcher with rimmed pot platform. A good construction

1760   *£700*   *£1,000*

799 A step ladder type pot holder of Sheraton design in mahogany with ebony inlaid stringing lines. Adapts well to mini cellar.

1810-1830   *£2,000 — £3,000*

Novelty gatelegs might be a better title for these small side tables which sometimes have slightly unusual methods of supporting the flaps, shaping of the legs, or are just good quality. Quite apart from being attractive, these little tables are very useful as they can be folded and put away when not in use. For this reason they command a good price, especially when that glorious colour, which age and polishing (i.e. patination) can confer, is present.

800 First a fruitwood example. It has a main turned support at each end, showing baluster and bobbin forms, joined usually by a wide stretcher, which in this case is divided into two square sections for lightness of appearance. There is a wide sledge-shaped foot at each end for stability. The gates which open to support the flaps are flat with a fretted lower stretcher.

Late 17th century   *£1,800 — £2,500*

801 In this oak example the main columns are flat and fretted. There is a wider foot than in the previous example and again, two flatter stretchers. The flat gates are shaped to echo the end supports.

Late 17th century   *£2,000 — £3,000*

802 (left) A charming oak single flap table, almost only a stand, in which the same constructional system is used but all uprights are turned with baluster forms.

Third quarter 17th century
£2,000 — £3,000

803 (right) A really rare and charming ash 'coaching' example in which the gates are on a pivot so that the whole top can be folded vertically. It was probably taken in a coach for use on picnic stops.

c.1680   *£2,500 — £3,000*

805 A conventional but charming walnut table with carefully graded bobbin turning and a small thick rectangular top.

c.1660   *£1,500 — £2,000*

804 Small occasional gateleg with the typical turning of the period. The long square sections to the legs give the piece height. The small turned stretcher is a nice touch.

c.1690   *£1,200 — £1,600*

806 A pretty little bobbin turned fruitwood example with the additionally attractive feature of bobbin stretchers as well. The drawer is a long one and is supported underneath by a central stretcher which runs the length of the carcase.

Late 17th century   *£1,200 — £1,800*

807 A simple version of 800, though the turning is not as good. The base is a single piece and it is generally more wormy but it makes an interesting comparison.

Late 17th century   *£800 — £1,200*

TABLES — Pembroke

Named after the Countess of Pembroke, said to have been the first to order one. Pembroke tables appeared about 1750 but really became popular around 1780. There are therefore some rare museum quality Pembroke tables in the Chippendale styles. They were considered to be a small useful table, with hinged wooden brackets to support the flaps, a drawer at one end and a mock drawer at the other, for symmetry. Used for many purposes, including writing, they were largely superseded by the pedestal table at the end of the eighteenth century. The Edwardians admired them and one must be watchful for period examples which they improved by adding marquetry or painting.

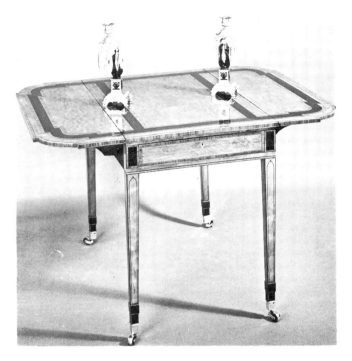

808 (above) A fine example in satinwood — considered the top of the scale for Pembroke table-building — with a broad inlaid band of purplewood and further crossbanding in kingwood. The shape of the flaps corresponds closely with that advocated by Sheraton c.1794. The square section tapering solid satinwood legs have collars at the ends and are mounted on brass castors.

c.1795   £20,000 +

809 (above) In satinwood with serpentine shaped flaps which, like the drawers, are cross-banded in kingwood. The inlaid shell on the top is generous in size, superb quality is emphasised by the ebonised edges and the gently curved apron below the drawer which compliments the shape of the flaps. Note the width of the original castors.

c.1790   £10,000 — £14,000

810 (right) Made in mahogany with the less popular turned and reeded legs, it is none the less very good quality. Note that the figured veneers on the flaps fan out to the edges to match the inlaid decoration. The flaps look even better down.

c.1795   £6,500 — £8,000

811 Further down the quality scale, but still very desirable with its broad satinwood inlay and white wood edging. The front is bowed and the top of the legs inlaid with a diamond pattern.

c.1795   £4,500 – £5,500

812 Well-chosen veneers with a black stringing line and cross-banded ends. A well-made table.

c.1795   £1,500 – £2,000

813 and 814 Two variations of the plain solid mahogany variety which continued to be made well into the nineteenth century — 'honest brown mahogany'. The one on the left has Chippendale moulded legs and a small satinwood stringing line. On the right the most simple type.

813: Left. c.1790   £800 – £1,000
814: Right. c.1800   £600 – £800

Architects' tables were large and solid; others were of lighter construction and designed to fit in with furnishings in the fine reception rooms. The best are to be counted among the most elegant furniture. Even the inelegant are loved — collectors love pieces that do things.

816 A much more simple reading table with adjustment by a series of notches, but none the less an elegant piece in the same rococo style as the first example. It has a good deep patination and one should not underestimate the desirability of metal fittings even when as simple as the band round the top of an elegant dark tripod. The band is, of course, part of the vertical adjustment fittings.

c.1760   *£3,000 — £4,000*

815 A superb Chippendale example of a mahogany reading table with elegant curved supports and well carved tripod legs. The small repetitive decorative design sets off the bottom edge of the table. It is almost identical to, if not the pair of, one in the Victoria and Albert Museum and as provenance or comparability are important, especially in high quality pieces, the price is substantial.

c.1760   *£8,000 — £12,000*

817 (left) The well-shaped feet and solid gun barrel turning suggest the date. Two slides either side provide space for glasses, spectacles, etc. The adjustable top, controlled from beneath for height, folds down to make a rectangular leather topped tripod table.

c.1770   *£2,500 — £3,500*

818 Again, elegance is the keynote of this superb piece which has two facing adjustable stands and folds down into a tripod table. The square box-like projection has two drawers, inlaid at the edges, which held rosin and hence the piece must have been a double music stand. The candlesticks are adjustable at three points. It is made in satinwood and cross-banded in a darker wood and again in rosewood at the edges. It has a lovely mellow colour and original patination.

c.1790   *£5,000 — £7,000*

Plate 105. This is one of two such tables at the historic Great Tew Park sale in May 1987, when Bullock and Morant became household names. The carving in walnut is wonderful; the bone structure at the top of the leg, for example, the detailing of the feathers on the wings. The girls have lost the Rowlandson-like features and are slimmer than Hope suggested and look a great deal better for it. The wings too are more finished. As with earlier published designs the craftsman has followed the published ideas but given them his own personal interpretation. A similar marble top cost 'at least' £550 in 1847. A view of home, portrait medallions and a super border of flowers and vegetables was probably made by Michaelangelo Barberi.

Morant has here created a superb sculptured piece of outstanding quality which at the Great Tew Park sale (1987) cost £82,500.

c.1841

Plate 106. Hope's design. Plate XXXIII.

Plate 107. A rosewood table with marble top, c.1830. The central picture of an antique temple with radiating segments of Spanish brocatello marble makes an excellent table. The carving is fine and the design good, but against the Morant example it pales.

£8,800 in 1988

Plate 108. A good looking rosewood sofa table from perhaps the first year of the 19th century, yet retaining the restraint of the early Georgian period. The use of satinwood as banding on the top, as crossbanding on the drawers (banding becomes crossbanding when it is on the edge, very thin banding is called stringing) and as decoration on the legs works well. The pedestals are the right thickness and the banding on the top just the right width. A fine piece.

Plate 109. Made at about the same time but later in feeling, this is a more stylish piece than the last example though interestingly they made about the same money on the day they sold.

The central chess board reverses to fit the rest of the top and the interior is fitted for backgammon; thus the drawers are dummy. The ends are a trifle thick and lack of a break where they spread is not in practice as elegant as it probably looked on the design sketch. The edges of the top are shaped to give a more interesting appearance when down.

Plate 110. A Regency maplewood and ebonised (as opposed to ebony) sofa table. The design looks thin; there is not enough body in the turned support and the large area of unrelieved black 'paint' is unfortunate. The applicated brass motifs do little for the piece.

Strong light has bleached out the right-hand edge of the flap, ebonising and all, and as always slight damage on the inside of the legs shows up against the black. Not a favoured model.
c.1815

Plate 111. No doubt about the date of this ormolu mounted and brass inlaid (the difference is that ormolu is gilded bronze which has a tin content which is not necessarily present in brass) rosewood sofa/games table. Even by neo-classical standards the hairy paw feet are oversized. The effect is heightened by build-up to the large supports. The supports that hold the end horizontal are inlaid with ormolu and become a decorative feature, one often associated with the later good quality examples.
c.1825

Plate 112. Not to everyone's taste, perhaps, but a carved rosewood centre table with style, accompanied by the self-restraint and sense of form that one might hope for from the 1830s.

The double ties of curved legs hold the marble top successfully and the tall, gracious finial fills the space well. The carver has supplemented the design, not tried to take it over.

Time has been good to this piece; the rosewood on the gadroon has faded to a glorious gold that harmonises with the marble and contrasts with the dark shades between. Rococo at its best and undervalued.

£5,000 — £7,000

Plate 113. A decade earlier than the previous example and showing a neo-classical approach to supporting a heavy marble top. The form, hairy feet, platform and huge centre pillar are typical, the decoration is well carved but not especially interesting. The marble is interesing but easily replaceable. One assumes the strong influence of the interior decoration market in the high price realised.

£31,000 in 1988

820 (right) A good design for a table which can be made into a reading table. The front drawer is, of course, false, as are the ones on the opposite sides, hence the piece qualifies for a centre table. The flexibility enhances the value. The fact that it is in partridge wood adds considerably to the interest, since, although the little piece is solid and heavy, it has specks of brown and dark red which, being mellowed, will give it a good tone.

c. 1790

£2,000 — £3,000

819 A well-made artist's table (perhaps strictly not quite big or solid enough for an architect's) with drawer under. The top comes down to make a not inelegant quatrepod. The ivory keyholes and reeded top to the legs suggest the date.

c. 1790 £3,500 — £4,500

821 (above) A mahogany adjustable reading table with feet and turned stretchers that seem to be anticipating a stack of folio ledgers or the weight of a collapsed bibliophile. Note the two fine tulip-shaped candle-holders with elegant curved supports.

c. 1820 £1,600 — £2,000

822 (left) A good, honest, Georgian mahogany reading table. It has tapering legs and slide and the usual adjustable top. From the point of view of design the small drawer bolted on the side seems an afterthought and detracts from the line of the piece.

c. 1790 £1,200 — £1,600

823 Shows a very good early form in oak, with cross-stretcher between the legs and ogee curves under the frieze edged by a small lip moulding. The simple drawers have a double-D moulding on the carcase around them and the legs show turned inverted cup or 'bell' forms which is a Dutch influence. The handles are period. Note the thinness of the top and compare with chests of the period and slightly earlier.

c.1700   *£2,000 — £2,500*

TABLES — side, lowboys (mainly cabriole leg)

Largely ignored in standard textbooks concerned with the development of furniture design is a delightful little group of tables which ranges from finely made town examples down (or should it be up?) to enchanting small country fruitwood or yew pieces; these are eagerly sought after but are often impossible to prize from the hands of dealers in country furniture. We have reserved the term lowboys for three or four drawered side tables often intended as dressing tables or for occasional use. As mentioned earlier, the dividing line between these and single drawer tables is often difficult to decipher. So we have produced this arbitrary distinction for the sake of convenience. On the question of fakes and improvements in general, little is done to these pieces. Some are veneered up which usually means walnut veneered top with oak legs or some other nonsense. However, when checking the underside note age on the bottom of the fretted front. It is not unknown for a large deep walnut veneered drawer front from an old bottom half of a tallboy to do service as a new front.

824 The classical Queen Anne walnut type — in fact of George I period — with veneered surfaces and solid cabriole legs ending in pad feet. The drawers are edged with herring-bone crossbanding and the top is quartered, inlaid with herring-bone and cross-banded. The handles may well be original.

c.1720   *£5,000 — £7,000*

825 Rather more flashily veneered in high quality figured walnut. The cabriole legs are scrolled at the top and end in pointed feet. The form of drawers shows a variant, with a single long top drawer and two smaller ones set beneath. The drawer edges are cock-beaded and there is an inlaid herring-bone line rather than crossbanding. The top is also quartered.

c.1730   *£7,000 — £10,000*
More valuable because more decorative than 824
which is a better table

826 A solid walnut example with inlaid boxwood and ebony stringing lines. Note how a slight lip extends from one foot up the inside leg along the bottom of the carcase and down to the other foot as if emphasising the clean outline of the design. The cabriole legs are with shells and the feet show very interesting carved 'folds'.

c.1730   *£3,500 – £4,500*

827 An attractive solid walnut example with good cabrioles all round, ovolo moulded drawer fronts and double half-round corners to the top (babies' bottoms). The bold brass handles are period if not original. As this has a very good colour it is a desirable piece.

c.1735   *£3,500 – £5,000*

828 The same top with half-round corners and tight quarter-round moulding of the period. This example is in oak and the cabrioles provide a problem; some collectors will find them attractive, others including this writer, will feel that they are poor-looking as though they have supported one of those large Chinese urns which weigh several hundredweights. Hence the wide price range.

c.1735   *£1,500 – £2,000*

830 An example of the glorious individuality that British country furniture can provide and certainly one of the very few pieces of humorous furniture which exist. How else can one describe these legs but as 'cobra cabrioles'? Apart from these extraordinary aberrations the piece has not too much in its favour. The arrangement of drawers makes it almost a writing table.

c.1730   *£700 – £1,000*
                              depending on one's sense of humour

829 A little cherrywood example. Note the same simple quarter-round moulding but ordinary corners. The drawer arrangement is unexciting and the cabrioles only just curve, nevertheless a pleasant country piece with glorious colour. Note the typical early decoration on the middle of the bottom rail.

c.1740   *£2,500 – £3,000*

In this section there are a lot of country or provincial pieces with the result that assessment of quality and hence value become more subjective than in the previous section. One may find a feature enormously attractive which to another collector has a glaring design fault. This is, after all, part of the fun of collecting but makes writing this section difficult.

831 In case anyone gets the idea that any cabriole is better than any pad foot this example will disillusion them. In pearwood with a glorious patination, attractive front fret and primitive drawer arrangement, it is a fine example of a country piece, the sort almost ignored up until the early 1960s.

1730-1740   *£2,000 — £3,000*

832 In walnut with a quartered top and oval inlay in the centre. One immediately notices the broad deep ogee moulding which is a typical late walnut period feature. The legs are straight with only slight moulding on the outside edge to relieve their rather dull appearance. One can see why the straight Chippendale legs are chamfered.

c.1740   *£1,500 — £2,000*

833 In terms of quality the Chippendale mahogany example deserves perhaps to come next. With a simple cock-beaded drawer arrangement, an attractive fret, and in a faded nut brown colour, this example is more elegant than the previous piece. The gap in the moulding is damage.

c.1760   *Assume well restored £1,400 — £1,800*

834 In oak, turned legs with pad feet. It makes an interesting comparison with the next example. This has a better fret, half-round corners on the top (but not the quarter-round moulding of many of the pieces in the cabriole section). In addition the drawers fit better, but that may be condition rather than design.

c.1730   *£1,200 — £1,500*

835 This example is, however, slightly smaller than the previous piece but the top has no moulding and the front is a little plain. The front incidentally is made out of two pieces of wood, a fact which does not necessarily detract but does indicate a less generous attitude as demonstrated by the mean fret. However if it had superb patination all would be overlooked.

c.1735   *£900 — £1,200*

836 Back to the Chippendale straight leg with a slight moulding to the outside edge. The drawers are marked with an incised line in an attempt to simulate cockbeading. The charming fret makes it a much more attractive piece.

c.1755   *£800 — £1,000*

837 A good wide overhanging top, genuine cockbeading and the side fret — in theory these should put this ahead of the previous example, but fail to do so because of the dull little fret. Notice that both examples have the same type of moulding, a version as seen in 832, but of necessity flattened out as the wood is thinner; 832 is walnut veneered on pine which was cheaper than oak so that a deep moulding was more feasible. Knobs here look later.

c.1755   *£700 — £900*

838 The neo-classical demand for the tapered leg has not helped this heavily designed oak piece (which incidentally could be the best technically constructed piece in this section). Frankly not very desirable;

1780-1810   *£600 — £800*

TABLES — side, early, single drawer

We have separated out lowboys or dressing tables and have defined them as having three or four drawers, while side tables are defined as having one or at most two drawers. The types are clearly related but side or centre tables are found well back into the early seventeenth century. However, for collecting purposes (i.e. availability) they start towards the end of the seventeenth century.

839 A charming fruitwood side table from the end of the seventeenth century with the typical column-shaped turnings that one associates with the mid-century. The square stretchers and thick top are also part of this design. However, the ogee fretted frieze indicates a later date.

c.1680   *If in fruitwood £1,500 — £2,000*

840 A superb olivewood oyster veneered side table with walnut spiral twist turned legs. The wavy stretcher is veneered on the top and the facing edge. This is a classic piece of the period. Note how the design is nearly identical to that for a chest on stand, and indeed one does see well-turned side tables with very poor tops (i.e. disposed stands often partly rebuilt), but this superb geometrically laid pattern could never have been intended for anything else than a side table top.

c.1680   *If legs original ££8,000 — £11,000*
                      If legs not original £3,000 — £5,000

841 Moving on a decade, this marquetry piece with well-turned legs shows a later form of stretcher arrangement, one that country makers seemed to prefer to the last example; at any event it was widely copied. Note the inverted acorn in the turning near the bottom of the leg. The quality of the marquetry — of green stained bone and other warm colours — is important.

c.1690   *£9,000 — £12,000*

842 Perhaps the country variant of the twists, though attractive, are only mere imitations of the original.

c.1700   *£1,800 — £2,500*

843 An oak variation of 841. One is tempted to say country, but the turnings are excellent quality, bold and imaginative: only the earlier type of moulding round the drawer front suggests that it was made out of the fashionable area.

c.1700   £2,500 — £3,000

844 A William and Mary design of crossover stretcher with slightly less interesting (though by no means bad) turning. One feels that the maker got into a mess at the bottom of the last round and didn't quite see what to do so left it. He could perfectly well have repeated the top pattern at the bottom if he had measured correctly *before* he started. Thick moulding on top and below drawer.

c.1710   £1,400   £1,800

845 An exuberant bobbin-turned stretcher structure derived from earlier pieces, c.1660, but the thick top with shallow moulding is of later date. A very popular design.

c.1690   £1,700 — £2,500

846 A much simpler fruitwood version of 845. Here the stretchers are of the normal type. The top and mouldings are very much the same and so is the date.

c.1690   £1,600 — £2,000

The introduction of the cabriole leg affected all furniture and, as we have seen with the lowboys, many interesting and very collectable examples were made. The development in design is predictable and clearly seen.

847 Shows a delightful walnut table of very high quality both in design and execution, with cabriole legs of exceptional form in which the feet are 'stepped' and the top contained within a fold backed by a scrolled shoulder under the frieze. The drawer is inlaid with an ebony and boxwood stringing line and cross-banded in cherrywood.

c.1710   *£3,500 — £4,500*

848 Shows a simpler, but still very high quality, version in cherrywood throughout, with cabriole front legs ending in pad feet and having a scrolled carving inside the knee. The drawer has an ovolo lip moulding and the back legs are the straight pad-footed type. A simple cross-band, also in cherry, decorates the edge of the drawer and top.

c.1720   *£2,250 — £3,000*

849 An oak table cross-banded in walnut on the top and drawer front. The cabrioles are very pronounced and end on pointed feet. The shoulder pieces fit in well and the piece has a strong sturdy look without being over muscular.

c.1740   *£1,750 — £2,500*

850 A high quality example in dark Cuban mahogany. Notice how the cabrioles are just that bit more restrained when compared with the last example. (By comparison with which, incidentally, it will weigh more than half as much again). The C scroll is well designed and executed and small carved decoration is appearing above it. Notice the quarter round moulding we saw in the lowboy section on walnut, early for mahogany. The frieze could be more exciting.

c.1740   *£2,500 — £3,500*

340

851 A pad foot example with frieze, the drawer is scratched around the edge to look like cockbeading which suggests a date a shade later than the piece might otherwise be.

c.1740 £700 — £900

852 A country elm piece which fails to excite. The legs are chamfered and the moulding is a broad quarter-round which is repeated on the outside of the leg. In burr elm with a good deep rich colour one might treble the price.

1760-1770 £350 — £500

853 New classical elegance, serpentine front and tapered legs. A reasonable quality example, almost Hepplewhite — see the small square near the bottom of the leg which is a typical feature.

c.1780 £800 — £1.100

854 Clearly from the restrained turned legs and the moulding a product of the early nineteenth century. In this design restraint is still the keynote; is there, one wonders, just the slightest hint in the tulip-shaped top of the leg that 'things' might soon be happening?

c.1800 £350 — £500

855 A console table. One can see Chippendale of the highest quality written all over it. It looks superb, the carving contrasts with the simple spindles which form a deep gallery. The length is over 4ft. A most impressive piece.

c 1760   *£7,000 +*

We join these two together because they are both rich man's furniture. Once furniture was treated as part of the architecture of the room, say with Adam and the neo-Classical movement onwards, such tables were used to decorate formal reception rooms.

A console is a piece of furniture, without back legs, which is screwed to the wall. It is not unknown for some suitably flamboyant small Regency table to get sawn in half to make a pair of Regency consoles.

A pier table is a rich man's side table — a pier being the gap between two windows — and above it one found the pier glass to help reflect as much light as possible. Again the table had to fit in with the general architectural scheme. They are now fairly rare and expensive pieces. We give a small selection below.

856 (above) A richly carved mahogany table in the style of William Kent, supporting a heavy marble top which it does without obvious effort though with a considerable show of muscle. Without the charm of the previous example it is, none the less, a most impressive piece and a pair would be very much more desirable.

c 1740   *£9,000 – £12,000*

857 A giltwood semi-circular pier table with a gouache painted top of very high quality depicting classical scenes. Slender tapered, reeded legs. The frieze with a simple but impressive line of interlinking circles with flowers inside. Clearly a piece of this kind, which is one of a pair, has to be valued very much in terms of the quality of the painting.

c 1760   *The pair around £25,000 +*

859 (right) Not strictly speaking a console table because it is free standing but often described as such. The scene 'Dolphin on the Rocks', is a common one and lends itself to decorative excesses. Carved wood gilded with an important painted hunting scene by a known artist.

c.1740
Pair £20,000 – £30,000

858 Faded and finely grained mahogany half-round (or in terms of this sort of furniture semi-elliptical) pier table. Sheraton decoration, good tapering leg.

c.1790   *Each £2,000 – £3,000*
                       Pair £6,000 – £8,000

The Sutherland table is a Victorian form of gateleg table with a particularly narrow centre section. It has the virtue that when the flaps are down the piece fits into a very small space. It is thus a useful occasional table. The earliest designs are by W. Smee & Son, from 1850 with the typical twin column ending. The single stem is first shown in 1864 and an example is illustrated left.

861 Square flaps are less common and the design books show several for the 1880s. This design of foot appears at that time. Spirals are shown for the late 1870s. Those here are well turned and the general quality of the piece is high. But why make a different turning for the gates? Economy?

c.1880   *£300 — £400*

860 The heavy rounded bun turned in the end column and the markedly carved feet pronounce a relatively early date. A good solid piece and not, by Victorian standards, very fussy. Booth shows a less solid but similar example in 1864.

c.1865   *£500 — £650*

862 Nowadays this would be a veneer merchant's waiting room table, but to the Victorians the use of segments of exotic stained woods was just another way of making impressive furniture. The fluting, thin line decoration and beading suggest the date.

c.1880   *Expensive because "flash" £450 — £650*

863 Another late example. Black and lots of turning for the sake of it without any idea of creating an overall design. Black is so unpopular that the best thing to do is to pop it in the stripper caustic tank.

c.1890   *£140 — £180*

The sofa table is a variation which was evolved from the Pembroke table and gets its name from its intended application, namely, to stand against a sofa. It is therefore long and thin with flaps at the end, whereas the Pembroke is squarer in shape, and so popular did it become that it gradually superseded the Pembroke. Although considered a typical piece of Regency furniture, the sofa table did in fact become popular at the end of the eighteenth century.

There are two distinct types, first those supported each end by a vertical member — or end standard as it is called — in a variety of forms and secondly, those with a central pillared support standing on a flat base which in turn rests on feet. The pillared support can of course vary considerably.

864 A high quality mahogany table, with satinwood cross-banding and satinwood veneered legs and cross-stretchers. The legs sweep out naturally from the end standards. There are false drawer fronts on the far side. The piece shows the late-Georgian restraint one associates with pre-Regency designs.

c.1790   *£15,000 — £17,000*

865 The early Regency has set in, but with equivalent quality and restraint in design. The piece is veneered in rosewood and the flap supports are carved with Egyptian heads and wings à la Thomas Hope of 1820 — the heads being fixtures. The legs still sweep elegantly out of the end standards but the feet make a vertical 'stop' in the curve not seen in 864.

c.1800   *£12,000 — £15,000*

866 The high leg of the Regency is seen clearly in this fine satinwood veneered piece which is cross-banded in rosewood. The classical motifs are inset in ebony and it is very good quality. Satinwood obviously helps the price, as does good grain arrangement.

c.1810   *£4,000 — £6,000*

867 A satinwood veneered attempt which is somewhat less successful than the first two examples. The end standard is wider, making the feet look small. The veneer runs in fairly strong straight figures across the top and the legs in a way which conflicts with the striped ebony and boxwood stringing lines on all the surface edges.

c.1800   *£4,000 — £6,000*

For convenience we have sub-divided vertically supported sofa tables into a). the earlier types, mostly without stretchers, shown on these pages, and b). those with stretchers, generally later or not always such good examples (see next section).

868 The variations in end standards can be considerable. This form, the lyre, is seen on a mahogany table which is otherwise a fairly plain piece. The main alternative form of lyre is a reversal of the form shown here. With a brass strip, this, if genuine, helps the price considerably. There is an ominous line towards the right-hand side of the near flap. If this is indeed a patch, take 20% off the price.

c.1820   *Assume no patch £4,000 — £6,000*

869 A fairly typical (if there is such a thing) Regency reeded leg support. The dramatic wedge-shaped end standards meet in a large circular centre section, with turned decoration, which looks like an oversize draught.

c.1820   *£4,500 — £5,500*

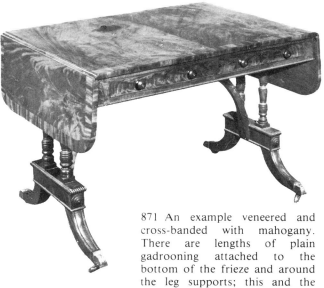

870 A plainer form of the previous example with simple reeded end standards terminating in carved paw feet. The sole decoration is the light coloured stringing line.

c.1825   *£3,000 — £4,000*

871 An example veneered and cross-banded with mahogany. There are lengths of plain gadrooning attached to the bottom of the frieze and around the leg supports; this and the rather aimlessly turned pillars would suggest a later date, while the solid legs with the inset line an earlier one. It has the same strange arch support as 867.

c.1830   *£2,000 — £3,000*

345

Next come sofa tables with end standards and stretchers. These can be sub-divided, as can be seen below, into those with cross-stretchers and those with double pillars. One of those sections in which quality varies dramatically. Condition, too, is important. Patches on the top affect prices dramatically.

872 Not a conventional sofa table but it relates to the next piece so well that, logically, it falls in here. This table is breathtaking: superbly light in appearance, the reeded, tapered cross-shaped supports are perfectly executed. Compare the reeding on the legs of 758. The use of gilt and ebonised decoration is restrained and the more effective, for one's eye is drawn to the carved bandage by which the middle stretcher appears to be tied at the ends. It relates to a known type.

c.1800   *£40,000+*

873 A finely figured mahogany example in which mid-Regency classical motifs are used lightly. It has good, small, inturned paw feet — a device which surprisingly enough works, and lion head handles. The cross-shaped curving supports, beautifully reeded with stretcher to match, shows Thomas Hope's influence at its most felicitous.

c.1805   *£30,000+*

874 A further crash down on the quality scale and yet still a good sofa table. The design is successful if a trifle thick on the moulded legs which terminate in attractive unusual castors. The melons (?) which support the table are attractive as is the leaf carving beneath them. The top with reeded edges is in plain mahogany.

c.1830   *£4,000 — £5,000*

875 Double pillar rosewood, turned to give a slight bamboo effect. It is in rosewood with metal mounts both on the edge of the legs, between the pillars and on the fronts. The top is selected veneers cross-banded with satinwood and ebony stringing lines between them.

c.1810   *£6,000 — £8,000*

876 A very pleasant spirally turned mahogany example. Brass inlay on the leg and a simple satinwood stringing line around the top and drawer fronts. Simple round edges to the table top.

c.1820   *£5,000 — £7,000*

877 A faded mahogany table with ebony stringing line in the square classical form and banding used as the principal inlays to contrast with the satinwood edging to the table top. The stretcher has a restrained turning, while the pillars show later turning.

c.1825   *£3,000 — £4,000*

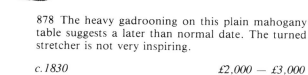

878 The heavy gadrooning on this plain mahogany table suggests a later than normal date. The turned stretcher is not very inspiring.

c.1830   *£2,000 — £3,000*

879 (right) A small mahogany sofa table of simple form. The maker was none too happy about getting the legs on to the pillar. They look what they are, two curves dowelled and stuck on to a rectangular piece of wood which in turn is built up like a Lego set into the top. Even the stringing line is a bit mean.

c.1830   *£1,200 — £1,600*

The final group of sofa tables is the one in which there is a central pedestal. These pieces are therefore linked with pedestal dining tables, for the same type of base was often used

880 In mahogany and remarkably similar to a design in zebrawood which can be dated exactly to 1810. The pillars are well turned and the decoration of split beading lines (fine around the drawers, slightly greater round the platform) is restrained. White stringing line is also used. The table edge is reeded and there is a thin line of crossbanding on the top.

c. 1810   £4,000 — £5,000

881 Another example with four pillar turning in which the knee has moved towards the peculiarly high Regency form. The piece is in rosewood and the pillars are well turned. A small amount of split beaded decoration and metal mounts on the leg. More cramped and not quite the quality of the first example.

c. 1815   £3,000 — £4,000

882 An example which illustrates the desire for show at not too much extra cost, and a type that became an obsession later on. Simply cut on a band-saw these solid mahogany supports are reeded to match the feet. The top, too, has the customary reeding around the edge and is cross-banded in the same wood. Not as good as it looks at first sight.

c. 1830   £2,500 — £3,500

883 (right) Down to two pillars. The same ringed decoration marks the place where the top of the legs don't pierce the platform. The turning on the pillars is getting somewhat aimless — a series of rings and the odd bulge, not like the careful baluster form of the first two examples.

c. 1830   £1,800 — £2,200

Plate 114. A wonderfully bold little mahogany tripod, c.1755, of a sort often referred to as a kettle or wine table. The baluster turning is finely carved with leaves but it is the legs which give it a superb bold posture. An excellent piece.

£15,000 — £20,000

Plate 115. A brass and mother-of-pearl inlaid mahogany tripod with scalloped moulded edge and raised centre. Pieces of this sort are usually attributable to John Channon who was making them in the 1740s when there was a vogue for them. Solidly made, it is, of course, shown in the tip-up position. The shapes are designed to hold plates, cups and saucers, etc. Eating meals from tripods and, later, Pembroke tables, when dining without company, was a common practice.

This table is made of the superb mahogany which is often seen on first rate pieces but is never (if such a word exists in discussing British furniture) found on inferior work.

The excellent photograph gives a very good idea of this early mahogany. It is very like red walnut, has a first rate colour, and often acquires a most wonderful patina. Note particularly the grain on the left-hand side (the nine o'clock position) which is typical of this fine wood. From the examples seen it was used only between about 1735 and 1750.

By contrast, Honduras mahogany, or baywood, has a pale yellow look. It was imported later in the 18th century, is light in colour and weight and one rarely sees it used in first-class furniture.

Plate 116. An elegant ormolu mounted rosewood and mahogany writing table, close enough to the French Empire designs to be an international piece. The use of ormolu stringing lines, the beautifully proportioned turned legs — see how they straighten after the collàr — mark this as a fine quality piece in a very expensive category.
c.1810   *£35,000 in 1986*

Writing tables with legs was a category we left out of the last edition. Commercially they are very important and, although simple in construction by comparison with many other pieces, they vary a great deal in quality. Prices are high.

Plate 117. A restrained design of good quality dating from the first years of the 18th century. The simple moulding has only a small beading at the bottom of the carcase to emphasise cleanly the break. The legs taper gently, giving an impression of strength without heaviness. The price is high for the work involved. Fakes will appear.

Plate 118. A library table in oak and holly wood by G.J. Morant, c.1816-1818, sold at the historic Great Tew Park sale. The very top of the designs which came from the neo-classical revival that Thomas Hope did so much to promote.

As a piece of furniture it is wonderfully made — there is huge muscular tension in the animal legs. The piece has good lines and a commanding presence achieved with a relatively small area of decoration.

Plate 119. An oak table attributed to the important A.W.N. Pugin. Strictly a centre table, c.1840, but included here because it comes broadly into this category and makes a strong contrast with the previous examples. The gothic taste crops up regularly — 1750 and 1810 are just two dates — but it was just the flavour that the fashion wanted. Pugin, sick of Regency excesses, went back to gothic essentials. This is one of his revised gothic designs. It has a strong simplicity, only the trefoils and quatrefoils provide ornament. You can see where the Arts and Crafts Movement found its inspiration.

Plate 120 is in mahogany, neo-
classical, and pays lip service
to these precepts. It is square,
has the classical arrangement
of legs, and the masks, faces,
paw feet and black paint are all
classical details. Even the
straight grain round the lion
mask handles is laid to
emphasise the uncompromising
square masculinity.

The two Carlton House writing tables on this page were made at very much the same time,
1810-1820, but at least in the design of the casework they are very different.

Plate 121 is in rosewood,
gloriously faded so that the
aggressive black markings
have gone down to a pleasing
texture running through the
soft brown tones which blend
in with the restrained brass
inlay and decoration. Even the
faded green leather of the
writing surface brings out the
colour of the metalwork.
Compare the brass rail on the
two pieces, the hard black
rings on the top of the legs of
the former against the soft lotus
leaves of the latter. The piece
presents a harmony of shape
and colour which is sadly rare
in pieces which nowadays
come on to the market.

352

884 (left) A bit of light relief. The vast base, heavily gadrooned, is supported by an equally substantial humanised version of the ball-and-claw foot. One would expect the top to be about 8ft. long, but in fact it is a normal sized sofa table, again gadrooned in calamander wood. The misalliance is condoned by two very elegant and beautifully reeded vase-shaped pillars with rims. It was sold at auction by a very knowledgeable specialist firm, so it must be right.

Early 19th century   *£1,400 — £1,800*

885 A robust turned and heavily carved centre pillar rosewood table. Plenty of brass inlay and a Regency knee with good stylised design. The edges of the table have a very refined beading. Rich effect without undue ostentation.

c.1810   *£3,000 — £4,000*

886 Equivalent to the previous example with a straight-sided pillar. Again plenty of brass inlay and some ebony in the leg which turns with the characteristic sharpness of the period. As can be seen, it has high decorative quality, but the drawback is its being mahogany.

c.1820   *When restored £3,000 — £4,000*

887 (right) A very simple example where the decoration is confined to a modest black stringing line on the side of the legs and a broader band on the top of the legs and the table itself. The two unimaginative rectangular pieces supporting the top affect the value.

c.1825   *£1,800 — £2,200*

TABLES —
tripods and candlestands to 1770

These evolved from candlestands which came to Britain at the Restoration. They were extremely useful and the design was adapted over the years to provide support for a wide range of objects from wine to books.

888 (left) A walnut spiral turned example with baluster form at the top. The rectangular sectioned S scroll legs meet on an octagonal platform which echoes the shape of the top which is quartered and cross-banded in walnut.

c.1680   *£2,000 — £3,000*

889 (right) Although a countrified version of the above with flatter feet and a burr elm top which has warped, the turning is excellent quality and has the thick snake-like coils at just the pitch which one associates with the best late seventeenth century work.

c.1690   *£1,750 — £2,250*

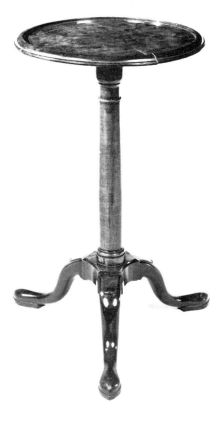

890 There does not seem to have been an identifiable 'Queen Anne' tripod style (for that matter there is not a 'Queen Anne' dining table), so one moves on from the rare turned base supported by three buns, c.1690, to the elegant walnut column stem table with a dished yew top. Note the remains of the platform still discernible where the legs meet.

c.1725
£1,500 — £2,000

891 The low feet and heavy barrel turned stem suggest an early date for this fine heavy, slightly squat, Cuban mahogany tripod table. It has the desirable 'birdcage' method of fixing top to stem. Notice that the pillars of the birdcage have the same barrel turning as the stem — this suggests originality.

c.1735   *£3,000 — £4,000*

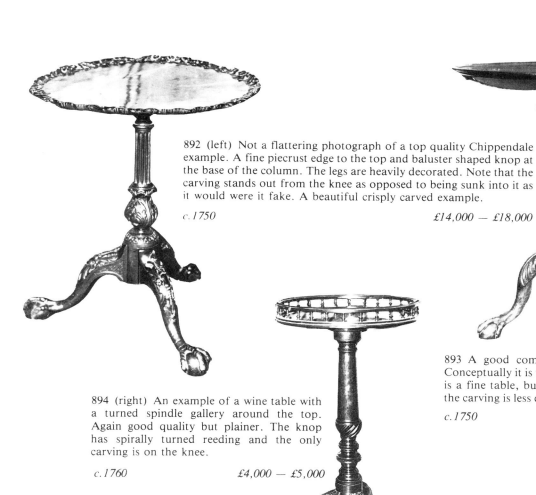

892 (left) Not a flattering photograph of a top quality Chippendale example. A fine piecrust edge to the top and baluster shaped knop at the base of the column. The legs are heavily decorated. Note that the carving stands out from the knee as opposed to being sunk into it as it would were it fake. A beautiful crisply carved example.

c.1750   *£14,000 — £18,000*

893 A good comparison with example 892. Conceptually it is the same design and indeed it is a fine table, but not of the same quality — the carving is less deep and the top rim is weak.

c.1750   *£7,000 — £9,000*

894 (right) An example of a wine table with a turned spindle gallery around the top. Again good quality but plainer. The knop has spirally turned reeding and the only carving is on the knee.

c.1760   *£4,000 — £5,000*

895 (left) Perfectly plain standard tripod shown in the stowaway position. Notice the good quality mahogany with a grain showing. No birdcage, which would help the price slightly.

c.1770   *£800 — £1,000*

896 (right) A Victorian attempt to copy the style of pieces in this section. The shapings of the legs and columns are an indication, but the vertical grooves in the upper part of the column and the finial under the base are the giveaways; Victorians loved these finials. A pretty table maybe, but not Georgian by any stretch of the imagination.

c.1870   *£200 — £250*

TABLES — smallish tripod and quadripod, 1800-1850

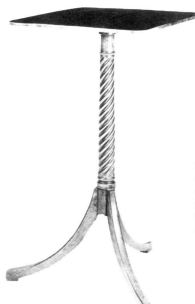

At first tripod tables followed the same form as the larger single tables but, with the inventiveness of the Regency period, individual designs emerged. The Victorians produced small tables with four small legs which strictly speaking do not belong in the same section but which, for the sake of convenience, have been included.

898 (right) A more decorative treatment of the same basic design. Sweeps to the top and bottom of the legs are emphasised with applied brass rosettes. The stem is tapered and ringed, the top has a rim. Value is enhanced by the fact that the height is adjustable. Anything which moves, adjusts or can be fiddled with seems to command a premium.

c.1815 £1,200 — £1,600

897 A turn of the century mahogany example, showing plain classical elegance. The legs have a clean simple curve and the stem is decorated with spiral reeding. The top is cross-banded in satinwood.

c.1800 £3,000 — £4,000

899 (right) If you look at page 218 you will notice that many high quality 'hairy feet' have wings or spurs at the back and one can see that they provide a good balance by supporting the base over a reasonable area, instead of looking as though they were screwed on at the end. This is a well-thought-out mahogany design, the sturdiness of which is justified by the heavy marble top.

c.1825 £10,000 — £15,000

900 (left) A novel little four-legged table — note its quality and the scroll behind the hairy feet. Curious that the carved Chippendale vase is retained on the centre column. The flaps have well-matched veneers which meet when the table is in the erected position, giving a fine effect. One of the best of its sort.

c.1830 £2,000 — £3,000

901 (right) It really is hard to be charitable about this horrible little table. Loudon (1833) had the same problem about a fairly revolting sofa table of the period. ''The justness of this criticism will appear more obvious, by applying it to the table...which has two supports more highly enriched by carving than those of any of the other pieces and yet has a plain top. This is in bad taste and ought not, in a work like the present, to be passed over without notice.'' Quite right. Not only is the top plain but out of proportion to the base and the decoration seems mindless.

c.1830 *Presumably somebody likes it, so* £800 — £1,200

902 Loudon would approve this design because both top and bottom have 'enrichments', but he might, like the present writer, be happier with it if the two sets of beading had been more of a size.

c.1830   *£300 — £500*

903 Typical small mahogany table of the period. Commercially not desirable. Not enough decoration for the Continental buyer and too small for a cheap dining table. Same design still offered by Light in 1881.

1830-1850   *£400 — £600*

904 A good papier mâché table with a delightful hop harvest scene painted on the top. If one can discover the artist or if it is by Jennens and Bettridge then the value will be more than quoted.

c.1850   *£1,200 — £1,500*

905 (below) A conventional papier mâché floral and gilt, with mother-of-pearl inlay, tilt-top table. Well decorated and elegant with the shape of the top helping to create an interesting piece. A good compact pedestal.

c.1840   *£500 — £700*

907 (below) Made over a considerable period of time, a form of simple table which was produced in huge quantities. The baluster-shaped turning on the pedestal is competent but attempts too much.

Basically 1830s   *£150 — £200*

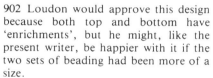

906 The use of iron was an obvious method of obtaining the maximum decoration as cheaply as possible. Once the mould was made presumably any number could be cast. Again the quality of painting is important. The price in this case is helped because the painting is topographical — shipping on the Clyde.

c.1850   *£1,000 — £2,000*

TABLES — work, with bags beneath

The work table fitted out with receptaces for needlework and embroidery implements as used by the ladies of the household, did not appear until the later part of the eighteenth century. Chippendale did not illustrate them, but Sheraton, true to form, showed a variety of ingenious designs. They must have been very popular, for every manufacturer or designer showed a wide variety right through the century.

908 Table-cum-firescreen — work could be done in warmth but the delicate skin shielded from the heat. It is in satinwood with ebony stringing lines, and has a fabric work bag beneath — sometimes on a slide for ease of access. A curious feature of this piece is the hollowed out inside edges of two of the legs — perhaps to fit over the corner of a particular fender? The most popular type of work table.

c.1795   *£2,250 — £3,000*

909 An example on a turned centre pillar and veneered in rosewood. It has brass ball-and-claw castors and brass decoration at the base of the pillar. The top lifts up and the drawers are false.

c.1820   *£2,000 — £3,000*

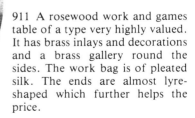

911 A rosewood work and games table of a type very highly valued. It has brass inlays and decorations and a brass gallery round the sides. The work bag is of pleated silk. The ends are almost lyre-shaped which further helps the price.

c.1820   *£3,500 — £4,500*

910 Thomas Hope at his best/worst. The Disney-esque paws jutting malevolently from heavy scrolls look as though they should belong to something prehistoric weighing about three tons. It has a slide and is in burr walnut.

c.1825   *£1,000 — £1,400*

912 A more modest mahogany William IV type on flat base with a simple top without drawer.

c.1835   *£600 — £800*

913 A work table showing the scroll-decorated end standards and finials under the top which one associates with the Victorians. The feet show the remains of the paw-foot design of the Regency. It is otherwise a simple piece, and very similar in design to one by T. King.

c.1835-1845   *£900 — £1,200*

914 High Victorian in style, with burr walnut veneers and a wooden veneered work 'bag' beneath. A type illustrated in manufacturers' catalogues in the 1870s and 1880s, but stemming from earlier designs.

c.1865   *£1,100 — £1,500*

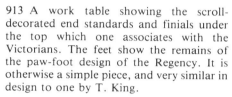

915 (left) A mahogany design with reeded baluster end standards and turned stretcher of a type illustrated by Loudon in 1833 and popular for some time afterwards.

1835-1845   *£550 — £750*

916 (right) A type introduced in the late 1850s as an elegant supported urn which settled down to this funnel shape by the 1870s. In walnut. The price depends on the quality of the interior fittings. Marquetry would help.

1875   *£600 — £800*

TABLES — work, without bags

Not all work tables had bags beneath. The selection shown here is of a type in which the drawers, fitted into a small table, were sufficient for needlework implements and materials.

917 (left) A Regency rosewood table with the lyre form built into its supports and brass inlays — enough to give any dealer a rush of blood to the head, for these lyre form pieces are very popular and fetch more than curved wood and brass rods justify.

c.1815
£2,000 — £3,000

918 A mahogany work table showing a distinct type with flaps and three drawers on a column support with a flat base on typical Regency feet.

1820
£1,200 — £1,800

919 (below) However, with more drawer space and more decoration than 918 this sort of design disaster can easily occur.

c.1840
£1,400 — £1,800

920 A burr walnut version of 918, with real drawers and an octagonal column which forecasts the piece in 921.

c.1830   *£1,200 — £1,500*

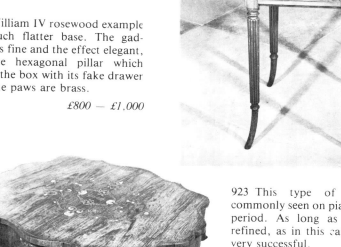

921 A William IV rosewood example on a much flatter base. The gadrooning is fine and the effect elegant, as is the hexagonal pillar which supports the box with its fake drawer front. The paws are brass.

1830   *£800 — £1,000*

923 This type of leg is more commonly seen on piano stools of the period. As long as the reeding is refined, as in this case, the effect is very successful.

c.1810   *£1,400 — £1,800*

922 More elaborate mid-nineteenth century in form, with inlays and delicate curved construction. Although of much less quality, it has a distinct design similarity to 727. Fittings are important.

c.1855   *£900 — £1,100*

924 (left) Made at the same time as the previous example, this piece owes more to Georgian than Regency forms. A little thin in the legs and the termination is not a success, but this is still desirable as a useful small piece.

c.1810   *£400 — £600*

925 (right) A simple little work table whose square shape and type of turning proclaim it as late in the century. The drawers are dummy.

c.1870-1880   *£300 — £400*

The long writing tables, often referred to as library tables, of the late Georgian, Regency and Victorian period have a marked design similarity to sofa tables of the early part of the period, except that they do not have end flaps. Perhaps designers produced one drawing which the retailer was happy to produce with or without flaps.

926 Shows a Sheraton style table in figured mahogany with rosewood crossbanding on end supports that are, clearly, late Georgian in design. There are drawers in the frieze, with false drawers at the ends, indicating that this really was designed as a centre table, to be viewed from both sides and ends.

c.1795   *£12,000 — £18,000*

927 A rosewood table with end supports of similar construction to the previous example except that scrolls have been included in the design, both at the bottom and the top of the support. The turned stretcher is, perhaps, decoratively intended.

c.1810   *£6,000 — £8,000*

928 A Regency rosewood example in which the legs sweep from the top to the floor. They are supported by a curved arch very similar to the first example. Metal decorations.

c.1830   *£6,000 — £8,000*

929 A very similar design to the previous example except that here rosewood cross-members are used in place of metal and of course it lacks drawers and so is simply a centre table. Note that the mouldings of these last three examples are simply cross-grain veneers, slightly rounded.

c.1830   *£2,500 — £3,500*

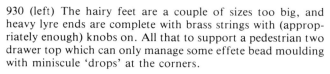

930 (left) The hairy feet are a couple of sizes too big, and heavy lyre ends are complete with brass strings with (appropriately enough) knobs on. All that to support a pedestrian two drawer top which can only manage some effete bead moulding with miniscule 'drops' at the corners.

c.1830   *£10,000 — £14,000*

931 Again in mahogany and a contrast to the previous example. The restraint in the design is obvious but one can clearly see the decoration gaining in importance. Typical of a whole group of stretcherless tables using designs of the period.

c.1830   *£7,000 — £9,000*

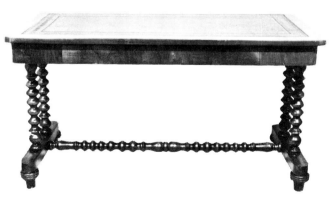

932 (above) Fussy it may be, but the parquetry top in exotic woods with bold corner finials goes well with the equally bold fretted base and stretcher to make a good solid ornate writing table. Rather hard to date with assurance because, looking through the *Pictorial Dictionary of Nineteenth Century Furniture Design,* one sees that the variations were being offered in the 1840-1860 period.

Say 1850s   *£3,500 — £4,500*

933 A bobbin turned version of a type more often seen in the design books as spiral turned. It produces decoration for less original cost than the previous example.

c.1840   *£900 — £1,200*

934 An extremely fine rent table with a central well shown open. A plain cannon turning and three well-shaped legs with decorative carving down the centre. The feet have a turned over scroll effect.

c.1790   *£10,000 — £15,00*

A round or multi-sided library table, with a number of drawers, supported on a central base, normally a pillar, is referred to in the antique trade as a 'rent' or 'drum top' table. By tradition they were used to keep account of rents paid and due, for some tables have initials on the drawer fronts. In some cases false drawers alternate with genuine ones, while others have false books or spaces for real books. They first appear at the end of the eighteenth century and command high prices.

935 A superb example almost identical with one illustrated by Sheraton. Extremely elegant on four ormolu paws. The applied moulding to the doors is typically neoclassical.

c.1795   *£20,000+*

936 By comparison with the previous example, not so successful for it is let down by the unrelieved square plinth. It has, however, inlaid initials on each drawer. It is veneered in good quality mahogany on a square stand with door. The only additional decorative treatment is a white stringing line.

c.1800   *£20,000+*

937 An octagonal library table in faded mahogany with four well-moulded legs. A good example of this popular type.

c.1800   *£6,000 — £8,000*

938 A typical late Georgian round library table with blank spaces instead of false drawers. The four reeded legs show a well-balanced curve.

c.1790 £6,000 — £9,000

939 A slightly later example, though the similarities with the previous example are strong. The same flat moulding and tooled leather top. The higher knee provides the clue to the date.

c.1800 £6,000 — £8,500

940 Another bad attack of Regency knee with the applied turned pieces on either side. The legs are no longer reeded and the general effect lacks elegance. However, the piece is in rosewood which does help the price though the cracks across the top, if indeed that is what they are, would depress it.

c.1825 £6,000 — £8,000

941 Almost an occasional table because it is small but the drawers suggest it should go into this section. The price is less because of its size but this is no reflection on its excellent quality.

c.1790

If right £3,000 — £5,000
More likely wrong £1,000 — £1,500

TABLES — writing, Carlton House and similar

A 'Carlton House' writing table appears in Gillows' *Cost Books for 1796*, described as a 'Ladies Drawing and Writing Table' and is also illustrated in the *Cabinet Makers Book of Prices 1788*. They are, naturally, associated with the late Georgian and Regency period — Carlton House was a London residence of the Prince Regent but the square tapering legs are what we now associate with Sheraton. These writing tables are usually made in satinwood or mahogany, were made throughout the nineteenth century, and are still being reproduced today.

942 An illustration of a top dog of the breed, in satinwood with inlaid decoration of musical and armorial instruments, as well as scroll and leaf forms. The inlays perhaps betray its provenance, for it is in fact a copy of the original table.

Late 18th century   £30,000+
Late 19th century   £7,000 — £9,000

943 This mahogany table is perhaps more faithful to the restraint of the original strain. It has stringing lines as its principal decoration apart from inlaid oval panels of satinwood.

c.1910   £8,000 — £12,000

944 A simpler version in rosewood, decorated with brass beading and gallery.

c.1820   £20,000+ (satinwood)
£9,000 — £10,000 (rosewood)

945 Edwardian, but its origins are clear — the Edwardian love of Sheraton design has become much appreciated recently, both aesthetically and materially.

Early 1900s   £3,500 — £4,500

The writing table with some sort of structure at the back is clearly a continuation of the fall front bureau design, which inexplicably had gone out of fashion by the start of the nineteenth century.

946 The sharp curve at the ends provides the clue to the date of this 'inlaid writing cabinet' even if it did not have the very Sheraton inlays, tapered legs, tambour slides and handles. A good elegant piece with what looks like an adjustable writing slope. Overseas demand is still amazingly indiscriminating, hence the small difference in price.

c.1805   *If period £9,000 — £12,000*
      If Edwardian   *£4,000 — £6,000*

947 The piece looks wrong. A deep heavy top resting on thin legs. Look at the previous example, it has less superstructure and the legs if anything are thicker. What goes in the top anyway? Books would break it and porcelain would be at grave risk as the piece is fitted with castors. On the side of the base there is a broad band of inlay with none on the top. One would want to inspect this piece very carefully.

c.1810
Assuming right
£700 — £950

948 Here is a case where the whole piece looks right. Both in the design and in the manner and distribution of decoration. Curved reeded legs and a bold stretcher suggest the date. The drawer slides in and a cover pulls from the back to make the front flush, while the tambour slide comes down to cover the drawers and pigeon-holes. A useful piece.

c.1830   *£3,000 — £4,000*

949 A very much simpler version of the previous piece. Here the panelled front (an inelegant feature with the top of the hinges exposed) folds back to knock objects off the galleried top, while the thin front folds out to be supported by lopers in the manner of a bureau. A curious feature is the slide at the side, but it too is thin. It says it is Sheraton but one doubts it. More likely Edwardian.

Early 1900s   *£800 — £1,000*

TABLE FURNITURE
spice cabinets, slopes and bible boxes

This covers a wide range of objects such as needle and stump work. However, we are concerned with furniture, so will confine ourselves to three of the main categories available to the collector: table cabinets (or more commonly spice boxes), slopes and bible boxes, the latter being used for small objects although the term bible box sticks. The illustrations for the bible box section are taken from a very much longer article by J.P.J. Homer in *Antique Collecting*, Vol. 13, No. 8.

950 These pieces are popularly known as spice cabinets though table cabinet is the correct term. This example is Dutch or Anglo-Dutch, an identity suggested by the sledge feet. It is in chestnut and has geometric mouldings arranged on the doors with quarter applied pillars to give a small arch effect. The capitals, however, are missing. A secret drawer removed by pulling forward one of the drawer dividers is a good touch. With fine patination.

c.1670   *£1,400 — £1,800*

951 (above) At the other end of the quality scale a more simple oak example of the same design. The front door is panelled but the rest of the cabinet is of nailed construction with no moulding. Interesting to note that the arrangement of the drawers on these first two pieces is identical. Very good colour.

Late 17th century   *£350 — £450*

952 While one tends to think of spice cupboards as early, they continued to be made with very much the same arrangement of drawers. This is still in oak but veneered in two sheets on the door to give the decorative effect. This, the crossbanding and curved corners mark it down as a product of the walnut period.

c.1735   *£2,000 — £3,000*

953 A well-carved writing box or slope. The carving is of the deep early geometric type and executed with considerable confidence. The front side shows early foliage type arcading. The apparently late date is justified by part of the coat of arms of the Commonwealth — a cross and harp carved on the top.

Mid 17th century £700 — £1,000

954 By complete contrast a plain oak example with moulded edges to the lid and the base. A simple piece.

c.1680 £200 — £300

955 A superb early box with geometrically designed chip carving and dated 1658. Original pin hinges now replaced by straps. A superb box with fine patination.

1658 £700 — £900

956 'John Cox His Box 1611'. The sort of inscription plus the pleasing sweep of the carving make this box very collectable. There is also punch decoration to its borders.

c.1611 £600 — £800

957 A large box size (2ft. 4ins.) with a very attractive design of two birds. The contrast between the scaly neck feathers and the formal rendering of the long tail feathers is well executed. Originally it had three flimsy pin hinges, now replaced with two straps. There is still a pivoting lid on the inside.

c.1670 £500 — £700

958 A medium sized early box decorated with guilloche carving above nulling (both very competently executed) as well as punched decoration. The lock is unusual in that the key protector moves upwards, releasing a pin which allows another larger section to slide sideways.

c.1650 £600 — £800

959 A small box dated 1684 with carved roundels. No mouldings or scratch mark on the lid and the carving does not have the air of assurance present in 957.

c.1684 £350 — £550

TEA CADDIES

One of the many subjects that would justify a book. Yet, in terms of what is normally offered for sale, the range is surprisingly small. Broadly, shape and materials are the main constituents of value and we show below a typical selection. A bit of silver mounting or unusual inlay helps the price, but don't expect the original glass bowl where there is a space for one.

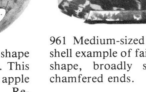

962 Fine marquetry caddy, mahogany ovals, satinwood fluting, cross-banded in rosewood — a beauty.

c.1790   *£600 — £900*

960 Tea caddies in the shape of fruit attract attention. This super little example is an apple made in applewood. Reproduced late nineteenth century.

Late 18th century
£1,500 — £2,200

961 Medium-sized tortoiseshell example of fairly ordinary shape, broadly square with chamfered ends.

c.1830   *£400 — £500*

963 A typical yew wood example of sarcophagus shape.

1800-1830
£200 — £300
but in mahogany
£90 — £120

964 The same shape but clearly later with the beaded edge which gives the date. Mother-of-pearl decoration.

c.1825   *£80 — £100*

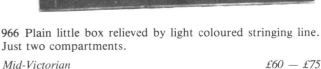

965 A more simple mahogany example with boxwood edge and keyhole cover.

c.1830   *£70 — £90*

966 Plain little box relieved by light coloured stringing line. Just two compartments.

Mid-Victorian   *£60 — £75*

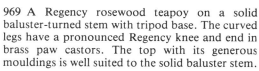

TEAPOYS

A Regency invention. Tepai is Hindi for three-legged or three-footed. Tepoys cover any sort of tripod supporting a container for tea and the cut glass bowls seen in the commonly found tea caddies. In construction they are closely linked to work tables and one often sees designs which could be either.

967 A mahogany teapoy on pillar-turned column and four curved legs, each with a scrolled 'knee' and brass paw castors. There are ebony stringing lines inlaid into the legs and base as well as around the top edges. Not really a very successful design. The base is solid, the top heavy, but the top of the stem is a shade too thin. Compare it with the others on this page.

c.1810   *£1,000 — £1,400*

968 A good quality mahogany teapoy with turned and fluted column on a flat platform base. The scrolled feet are raised on 'gadrooned' circular buns echoed in the base of the column. Note the figuring of the mahogany used for the convex top and its lid. The two glass bowls from the interior are missing but the lids for the tea compartments remain.

c.1830   *£800 — £1,200*

969 A Regency rosewood teapoy on a solid baluster-turned stem with tripod base. The curved legs have a pronounced Regency knee and end in brass paw castors. The top with its generous mouldings is well suited to the solid baluster stem.

c.1825   *£900 — £1,400*

970 A plain mahogany teapoy with a flat platform base on turned feet. The centre column is plain turned and the only decoration to the top is the bead moulding around the edge of the lid.

c.1835   *£400 — £600*

971 A high quality walnut teapoy ascribed to T.H. Filmer, Berners St., Oxford St., London. The basically baluster shape of the centre column has been elaborated by the spiral twist turning with an interesting broadening to the base. The top is veneered in burr walnut, while the rest of the piece is made from the solid. A type increasingly respected.

c.1845   *£1,400 — £2,000*

972 This small wine cooler made in sycamore with, most important, a good colour and brass bands, and with its original tin insert, has attractive mouldings. It is very useful for flower decoration and even cooling wine.

Late 18th century
£600 — £800

Treen can be described as a smallish wooden object normally made for a specific purpose which is attractive enough to be collectable. It therefore embraces a vast number of objects and anyone who becomes fascinated in this subject will wish to read Edward H. Pinto's *Treen and Other Wooden Bygones*. Obviously we cannot go into the depth of detail which has been possible in most other sections of this book but there are so many delightful objects to be found that it would be a pity to leave this subject out. There are moreover certain features which influence price and it seems sensible to discuss them to help new collectors understand values.

One might define the main desirability features as: firstly, attractiveness with utility; secondly, quality of workmanship; thirdly, grain or colour of wood, and lastly, quaintness or just decorativeness. More than in any other sections of the book there are no absolute standards and so value is a highly subjective matter, hence the wide ranges given. What is important is that *you* like it. We give some fairly expensive items in this section but do not be put off if you only want to spend a pound or so, there are still small interesting pieces to be found.

973 A unique antique cricket bat trolley. It might pass the quaintness test but is bulky and most important it does nothing practical. Now imagine that originally the side was hinged and a shelf swung out with holes for cricket balls, which would hold glasses, and there was room for bottles at the base, then it would have quite a different value. Makes adjusting, adapting, call it what you like, so profitable.

Early 19th century
As is £700 — £900

If, as imagined above, plus a suberb patination, £4,000 — £5,000

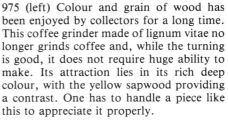

974 The next of the desirability features, that of quality workmanship without current use, covers a very large area of carved and sculptured figures. This example of a carved plane, with a superb cherub beautifully executed, stands on its own decoratively.

17th century £600 — £800
If it has a name stamped on it £2,000+

975 (left) Colour and grain of wood has been enjoyed by collectors for a long time. This coffee grinder made of lignum vitae no longer grinds coffee and, while the turning is good, it does not require huge ability to make. Its attraction lies in its rich deep colour, with the yellow sapwood providing a contrast. One has to handle a piece like this to appreciate it properly.

18th century £500 — £700

976 (right) This carved mangle board illustrates another area where quality of workmanship is high and where the piece can be admired for what it is rather than what it now does.

18th century £300 — £400

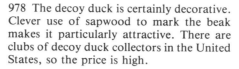

978 The decoy duck is certainly decorative. Clever use of sapwood to mark the beak makes it particularly attractive. There are clubs of decoy duck collectors in the United States, so the price is high.

19th century   *£400 — £600*

977 A more simple example of a lignum vitae string box — some have blades to cut the string if you pull at an angle. One can see the sharp contrast of the wood and visualise the intensity of colour.

Mid-19th century   *£250 — £350*

979 Quaintness, which is perhaps better described as 'obvious age', is clearly apparent in this simple Irish lamhog carved from solid willow. Doesn't it look old? How does one value such a piece?

17th century?   *£300 — £400*

980 (left) A turned long pole supporting an oil lamp on a base of three simple sledge type feet. The key to its desirability is that it is in yew. Not the pinky red tinge of the late eighteenth century but the nut brown of the seventeenth century that sends a 'yew freak' fumbling for his cheque book.

Late 17th century   *£600 — £800*

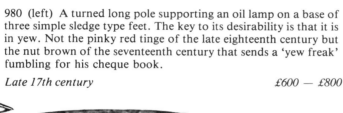

981 (left) A 9ins. boxwood chalice simply turned, with decoration of bands and triangles around the top alternately filled with crude cross-hatching. Well-turned below like an early brass candlestick. It cost £1 in 1968. British Rail Pension Fund please note that maximum percentage increases in value often go hand in hand with low initial price.

Late 17th/early 18th century
£300 — £400

982 (right) Quaintness, it is suggested, can exist not necessarily in the piece itself but in the associations it produces. This is a 16½ins. high oak pillarbox from the hall of a country house. A handwritten note states the delivery and despatch times, starting with 6 a.m. High price because almost identical to one in Pinto. But it is possible to find something similar at £40 + .

Late 19th century   *£400 — £600*

VICTORIAN 'CARVE UPS' — and related pieces

The better off late Victorians had plenty of leisure. Wood-carving was a popular hobby and as oak was an ideal victim one finds 'Do It Yourself' magazines advising "Take an old chest, knock out the carved panels and put to one side, cut off the legs..."

Ten years ago such furniture was nearly worthless but some elements of overseas buyers, unbiased by a background of antique collecting, purchase pieces purely for their decorative quality and see them in terms of their cost to make now. This logical approach has resulted in some 'carve ups' being worth more than their unscathed brethren (some 30 hour duration oak longcase clocks are a case in point). Understandably the purist regards this phenomenon with the same bewilderment that one might attribute to African natives gathering fertility gods for Victorian ethnographical collectors when they discovered that they were paid less for the ones with large genitals. The crude analogy has more serious overtones. Overseas buyers have immense financial muscle and can influence prices dramatically, but rarely in a predictable direction.

983 This imposing looking piece is made from two chests. The bottom one was a fine James I inlaid piece of rather large proportions which had Victorian gadrooning added and raised on stilts while the originality of the top consisted merely of the panels. The bunches of grapes, the leafy side rails and of course the gadroons are — in the happy auctioneer's phrase — 'by a later hand'. The turned supports are new. There was, however, a slight functional problem in that there were no doors to the bottom half, one had to lift off the entire top to gain access.

Assembled late 19th century   *£700 — £900*
If split and sold as two chests £900 — £1,200

984 An oak bureau with a well, c.1710, which was 'carved up' in a very sympathetic manner, that is, not crudely to look quaint, see 987, or too fiddly to be genuine, see 989. Indeed it is this quality of work when added to an original piece of carving that can be very difficult to detect. Now too valuable to be veneered in walnut as used to be the case up to about 1970 when they were worth £50 — £80.

Carved late 19th century   *£1,200 — £1,600*

985 (right) A good court cupboard dated 1725 aesthetically ruined by Victorian carving. The motifs of kings and knights are typical.

Carved late 19th century   *£1,000 — £1,400*

986 Detail of a wainscot chair on which a replacement cresting to the top rail has been fitted. Look at the two large scrolls and the leaves falling down on either side. This has more in keeping with the eighteenth century (see the walnut chair section) than the crudely cut flower of the central panel below.

Added late 19th century   *For value see 104*

987 Fortunately not all Victorian carving was foisted, cuckoo like, on older pieces. This joke was made up out of old wood and provides a good example of the quaint medieval school. The same wizards, kings and knights appear but much more crudely. The seahorse-like kissing couple and the monsters which make up the seat rail and arms are typical. Anybody even slightly acquainted with medieval chairs realises that they did not have a rake to their backs like those shown in the panels.

Late 19th century   *Incredibly £500 — £700*

988 Perhaps such an early design does not belong in this section. It is, however, of a type which was sometimes adapted from fragments of earlier pieces and indeed it would be incredible if they had not undergone some repair. In this case the two rails either side of the door must have moved slightly, as the dowels which should be directly above them appear to have shifted slightly to one side. The absence of a top moulding is normal. These pieces show signs of great age, decay and of the repairs to their legs. It is not unknown for out and out fakes to be manufactured.

If right £12,000+
But more probably wrong £1,000 — £1,400
(according to who you think you can fool!)

989 Carving of the highest quality is seen on this chest dated 1888. It is not that the quality is too high but just that the treatment is wrong. The chain of guilloche circles in the centre panel moves in at the corners to allow for the spandrels of leaves. The flowers curve too prettily and grow conscious of the space they have to fill. It has more Kate Greenaway in it than 17th century. It lacks the boldness of the early period. Compare with 296 and 104.

c.1888   *£400 — £600*
                    More if the date had been 1688

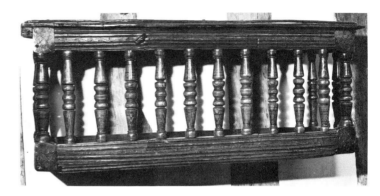

The turner's art has been slightly neglected in this book. Those extraordinary chairs made almost entirely of turned parts are rather specialised but one does, however, still see wall cupboards which have turning for their main decorative feature.

990 A fine quality example of a turned wall cupboard. Only the top, bottom, shelf and door supports are not turned. The principal design used in making the spindles is a variant on the baluster form with a ridge cut at the widest point to lighten the appearance. Made in ash, it is unusual in being constructed entirely without a joined frame. A fine collector's piece which is reflected in the price.

Late 17th century   £4,000 — £5,000

991 A small oak spindle wall cupboard. The frame is joined and decorated with simple groove moulding and punch marks of various shapes. The top and bottom are nailed on and the top has extra strip to prevent objects slipping forward. The design of turning is again broadly baluster shaped with three central bobbins. The centre four spindles and a horizontal split of the top and bottom rail form the door. Good patination.

Late 17th century   £2,000 — £3,000

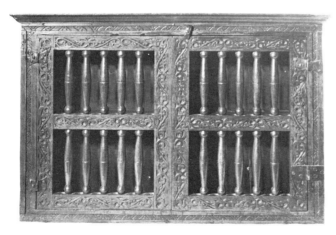

992 A form of hutch or food cupboard. This form is little removed from a cupboard with the panels removed and spindles substituted. Neither the carving nor the form of the spindles demonstrate any great quality.

Late 17th century   £1,500 — £2,500

993 The form of hanging cupboard is even more apparent. The spindles, of primitive form, now occupy even less space than in the previous examples. This should not, however, disguise the fact that this is a well-made, beautifully coloured and *small* example of oak furniture.

c.1720   £1,000 — £1,400

WASHSTANDS

Like the night table the washstand, designed to hold the jug and basin set, is now technically obsolete. The question of value is therefore influenced by the use to which they can be put.

The first three examples are extremely decorative and are the corner variety. The four-legged washstands tend to have their galleries lowered, or replaced with brass frets. Complete with inset red tooled leather the price is at least doubled.

994 A rather fine fruitwood eighteenth century washstand on three cabriole legs. With pillar uprights supporting the triform centre section with two drawers and, above, a circular basin holder. Note the dished base, designed to hold a jug or basin.

1770-1790　　*fruitwood £900 — £1,200*
　　　　　　　mahogany £1,200 — £1,800

995 (above) A mahogany corner washstand with arched back and three drawers but no undertier.

1790-1810　　　　　*£600 — £900*

996 (left) A mahogany corner washstand with splayed legs and a shaped back to the basin shelf which is inlaid with stringing. Note also the drawers and shaped stretcher, dished centrally to hold a jug (an undertier, technically).

1790-1810　　　　　*£600 — £900*

997 A late Georgian mahogany washstand on turned legs, with two cock-beaded drawers and shaped back and sides in solid mahogany, which is thin enough to give an appearance of lightness without being flimsy. Compare turning in 182.

c.1830
　　　　with turned legs £500 — £700
　　　　with tapered legs £800 — £1,200

998 A Victorian mahogany washstand which is similar to the previous example but the legs have lost the elegance of turning and the drawers are simple, without cockbeading. The high backs are sometimes found cut down and leather can be inserted to make a writing table.

c.1860

　　　　　　　　£300 — £400

WHATNOTS

A whatnot is a term usually applied to a shelved piece of furniture for incidental use, with or without a drawer and either mobile (on castors) or fixed. Examples date from about 1800 and have the usual characteristic turned uprights with collars or 'bamboo' double-collared designs. Later, like Canterburies, they exhibit Victorian features such as scrolled fretted carving, burr veneers and bulbous legs. A fitted drawer adds to the value, while a pair of large (preferably over 5ft.) Georgian whatnots would command a very high premium.

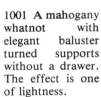

999 A large mahogany whatnot of four shelves with a drawer at the bottom and a three-sided gallery on top. More decorative examples are to be found.

1810-1830　　　　*£1,000 — £1,300*

1001 A mahogany whatnot with elegant baluster turned supports without a drawer. The effect is one of lightness.

1810-1830
£700 — £900

1000 (above) A mahogany whatnot with a turned gallery to the top shelf and a central drawer. The gallery helps the price.

1810-1830　　　　*£700 — £900*

1002 (left) A rosewood whatnot with spirally turned uprights and a (broken) fretted gallery to the top. The drawer adds to the price but the effect is much heavier.

1820-1840　　*In good condition £450 — £600*

1003 (right) A walnut corner whatnot of elaborate turning and fretted decoration. The top fretwork is broken. Very much the heavy Victorian appearance.

1840-1860　　*In good condition £450 — £600*

1004 A typical George III mahogany octagonal cellaret, bound in brass, on square reeded legs with fretted brackets at the top corners.

1790-1800   *£5,000 — £7,000*

WINE COOLERS — or cellarets, 1790-1830

A cellaret, or wine cooler, was quite an important piece of furniture for those who had not yet acquired an Adam sideboard where the wine could be stored in a pedestal cupboard.

The wine cooler was the receptacle in which the wine was stored before use at the table — a sort of distribution stop between cellar and wine glass, but, more importantly, a means of cooling those wines which had to be served chilled. Certainly many of them have metal liners.

The wine cooler appears to have enjoyed a relatively brief and later Georgian boom after which the Victorians seem to have established, in their more commodious sideboards and cabinets, a means of keeping the wine from sight without a separate container.

As many of them contain relatively little workmanship in proportion to their market value, they have been hugely faked especially the simpler (i.e. easier) Georgian variety.

1005 Brass bound mahogany octagonal cellaret on square tapering legs. Less brass and decoration than the previous example.

1790-1800   *£4,000 — £5,000*

1007 Oval Sheraton satinwood cross-banded in tulipwood, on tapering legs with collar. Maximum use has been made of the contrasting direction of the grain.

1790-1820   *£4,000 — £6,000*

1006 Brass banded oval version on stand with square tapering legs inlaid with a stringing line. Nice flat period leather castors. If this was much shallower and was detachable with a brass handle, it would be an oyster bucket.

1790-1810   *£3,000 — £4,000*

1008 Highly decorative carved mahogany oval cellaret with reeded tapering columns and lid. The classical decoration is in the Adam manner.

1790-1820   *£5,000 — £7,000*

1010 Mahogany sarcophagus-shaped wine cooler with lion-mask handles and reeded moulding, on splayed feet.

1800-1820   *£1,500 — £2,000*

1011 Mahogany inlaid with boxwood and ebony stringing on serpentine bracket feet. It looks out of proportion because the front legs are propped up for the photograph.

1790-1820   *£1,200 — £1,600*

1009 The mahogany equivalent of example 1007. Cross-banded on the top and inlaid with brass handles, Plain legs with brass castors.

c.1790   *£3,000 — £3,750*

1013 Brass bound oval cooler on stand with 'Hepplewhite' scrolled legs in the French manner. The top edge is gadrooned.

c.1790   *£3,500 — £4,500*

1012 Mahogany bow-fronted and inlaid with stringing lines of various colours. Underneath there is a separate drawer. The out-of-proportion feet suggest a piece after Hope.

c.1830   *£1,700 — £2,300*

1014 Mahogany wine cooler on stand, with turned legs and collars.

1800-1820   *£1,000 — £1,500*

1015 Mahogany Sheraton cooler with lion-mask handles, inlaid shell motif, black stringing. On splay feet with castors.

1800-1820   *£2,500 — £3,500*

Photographic Acknowledgements

The photographs which appear in this book are derived from a large number of sources over a long period of time. I would like to thank the following auctioneers for their help and assistance. They are, in alphabetical order:

Bearnes Salerooms
Chas. Boardman & Son
Bonham's
Burrows & Day
Button, Menhenitt & Mutton
Christie's
Christie's South Kensington
Churchman Burt & Sons
Cranleigh Salerooms
Dreweatt, Watson & Barton
Hy. Duke & Son
Alan Fitchett & Co.

Garrod Turner & Son
Graves, Son & Pilcher
Humberts, King & Chasemore
King & Chasemore
Lacy Scott & Sons
May, Whetter & Grose
Messenger, May Baverstock
Moore, Allen & Innocent
Neales of Nottingham
Olivers
Osmond, Tricks
Outhwaite & Litherland
Parsons, Welch & Cowell

Phillips
Phillips in Knowle
Phillips of Scotland
Restall, Brown & Clennell
Riddett & Adams Smith
Russell, Baldwin & Bright
Sotheby's Belgravia
Sotheby Parke Bernet & Co.
Henry Spencer & Sons
Waddington, McLean & Co.
Weller & Dufty
Woolley & Wallis

Photographs supplied by dealers and some private collectors have been extremely valuable, if not actually appearing in the book, at least in enabling me to examine the permutations that exist. Some were taken by the Club at antiques fairs and shops and, wherever possible, the names of the dealers have been included below. Again in alphabetical order:

Philip Andrade
Arnold and Walker
Hazel Bakers Antiques
Barlow Antiques
John Bly
Wilfred Bull
Tom Burn
Anthony Butt Antiques
Cedar Antiques
Chilham Antiques
Cirencester Antiques

Compton-Dando
John Creed Antiques Ltd.
Thomas Crispin Antiques
Doveridge House Antiques
Foster Antiques
David Gibbins
Harcourt Lacey
J.P.J. Homer
Jose Hornsey
Anthony Hurst Antiques
Lita Kaye of Lyndhurst

H.W. Keil
Mallett
Betty Meysey-Thompson
Partner & Puxon
Pembroke Antiques
A.T. Silvester & Son Ltd.
Spink & Son Ltd.
Pamela Streather
Thistle Antiques
Charles Toller
A.G. Voss
Leslie Wenn

There is no doubt that one of the finest collections of antiques in the world is assembled annually at The Grosvenor House Fair, more correctly known as The Grosvenor House Antiques Fair. It is in this treasure house of quality that one can purchase superb pieces. Among the many firms that have taken part are the following, some of whose publicity photographs have been included:

Norman Adams Limited
Barling of Mount Street Ltd.
Arthur Brett & Sons Ltd.
Michael Foster
Glaisher & Nash Ltd.
W.R. Harvey & Co. (Antiques) Ltd.

Hotspur Ltd.
John Keil Ltd.
Mallett & Son (Antiques) Ltd.
Trevor Micklem Antiques
Neptune Antiques
Ronald Phillips Ltd.

Prides of London
Randolph
Stair & Co. Ltd.
Temple Williams Ltd.
Trevor Antiques

Finally the Fine Art and Antiques Fair held annually has recently established itself as an excellent market place for fine quality. Among the publicity photographs which were used we wish to acknowledge the following:

Norman Adams Ltd.
Biggs of Maidenhead Ltd.

Cirencester Antiques
The General Trading Company

Harrods Limited
H.W. Keil Ltd.

Third Edition. We are grateful to Christie's and Sotheby's for the use of colour transparencies taken from their sales catalogues over the past few years.

If by accident I have included photographs without having made acknowledgement, I apologise in advance. Some labels are missing from the back of the photographs.

Glossary
Cabinet Makers, Designers and Manufacturers

Adam, Robert and James. Two of the four sons of a Scottish architect, William Adam, all of whom followed their father's profession. Robert Adam is generally acknowledged to have taken the leading part in the production of the *Works on Architecture* produced with James. Robert was born in 1728 and died in 1792. He was in Rome in the 1750s and instigated a Classical Revival based, like William Kent, on an overall concept of design covering a house and all its furnishings. Syon House, Osterley and Kenwood are examples. He was most influential after 1765 and much of the finest furniture in the second half of the eighteenth century was produced under the influence of his design. The Classical Revival gradually superseded the Chinese, Rococo and Gothic tastes which are noticeable in Chippendale's 'Director' of 1754 and, in later years, Chippendale carried out work in the style of Robert Adam.

Boulle, André Charles. A French artist of the Louis XIV period, after whom a form of marquetry made from shell and metal was named. Boulle (or Buhl) furniture was also popular in the Regency period in England but it is thought that the English marquetry of the William and Mary period was influenced by the French Boulle designs. See 644.

Boulton, Matthew. Famous for his collaboration with James Watt on the steam engine, but his Birmingham foundry also produced metal ormolu mounts for furniture from 1762.

Chippendale, Thomas Not very well documented personally, but famous for his book of designs *The Gentleman and CAbinet Maker's Director,* first published in 1754, and for his work as a cabinet maker and carver, particularly in mahogany. The book starts with the five classical orders, but rapidly reflects the contemporary taste for Chinese, Rococo and Gothic styles. It is suggested that Lock and Copland's book *New Book of Ornaments* of 1746 was a source of Chippendale's. A very important book, Chippendale's 'Director' as it is called, is now used to describe the styles of domestic furniture illustrated therein, although some of the pieces were never made.

Chippendale styles cover the years 1740 to 1760 and, of course, many later reproductions. Apart from his grand furniture in the Chinese, Rococo and Gothic manner, he is associated with the more severe straight square leg which superseded the cabriole on chair legs in the 1740s and onwards. In later years the firm of Chippendale carried out work for and in the style of Robert Adam. See illustrations for typical chairs of the 1740-1760 period.

Clay, Henry. Originator of papier mâché furniture, about 1772. Made by building up layers of paper with pitch and oil over an iron frame. Usually finished by painting and decorating with inlay.

Cobb, J. With his partner, William Vile, the firm of Vile and Cobb were justly celebrated in the years 1755-65. They were cabinet makers and upholsterers to George III and pieces by them remain in the Royal collection. Cobb was originally the upholsterer until Vile's retirement in 1765.

Copland, M.A. A designer, with Matthias Lock (q.v.).

Edwards and Roberts. A Victorian firm who specialised in eighteenth century reproductions.

Gillow, Robert. Gillow's of Lancaster were in business in the mid-eighteenth century — Hepplewhite was a Gillow apprentice — and continued on throughout the nineteenth century. Robert Gillow came from Lancaster, where the furniture for the Oxford Street branch in London was made. The firm's Cost Books from about 1790, with their designs, are now in the Westminster Public Library. The first reference to a Davenport occurs in their Cost Books — "To Captain Davenport, a desk".

Haigh, Thomas. Was a partner of both father and son Chippendale.

Hepplewhite, George. Died in 1786, but his *Cabinet Maker and Upholsterer's Guide,* published posthumously in 1788, greatly influenced many cabinet makers. He is well known for his chairs, for the splayed curved foot, which replaced brackets on chests, and for much inlaid decoration on furniture. He used classical motifs a great deal, which were similar to those of Adam.

The shield and oval back chairs are particularly associated with Hepplewhite, as is the Prince of Wales feathers motif (see 157), but he also published many other designs, including squarer backs of chairs, which we now associated with Sheraton. Knife boxes, cellarets, sideboards and particularly serpentine and bow-fronted commodes appear in Hepplewhite's designs; so do square chests of drawers with both bracket and splayed feet.

Holland and Sons. A celebrated nineteenth century firm who produced French and English eighteenth century reproductions.

Hope, Thomas. Scholar and architect who published a book *Household Furniture and Decoration* in 1807. His designs were of formalised classical type with much zoological decoration and drew on nearly all the ancient civilisations for their forms.

Ince, William. Partner in the firm of Ince and Mayhew, of high reputation, who published a book of designs, the *Universal System of Household Furniture* in 1759-63. Ince was actually the designer, Mayhew apparently being the business man. Chinese and Gothic designs, with frets, are prevalent in their book. The firm continued in existence until the early nineteenth century.

Jennens and Bettridge. Obtained a patent, in 1825, for decorating papier mâché with pearl-sheen inlay, a feature used on papier mâché furniture for some considerable years afterwards.

Johnson, Thomas. A mirror man, contemporary with Chippendale and described as a carver, c.1755, of Grafton Street, Soho, who produced a design book of very intricate rococo frames and console tables.

Kent, William. Architect, born in Yorkshire in 1684. Went to Rome in 1710 and returned to assert Classical values upon house and furniture in a somewhat grand manner. The broken pediment, the supporting eagle, festoons of fruit, ball-and-claw feet, all on a gigantic scale, are the hallmarks of William Kent. He died in 1748, but had considerable influence in the early mahogany period of 1730-1745.

Langley, Batty and Thomas. Produced a book, *The City and Country Builder's and Workman's Treasury of Designs* in 1740, a manual for craftsmen containing mainly architectural designs in the prevailing Classical, Chinese, Rococo and Gothic tastes.

Langlois, Peter. A cabinet maker who supplied furniture for Syon House and Strawberry Hill, 1760-1770, and who worked a good deal in the Boulle (q.v.) manner.

Lock, Matthias. Lock published several books of designs, starting in about 1740 and, with Copland, produced a *New Book of Ornaments* in 1746. It is thought that, since they worked for Chippendale, he copied their designs for his own famous 'Director'. Subsequent publications by Lock were more in the Adam style.

London, J.C. Published his *Encyclopaedia of Cottage, Farm and Villa Architecture* in 1833.

Manwaring, Robert. Published another book of designs in 1765, *The Cabinet and Chair Maker's Real Friend and Companion,* containing many designs for chairs, some of them rather clumsy.

Mayhew, Thomas. See Ince, William.

Seddon, George (1727-1801). A cabinet maker whose firm was large and which covered nearly all trades.

Shearer, Thomas. Cabinet maker and author of *Designs for Household Furniture,* 1788. A contemporary of Hepplewhite and Sheraton, but his designs are nearer to Sheraton in style.

Sheraton, Thos. Not a cabinet maker but a publisher of designs, Thomas Sheraton produced, starting in 1791, *The Cabinet Maker's and Upholsterer's Drawing Book* using many of the same motifs as Adam and Hepplewhite. He is associated with squareness: square chair backs and tapering square section legs. Inlays and painted decoration were also used. Many quite complicated dressing, writing and Pembroke tables appear in his designs, which include the Carlton House writing table, cylinder and tambour tables, washstands, kidney-shaped, games and sofa tables.

Smith, George. Cabinet maker and author of *A Collection of Designs for Household Furniture and Interior Decoration,* 1808.

Vile, William. *Senior partner in the firm of Vile and Cobb, probably the most famous of the period 1755-65. See also Cobb.*

Wright and Mansfield. A firm of cabinet makers of the period 1860-1886 who made fine classical eighteenth century designs of Adam and Sheraton inspiration.

Chronology

Monarch	Date of Reign	Period Appellation	Collective Period Description	Publications and Events
James I	1603-1625	Jacobean		1754 Robert Adam b.1728 c.1792.
Charles I	1625-1649	Carolean	**Oak period** to about 1670	T. Chippendale *Gentleman and Cabinet Maker's Director.* 1st Ed.
Commonwealth	1649-1660	Cromwellian or Commonwealth		
Charles II	1660-1685	Restoration		
James II	1685-1689	Restoration	**Walnut period** 1670-1730	1763 Ince and Mayhew *System of Household Furniture.*
William & Mary	1689-1694	William & Mary		
William III	1694-1702	William III or William & Mary		1766 R. Manwaring *Chairmaker's Guide.*
Anne	1702-1714	Queen Anne		
George I	1714-1727	George I — early Georgian	**Early manogany** 1730-1770	1788 A. Hepplewhite *Cabinet Maker's and Upholsterer's Guide.* 1st Ed.
George II	1727-1760	Early Georgian		
George III	1760-1811	Later Georgian	**Later mahogany** 1770-1810	1791 Thomas Sheraton *Cabinet Maker's and Upholsterer's Drawing Book,* 1st Ed.
George III (Regency)	1811-1820	Regency		
George IV	1820-1830	Regency	**Regency and William IV** 1810-1840	1807 Thomas Hope *Household Furniture.*
William IV	1830-1837	Late Regency or William IV		
Victoria	1837-1901	Early Victorian up to 1860	**Victorian** 1840-1900	1808 George Smith *Household Furniture.*
		Later Victorian 1860-1901		
Edward VII	1901-1910	Edwardian		

Trade Terminology

The terminology of the antiques trade can sometimes be confusing. Here is a short, light-hearted list of common terms often used by dealers. It was kindly contributed by Christopher Hurst of Anthony Hurst Antiques, Woodbridge, Suffolk, and subsequently added to as other definitions were forthcoming.

'As bought'. *As purchased — a phrase used to exonerate the vendor of any moral or legal responsibility with regard to the item he is selling (e.g. 'What is it?' 'Not sure, sir, but it's as bought.'). Much used by Irish knockers. Auctioneers use similar terms, 'As found' or 'With all faults'.*

'Bought in'. *Bought by the auctioneer on behalf of the vendor, as the price bid was not considered sufficient. Normally not up to the predetermined reserve agreed by the seller and auctioneer.*

'Boys, the'. *The dealers regularly attending a local auction, sometimes members of a loosely organised ring; to 'take it away from the boys' at auction is to bid higher than the ring, thus cutting them out (e.g. 'The boys weren't happy' — the local ring were unable to buy any goods cheaply to re-auction amongst themselves).*

'Breaker'. *A piece of furniture in which the wood is more valuable for use in repairs or re-manufacture than in its original form.*

'Collector's piece'. *Originally a term to describe a fine piece that only a connoisseur would appreciate; often now debased to the sort of thing that only an eccentric enthusiast on the subject would want; normally overpriced, and often totally undesirable.*

'Come right'. *A defensive expression used by a buyer of an item for which he has paid over the current market value, implying that it will in time prove a good investment or 'come right'.*

'Commercial'. *1. Not necessarily a fine or completely original piece, but readily saleable. 2. The description of a dealer's goods as 'commercial' is not a term of approbation and is often used by a specialist of another dealer who is more financially successful.*

'Cost'. *The fictitiously large amount alleged to have been paid for a piece to justify the price being asked.*

'Cut down'. *The conversion of a large piece into a smaller, more saleable, and usually more expensive, item.*

'Desirable'. *Combining all or most of the good points normally associated with a piece of its type.*

'Estimate'. *The price suggested by the auctioneer as the amount a lot is likely to fetch. Usually a tortuous compromise between the need to prove to the vendor the auctioneer's competence as a valuer and an effort to persuade as many potential buyers as possible to attend.*

'Fit up'. *The interior fittings of a secretaire or bureau which, when closed, are not on view.*

'Flashed up'. *Unnecessary and usually recent embellishment to turn a rather dull item into something with more immediate appeal. (See 'Improvement'.)*

'Flea market'. *A collection of stalls where the variety of pieces sold is very considerable, often rubbish, and usually overpriced. Prices asked are normally subject to negotiation.*

'Forward-buying'. *The purchase of goods, sometimes at top prices, with the expectation of the market rising in the future.*

'Fresh'. *Unseen by dealers in the locality.*

'Furnishing piece'. *An article which will sell more for its decorative or functional value than for its originality; often used for goods that are not quite 'right' (q.v.).*

'Goods'. *Antiques.*

'Growing roots'. *Used of items on sale, often in the same place for a considerable period of time.*

'Half age'. *Not nearly as old as it looks at first sight; applied particularly to Victorian copies of furniture of eighteenth century and earlier designs. (See 'Old English'.)*

'Hammer price'. *The auction price.*

'Harlequin set'. *See 'Matched'.*

'Hawking'. *A possible vendor, usually private, taking goods from one shop to another, asking for offers, and usually claiming ignorance of the worth of the article for sale.*

'Honest'. *A piece which is 'right', but simple in construction or decoration.*

'Important'. *An all-embracing word often used by provincial auctioneers to describe a piece which they feel might have more potential than they understand (similarly magnificent, very fine, scarce, rare, superb, unusual, desirable, etc., etc.).*

'Improvement'. *Work carried out to make the piece appear of better quality, or of an earlier or more desirable period, than is the case. Usually involving the addition of crossbanding, inlay, stringing, or brass embellishment.*

'In the book'. *Not common in furniture: an attempt to establish an immediate provenance for a piece otherwise hard to compliment by reference to standard works, or indeed any printed source. An attempt to confer immediate acceptance and respectability.*

'Investment item'. *Used descriptively by a dealer of something for which he has paid too much.*

'Irish'. *A useful blanket term used to describe heavy and ill-proportioned furniture, usually eighteenth century mahogany.*

'Knocker'. *One who calls on a private house uninvited and tries to buy goods, usually below current market value.*

'Knocking down'. *At auction, the selling of an item.*

'Knocking out'. *The selling of goods at very small profit, very quickly, with the object of (a) bringing in money quickly or (b) disposing of a piece for which one has paid too much.*

'Leaving something in it'. *Underselling an item so there is (allegedly) a quick profit to be made by the buyer.*

'Likely'. *An item that might prove on close examination to be better than at first glance; not usually a run-of-the-mill item.*

'Looker'. *A serious buyer without the funds to acquire any goods.*

'Lump'. *A piece of furniture but normally heavy; often late and rarely very desirable.*

'Made-up'. *A piece constructed from old wood or materials — not necessarily with any intention of deception.*

'Marquee'. *A large canvas structure which when erected above goods in a country area, preferably in the grounds of a large country house where an auction is taking place, enhances prices beyond all reason.*

'Marriage'. *The joining together or assembling of two pieces which did not start out life together.*

'Matched'. *Similar items assembled into a nearly matching set.*

'Messed around'. *1. A piece which has been altered with a view to improving its value. 2. Badly restored.*

'Non price'. *Much too much to pay for a reproduction, copy or marriage. For example, a good Queen Anne walnut chair with arms might be worth £3,000-£5,000 and a copy £250-£500. To see one priced £1,800 would be a non price.*

'Old English'. *Meaningless auctioneer's description of something that is wrong and which everybody with any knowledge (including the auctioneer) knows is wrong; usually applied to nineteenth century or later copies of oak furniture.*

'Old friends'. *Ironic — pieces of whose company one has tired, either items that reappear regularly at auction or items in a shop that have hitherto failed to find a buyer.*

'Period'. *An all-embracing word much beloved of the trade, and normally used on its own, e.g. 'Is it period?' (i.e. 'Was it made at the time the design would suggest, and not later?').*

'Provincial'. *1. Pieces made outside the main fashionable production centres, usually less sophisticated but often desirable. 2. A pejorative word to describe ill-proportioned and often country-made furniture.*

'Right'. *A piece which proves, on examination, to be of the period which at first sight it seemed to be, and in most important respects is original. Frequently used by antique dealers. (See 'Wrong'.)*

'Ring'. *A group of dealers who agree not to increase the price at auction by nominating one of their number to bid. A piece so bought is re-auctioned privately afterwards and the difference in value split as agreed between the participants. There may be several opposing rings at one auction. (Illegal under the Auctions (Bidding Agreements) Act 1969.)*

'Rooms, the'. *The large auction houses, especially in London. Often used pretentiously in the provinces by those who would like their intimate familiarity with the London auction houses to be assumed.*

'Rough'. *Damaged or in poor condition; unrestored.*

'Runner'. *One who makes his living by transporting pieces between dealers with a view to making a margin from the prospective sales, usually selling from his vehicle.*

'Shine'. *The effect of hard polishing over a short period of time. Not to be confused with patina.*

'Shipping goods'. *Items regularly sent abroad, and not usually regarded as being of high quality; bought usually in bulk and often of undeterminate age and/or originality.*

'Showing strength'. *Used particularly at auction of a dealer who is prominent in the bidding — sometimes with the object of being admitted to a 'ring' (q.v.).*

'Six plus two'. *Refers to a set of eight chairs, two of which have arms while the remainder do not.*

'Skin'. *Patination and polish; general appearance of surface.*

'Sleeper'. *A piece which has been untouched for many years and is therefore more desirable than something recently restored.*

'Solid'. *Made out of the solid wood as opposed to veneered.*

'Speculative'. *May or may not have considerable value, normally the latter.*

'Stalk'. *A pedestal table with missing top (East Anglian).*

'Standing in'. *Being admitted to or joining a ring — either for one specific lot or an entire sale.*

'Stolen'. *1. Goods illegally obtained as generally understood. 2. A very cheap purchase (see 'Touch').*

'Through the mill'. *Restored, often extensively and sometimes badly.*

'Touch, a'. *A cheap item with a good profit ('a useful touch': an even better profit might be envisaged).*

'Trade, the'. *Antique dealers collectively.*

'Trade price'. *Cost of an item to a dealer, usually less than the marked ticket price (e.g. 'What's the trade on...?').*

'Trotting'. *1. At auction, the artificial increase in bidding with the intention of raising the selling price (running up). 2. Also used of runners (q.v.) taking their goods from place to place in the hope of finding a buyer.*

'Unseen'. *Bought without considered examination, often in the early hours with the aid of a touch.*

'Wrong'. *1. Faked, or so heavily adapted from what the piece originally was that it now pretends to be what it is not. 2. An out-and-out fake. 3. A piece that although possibly desirable has had a considerable amount of restoration, addition or alteration.*

Short Critical Bibliography

During the 1980s Sotheby's and Christie's, followed by other auctioneers, have increasingly illustrated the lots they sell. The availability of thousands of photographs has led to a spate of books heavy on pictures but weak on texts; the pictures by themselves are insufficient for a full understanding of furniture.

GENERAL

The Dictionary of English Furniture — Ralph Edwards
> The 1954 revised edition in three volumes was the classic work on the subject, but covers mainly quality furniture to the start of the nineteenth century. Nevertheless it remains the key work. Available Antique Collectors' Club paperback, original published by *Country Life,* 1954.

The Journal of the Furniture History Society — published annually
> The focus for research on British furniture follows a history of art approach and tends to concentrate on narrow subjects of academic interest. C/o Victoria and Albert Museum, London.

Antique Furniture — John C. Rogers, revised Margaret Jourdain
> A cabinetmaker's approach to antique furniture. Very compact and sound. Long out of print.

Authentic Decor — The Domestic Interior 1620-1920 — Peter Thornton
> Shows contemporary illustrations of interiors worldwide in their original settings, not just furniture but how it was used. Weidenfeld & Nicholson, 1984.

World Furniture — Edited Helena Hayward
> Remains the best general introduction to world furniture. Hamlyn, 1965.

SPECIFIC PERIODS

Early Furniture

Oak Furniture — The British Tradition — Victor Chinnery
> The classic text on British oak furniture to the end of the eighteenth century. 1,000 illustrations. Antique Collectors' Club, 1979.

18th Century

Pictorial Dictionary of 18th Century Furniture Design — Lisa White
> A valuable collection of some 4,000 illustrations from 18th century and early 19th century sources together with notes on designers. Antique Collectors' Club, Autumn 1990.

18th Century English Furniture — The Norman Adams Collection
> The pieces sold by a leading dealer over sixty years of business provide a good survey, well balanced between art history and the interests of collectors; discusses patina. Antique Collectors' Club, 1983.

Walnut Furniture to 1750

Not a favourite period for researchers, perhaps because of the paucity of documentation. The most useful specialist book remains:

Old English Walnut and Lacquer Furniture — R.W. Symonds
Herbert Jenkins, 1922.

After 1740

The designers increasingly make their presence felt and much work has been done on individuals of which the major work is:

The Life and Work of Thomas Chippendale — Christopher Gilbert
A scholarly assessment. Trefoil, 1978.

19th Century

The Price Guide to Victorian, Edwardian and 1920s Furniture — John Andrews
The companion volume to this work, containing the same blend of down-to-earth advice and discussion of quality. Price revision annually. Antique Collectors' Club, 1980.

Regency Furniture — Frances Collard
The standard work. Antique Collectors' Club, 1985.

The Pictorial Dictionary of 19th Century Furniture Design
Contains by type over 4,000 illustrations from some forty-five of the major design books of the period. Antique Collectors' Club, 1977.

Victorian Furniture — R.W. Symonds and B.B. Whineray
The excellent seminal work on the subject. *Country Life,* 1962.

Victorian Furniture 1840-1880 — Rosamund Allwood
Covers the period before the Arts and Crafts Movement. Dominated by revivals of styles — Gothic, Rococo, 'Old English', etc. Antique Collectors' Club, late 1990.

Vernacular Furniture

Regional Chairs — Bill Cotton
The first modern scientific study of the subject, providing accurate identification of hundreds of hitherto unknown makers. Antique Collectors' Club, Spring 1990.